THE
FIRST DAYS
OF SCHOOL

HOW TO BE AN EFFECTIVE TEACHER

HARRY K. WONG   ROSEMARY T. WONG

" Your book taught my son how to teach. "

John Hattie

HARRY K. WONG PUBLICATIONS, INC.
www.EffectiveTeaching.com

This book is printed on environmentally friendly paper. Join us in making a choice to save the planet.

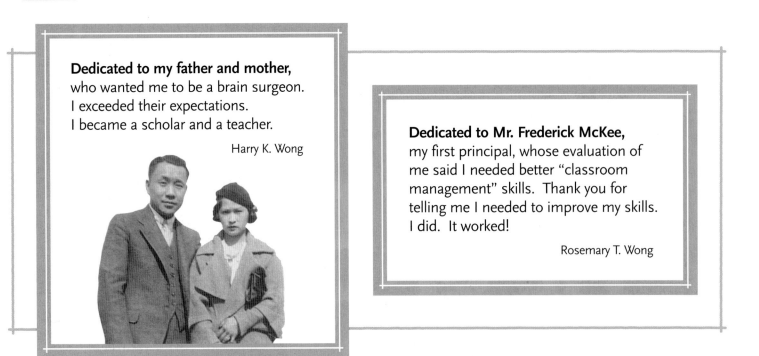

Dedicated to my father and mother,
who wanted me to be a brain surgeon.
I exceeded their expectations.
I became a scholar and a teacher.

Harry K. Wong

Dedicated to Mr. Frederick McKee,
my first principal, whose evaluation of
me said I needed better "classroom
management" skills. Thank you for
telling me I needed to improve my skills.
I did. It worked!

Rosemary T. Wong

Cover Images: Thank you to the real teachers in real classrooms who have shared with us how they are making a difference in the lives of their students. From right to left: Sarah Jondahl, Jeff Gulle, Nile Wilson, Chelonnda Seroyer, Elmo Sanchez Jr., Stacey Allred.

ISBN: 978-0-9764233-8-6
Library of Congress Control Number: 2018903809
15 14 13 12 11 10 9 8 7 6 5 4 3 2
Printed in Canada by TC Transcontinental Printing

Executive Producer: Rosemary T. Wong
Graphic Designer: Mark Van Slyke
Editor: Katharine Sturak
Original DVD Sleeve and Disc Design: David Bawiec

www.HarryWong.com
Your Success. Our Passion.

Visit us to
- find our proven resources for developing effective teachers
- view our digital offerings
- enhance your professional development with our free resources
- learn more about how we are helping children realize their potential

HARRY K. WONG PUBLICATIONS, INC.
943 North Shoreline Boulevard ▪ Mountain View, CA 94043 ▪ T: 650-965-7896 F: 650-965-7890 ▪ www.EffectiveTeaching.com

About the DVD, *You Have Changed My Life*

The Presentation

When was the last time you saw an in-service presenter get **three** standing ovations in just forty-five minutes? In Lakeland, Florida, 1,300 educators were teary-eyed and emotionally proud as a student (now 40 years old) told how a teacher changed his life. One teacher was sobbing so uncontrollably that Rosemary had to reach over to comfort her. In *You Have Changed My Life*, William Martinez tells of his life and transformation in story, song, and American Sign Language as he pays tribute to the teaching profession.

Because of a Teacher

William was raised in a silent home with a single-mother who could not speak or hear. He attended close to twenty elementary schools, failed nearly every class in those schools, and was held back several times. Then, his eighth-grade music teacher, Norma Freeman, turned his life around. Because of her, as William says in the presentation, "For the first time in my life, I was a something."

Because of a teacher, he pulled his academics together, attended and graduated from college, performs worldwide, and is a member of Actors Equity.[1]

His voice in song is magnificent. His acting is superb and his personality, endearing. His presentation is Hollywood quality, with music orchestrated by Grammy nominee, David Bawiec.

**Because of a teacher,
he became the unique, magnificent performer he is today.**

William's DVD, *You Have Changed My Life*, is in the back of this book. Watch it and aspire to be that one teacher who is the difference in the lives of students.

> *William Martinez's program was absolutely one of the most powerful educational presentations that I, as a fourteen-year teacher, have ever witnessed. His theatrical talent is better than Broadway, but his ability to convey to educators the importance of teachers, the arts, and how they impact a child, is phenomenal. I laughed, cried, and was thoroughly entertained, but most importantly, could feel how the life of a student was changed forever, all because of a teacher who cared.*
>
> Dana Maharrey
> Tupelo Public School District,
> Mississippi

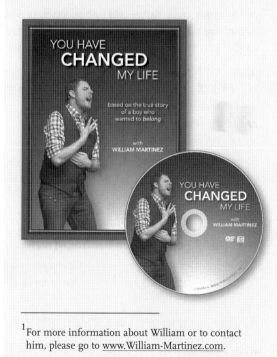

[1] For more information about William or to contact him, please go to www.William-Martinez.com.

CONTENTS

Unit A Basic Understandings—The Teacher

The successful teacher must know and practice the three characteristics of an effective teacher.

Unit B First Characteristic—Positive Expectations

The effective teacher has positive expectations for student success.

Unit C Second Characteristic—Classroom Management

The effective teacher is an extremely good classroom manager.

Unit D Third Characteristic—Lesson Mastery

The effective teacher knows how to design lessons to help students achieve.

Unit E Future Understandings—The Professional

The teacher who constantly learns and grows becomes a professional educator.

DVD *You Have Changed My Life*

The story of how a teacher can impact the life of a child told in story, song, and American Sign Language.

About the Authors

Who are Harry and Rosemary Wong?[2] Many have described the Wongs as new teacher advocates, motivational speakers, inspirational leaders, writers, classroom management gurus, rock stars, connectors, angels, encouragers, cheerleaders, and enthusiastic, down-to-earth, patient, and real. However, the phrase the Wongs take most to heart is,

They are teachers . . . and so proud of it.

> *Success in life is not in knowing the right answer; it's in knowing how to ask the right question.*
>
> Harry K. Wong

> *A simple smile opens the door to opportunities of caring, kindness, and boundless fulfillment.*
>
> Rosemary T. Wong

[2]For more information about the Wongs read About Us at www.HarryWong.com.

Teachers Teach Students

Schools exist for one reason only—for students to learn and achieve. The noblest of all professions is teaching. The success of each child hangs upon the effectiveness of that teaching.

The single greatest effect on student learning and achievement is the effectiveness of the teacher.

Decade after decade of repeated studies, and common sense and experience if you are a parent, has shown that **the single greatest effect on student achievement is the effectiveness of the teacher.** It is astounding what effective teachers can do for students. More can be done to improve education by improving the effectiveness of teachers than by any other single factor.

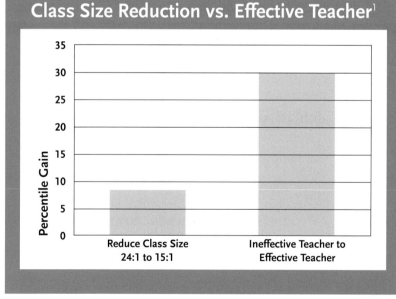

Class Size Reduction vs. Effective Teacher[1]

The skills of an effective teacher produce greater student gains than reducing the number of students in a classroom.

[1] Michael Barber and Mona Mourshed, "How the World's Best-Performing School Systems Come Out on Top" (McKinsey & Company, September 2007).

⭐ **THE KEY IDEA**

The successful teacher is proficient in the three characteristics of effective teachers.

Everyone Nodded and Continued to Work

THE First Days of School saved me from walking out of a teaching contract ten years ago. I had transitioned from teaching first grade to eighth grade, and at the end of the first week I went home in tears feeling like a dismal failure. Nothing was working. I spent the weekend devouring your book and within a few years I was Teacher-of-the-Year and students actually wanted to be in my eighth-grade English class.

Everyone has commented on how I always have such well-managed classes with students working and learning. I tell them I had applied the Wongs' strategies and procedures.

One day, there was some commotion we could all hear down the hall while my students were doing their bellwork. A student looked up and said something about how noisy those students were and wasn't that just awful?

Others nodded and everyone continued to work. More validation that effective management is truly the key!!

Jennifer Bergeron
Houma, Louisiana

Every teacher wants to be successful, and every teacher can be successful. It is the teacher, not programs or the latest technology, that creates successful classrooms. Do not be misled into thinking that programs, ideologies, and structural changes to the school, such as class size, will teach students. Programs and technology do not teach students.

Teachers teach students.

Programs cannot replace an ineffective teacher. A trained, confident, and effective teacher will enhance the quality of any program or use of technology.

All teachers come into teaching believing that they can make a difference in the lives of young people. They do more than make a difference; **they ARE the difference in the lives of their students.**

The Effective Teacher

The subtitle of this book, *How to Be an Effective Teacher*, states the intended outcome of reading the book. The title of the book, *THE First Days of School*, says you must be ready for the students *before* they enter your classroom. It is the effective teacher who knows what to do on the first day of school. Ask any sprinter. How you come out of the starting blocks will determine the outcome of the race. **This book will show you how to be <u>effective</u> from the start.**

Effective Teachers Produce Results

Successful people are effective people; that is, they know what they are doing and they produce results. The key word is EFFECTIVE.

ef • fec • tive   (ef-fec'-tive)

Definition: successful in producing a desired or intended result

How often have you walked out of a bank, office, restaurant, or repair shop with a smile, and someone asks, "Why are you smiling?" And you reply, "I like to go in there because they know what they are doing. They produce the results I want."

Effective people have the power to do an action perfectly and produce intended and expected results. In sports, the result is to produce winning games. In business, it is to produce profitable sales or excellent service.

People who do things right are **EFFICIENT**. They work in a well-organized and competent way. And people who do things right over and over again, consistently, are considered **EFFICTIVE**.

> **Efficient and effective teachers know what they are doing and do things right consistently.**

Effectiveness has to do with **DOING**. To be effective, you must be constantly working toward improved performance.

Effective Teachers Know What to Do

Simply put, effective teachers know how to do things right consistently. In turn, effective teachers teach students how to do things right consistently. (See Chapter 15 and Chapter 16.)

The effective teacher knows these things:

- What to do on the first days of school
- How to start a class so that students are immediately engaged in their work
- How to quiet a class in fifteen seconds or less *please!*
- How to implement a classroom management plan— not a behavior plan, but a management plan
- How to get a class to work cooperatively
- How to have students pass in papers in a matter of minutes without the students creating a disturbance during the process
- When to ask questions during a lecture, assignment, or classroom activity
- How to give an assignment that will increase the number of students who will do the task
- How to conduct formative assessment and summative assessment and the difference between the two

When you know how to teach efficiently and effectively, you affect lives.

Be Efficient and Effective
EFFICIENT: Doing Things Right

"My, he's an efficient waiter!" This may refer to a waiter who fills your water glass without you having to flag him down and ask for it. He does things right, so that you get efficient service and enjoy your meal.

"She is an efficient teacher!" This may refer to a teacher who knows how to take roll without wasting classroom time so as to move on to the lesson for the day. She does things right, so that the classroom runs efficiently.

EFFECTIVE: Doing Things Right Consistently

"She runs an effective office!" This refers to someone who does the right things or makes the right decisions repeatedly, so that the office is effectively run.

"He is an effective teacher!" This refers to a teacher who does things right consistently, so that he has an effect on the lives of his students.

Effective Teachers Affect Lives

Teachers who are efficient and effective are more capable of affecting the lives of students than teachers who are not. **Research has found, again and again that, more than any other factor, an effective teacher is the strongest predictor of student achievement.**

The effective teacher is one who is able to produce intended and expected results.

Effective teachers and school principals produce results in student learning, growth, and achievement.

- **Learning** is acquiring basic knowledge and skills. Learning can also include acquiring behaviors, values, and understandings.

- **Growth** indicates quantity or progress over time, such as acquiring more information and skills, and being able to synthesize and apply the information and skills.

- **Achievement** is when a student is able to demonstrate an act of accomplishment or attainment, such as producing a report, writing a poem, welding pieces of metal, singing a song, or solving a problem. **Achievement is not necessarily linked to or measured by test scores.**

Effective teachers know how to manage their classrooms. They know how to achieve student success by employing effective practices and procedures. They teach for mastery, and have high expectations for their students. **Student learning is their mission, and their mastery goal is student achievement.**

The Three Characteristics of Effective Teachers

The purpose of *THE First Days of School: How to Be an Effective Teacher* is to teach YOU to be an effective teacher. It is not a book that promotes some philosophy, ideology, program, or initiative. It is based on current research and reflects the best and most practical classroom practice.

There are three, well-researched, and well-known characteristics of effective teachers.

You return to your favorite hairdresser because of the consistent results you have come to expect each time you go there. Likewise, you choose doctors because they are able to produce results.

The Three Characteristics of an Effective Teacher

1. Has positive expectations for student success
2. Is an extremely good classroom manager
3. Knows how to design lessons for student mastery

Schools and school systems can use the three characteristics of effective teachers to form the framework of a professional development program to train teachers to be effective.

These three characteristics of effective teachers have been validated by <u>over fifty years of research</u> by researchers such as Thomas Good, Jere Brophy, Robert Pianta, and Charlotte Danielson, among many others.

Thomas Good and Jere Brophy first published their book, *Looking in Classrooms*, in 1973.[2] They identified the three characteristics of effective teachers and used these characteristics to show how teachers can foster student learning and achievement. We were introduced to the work when the book was in its third edition.

Four decades later, the book is in its tenth edition and the authors' research still remains valid. They identified the three most important characteristics of effective teachers:

1. They have POSITIVE EXPECTATIONS for student success.

2. They are extremely good CLASSROOM MANAGERS.

3. They know how to teach a lesson for student LEARNING and MASTERY.

Robert Pianta at the University of Virginia's Curry School of Education developed the Classroom Assessment Scoring System (CLASS) and reached the same conclusions in 2008, matching those of Good and Brophy. After examining more than 3,000 classrooms, Pianta concluded that these are the three most important factors in effective teaching:

1. Emotional support

2. Organizational support

3. Instructional support[3]

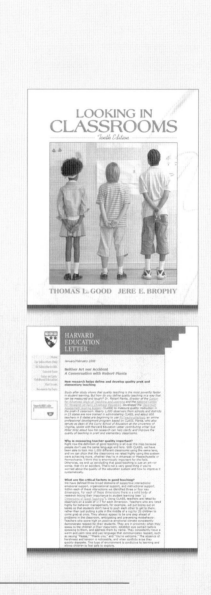

[2] Thomas L. Good and Jere Brophy, *Looking in Classrooms* (Needham, MA: Allyn & Bacon, 2007): 313–314.

[3] Sue Miller Wiltz, in conversation with Robert Pianta. "Neither Art nor Accident: New research helps define and develop quality preK and elementary teaching," *Harvard Education Letter*, vol. 24, no. 1 (January/ February, 2008): 1–3.

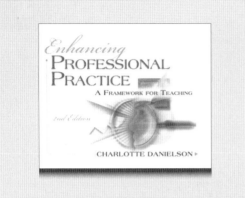

Charlotte Danielson's *A Framework for Teaching*[4] lists four domains of professional practice. By combining her first two overlapping domains, the result matches the characteristics previously enumerated.

> Domain 1 – Planning and Preparing the Classroom Environment
>
> Domain 2 – Instruction
>
> Domain 3 – Professional Responsibilities

The same three characteristics are the hallmark of every successful enterprise and every successful classroom.

In a successful business:

1. The customers are well treated.
2. The place is well managed.
3. The merchandise is well selected.

In a successful classroom:

1. The students are well treated.
2. The classroom is well managed.
3. The lessons are well delivered.

A successful business

A successful classroom

The three characteristics of an effective teacher apply to every teacher. They are well researched; they are tried and true; and you can easily learn how to become a very effective teacher by using them.

[4]Charlotte Danielson, *Enhancing Professional Practice: A Framework for Teaching*, 2nd ed. (Alexandria, VA: Association for Supervision and Curriculum Development, 2007).

Positive Expectations—Unit B

Having positive expectations simply means that the teacher believes in the student. **The teacher expects that the student can and will learn.** For student learning to take place, it is essential that the teacher exhibit positive expectations toward all students.

The belief in positive expectations is based on the research that the student will produce what the teacher expects him or her to produce. If you believe a student is a low-level, below-average, slow learner, the student will perform accordingly because these are the expectations you transmit to him or her. If you believe a student is a high-ability, above-average, capable learner, the student will perform at that level because these are the expectations you transmit to him or her.

what does this have to say about equity?

The positive tone in Sarah Jondahl's classroom creates an expectation for success.

Effective teachers succeed not only because they have positive expectations for their students, but because they have positive expectations for themselves, too. **Effective teachers want to succeed and they do so when their students succeed.**

Positive expectations benefit the teacher, the student, and the overall classroom environment. **Unit B explains the importance of positive expectations and discusses ways to convey them.**

Classroom Management—Unit C

Classroom management consists of the practices and procedures that a teacher uses to maintain an environment in which instruction and learning can occur. For this to happen, the teacher must create a well-ordered environment.

Discipline has very little to do with classroom management. You don't discipline a store; you manage it. The same is true of a classroom. Discipline is behavior management (Chapter 17). It deals with how people behave. Classroom management deals with how things are done. **Unit C explains how to organize and structure a well-managed classroom so every student will know what to do to learn and succeed.**

**Well-Ordered Environment
+ Positive Academic Expectations**

= Effective Classroom

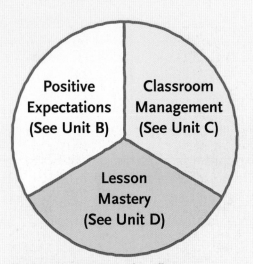

The three characteristics of an effective teacher and where to find them.

Lesson Mastery—Unit D

Lesson mastery refers to how well a student demonstrates that a concept has been comprehended, or performs a skill at a certain level of proficiency, as determined by the teacher. When a house is built, the contractor receives a set of blueprints from the architect. The blueprints specify the required degree of competency. The inspector who checks on the construction always looks at the blueprint first and then checks to see if the work meets the degree of competency specified.

Teaching is no different. To achieve student mastery, an effective teacher knows how to do four things:

1. Design lessons so that students learn a concept or perform a skill to lesson targets or objectives.
2. Create and use a lesson plan that delivers the instruction to teach to the lesson targets or objectives.
3. Use a rubric to assess for understanding, competence, and mastery.
4. Provide corrective action, if necessary, so students master the lesson objectives.

Student success depends on how well the teacher designs lessons and checks for mastery of the subject matter. **Unit D is on effective instruction. It explains how to effectively teach for lesson mastery.**

Effective Teaching Applies to All Teachers

What works in a kindergarten classroom, special education classroom, or high school classroom also works, with modifications, in any classroom.

Teaching is not covering chapters or assigning activities. Do not become enamored with presenting information, doing activities, and using the technology present in the classroom. Nothing is being achieved if there is no evidence that students are actually learning the lesson outcomes or objectives.

The purpose of school is learning. Teaching is not what you do to fill up a day. Teaching is the outcome you get from students.

Research consistently shows that of all the factors schools can control, the effective teacher has the greatest impact on student learning and achievement.

Decade after decade of educational theories, innovations, and fads have not increased student achievement. **The only factor that significantly increases student achievement is an effective teacher.**

Helping you become an effective teacher is the purpose of this book.

Going Beyond

The greatest impact on student achievement is an effective teacher.

The term *lagniappe* (pronounced "lan-yap," meaning "something extra") is used in Louisiana and Mississippi. It began as a little bonus that a store owner might add to a purchase, such as an extra donut (as in a baker's dozen), something for the road, or a complimentary dessert. Today it has become synonymous with the little extra things people do for each other.

When you see a **Go**ing **Be**yond or **"GoBe"** folder, go to **www.EffectiveTeaching.com** and access *THE First Days of School*. One of the tabs across the top of the page says **Going Beyond**. Open the tab to be taken to all of the GoBes in this book. Or, scan the QR Code on this folder for direct access to this same list of GoBes.

For immediate access to the information in any folder, use the QR Code reader on your mobile device and scan the code. (Readers are free in any App store.) With the book in hand and your mobile device ready, you'll have everything you need to be successful right at your fingertips.

Close to a Miracle

Stacy Hennesee's classroom was out of control. Then he experienced something close to a miracle. What he did can be found in the **Go**ing **Be**yond folder for Chapter 1 or scan the QR Code.

Students Work Without the Teacher Present

I visit eight schools in my role as an instructional coach. One day I complimented the principal of one of them (a middle school) on the orderliness of the school, but more importantly, on the sense of responsibility his students exhibited and the respect they exhibited for each other, the teachers, and the property.

They always seemed to know exactly what to do and how to behave and there was nothing coercive about any of it. I observed one day how a teacher sent two students, unattended, into the library to make up a test. The librarian wasn't there yet and the teacher had no idea I was present. The kids came in by themselves, took seats at tables far apart, and sat down facing the same direction. When each finished, they picked up their test and returned to the classroom—separately.

Kids constantly come into the library, without passes, just on trust. They check out books without dilly-dallying and without loud talk—and then they return to their classrooms. I sometimes leave my purse, my camera, my computer just sitting there on a library desk when I leave to visit a classroom. Never a worry.

After my time in the school, I had much to compliment the principal on. I asked him "how he did it."

He turned to me and said one word, "Procedures."

Sarah Powley
Lafayette, Indiana

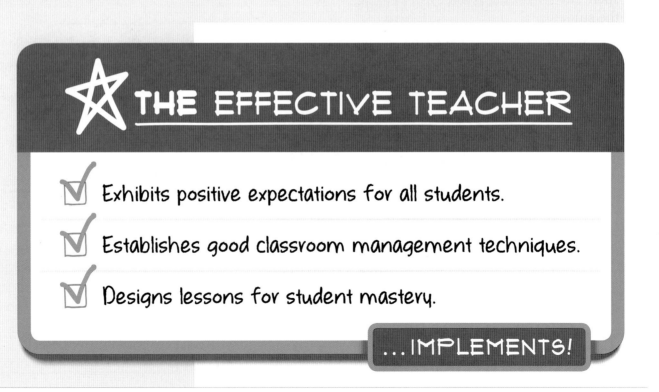

☆ THE EFFECTIVE TEACHER

☑ Exhibits positive expectations for all students.

☑ Establishes good classroom management techniques.

☑ Designs lessons for student mastery.

...IMPLEMENTS!

Success on the First Day of School

What you do on the first days of school will determine your success or failure as a teacher for the rest of the school year. Your desire to be an effective teacher will be defined by how you structure a successful first day that will set the stage for an effective classroom throughout the school year.

> **Successful teachers have a script or a plan ready for the first day of school.**

THE KEY IDEA

Your success during the entire school year is determined by what you do on the first days of the year.

College professor Douglas M. Brooks embarked on a project to videotape a series of teachers on their first day of school. He wrote his findings in an article entitled, "The First Day of School."[1] Watching the recordings, he made a startling discovery. The ineffective teachers began their first day of school by covering the subject matter or doing a fun activity. These teachers spent the rest of the school year chasing after the students.

Douglas M. Brooks
Miami University of Ohio

The effective teachers spent time explaining to students how the class was going to be organized and structured so they knew exactly what to do to succeed.

The Effective Teacher Rubric

It is highly recommended that you read page 301 in Chapter 22 early on to understand the three characteristics of an effective teacher and how they come together to determine your effectiveness and success in the classroom.

Effective teachers plan for success.

[1] Douglas M. Brooks, "The First Day of School," *Educational Leadership*, vol. 42, no. 8 (May 1985): 76–78.

The Effective Classroom Is Consistent

The most important thing to establish in your classroom the first week of school is CONSISTENCY. People in general like to know exactly what they are getting, what will be happening, and what they need to do. Students want a safe, predictable, and nurturing environment—one that is reliable and consistent. Students like well-managed classes and classrooms because there is no need to enforce rules and the focus is on learning.

Students, especially at-risk students, crave consistency because they come from home environments that lack consistency. In a consistent classroom, students know from day to day how the classes are structured and organized. If they break a pencil point, they know what to do. If they are tardy, or they need help from the teacher, or they must walk down the hall, or they need to transition from one activity to another, they know what to do and how to do it.

This is no different from the reasons why we go to our favorite stores, restaurants, or websites—they are predictable and consistent. Teams that win strive to achieve consistent results. We appreciate people and workers who are consistent.

Effective teachers have classrooms that are structured, organized, and CONSISTENT in how they are run. A consistent classroom is

- predictable,
- reliable,
- dependable, and
- stable.

In a consistent classroom the students know these two things:

1. What to DO because there are **Procedures**
2. What to LEARN because there are **Objectives**

Effective teachers establish classroom management procedures that create consistency. With consistency, effective teachers have classrooms that are calm, caring, thought provoking, challenging, and academically successful. A well-managed classroom is the foundation for learning in the classroom.

Hand in the Work

A student from a school in an at-risk community (these students are actually "at-promise") said, "I like coming to this school because everyone knows what to **DO**. No one yells at us and we can get on with learning."

The student is not talking about behavior, which is addressed in Chapter 17. The student is talking about **DOING**, or getting things done as explained in Chapter 15 and Chapter 16. Summarizing the importance of *doing*, a seventh-grade student said, "I have figured out how to succeed in school. Get the work done!"

Learning takes place when students know what to DO.

Unit C in this book may be the most important one for you to read and implement as you start your first days of school. **Unit C teaches you how to teach students what to DO.**

Effective teachers also have lesson plans with clear lesson objectives that promote student learning. Unit D gives precise guidelines on how to get your students to learn and achieve. **Unit D teaches you how to teach students what to LEARN.**

Effective Teachers Have Contingency Plans

If you watch football, you know that a coach scripts the first ten to twenty plays. As the game progresses, the plan is modified as the opposing coaches play out their respective game plans.

Pilots, too, have flight plans and as their flights progress, the flight paths may be modified based on weather conditions.

Effective teachers have a classroom management plan and from this plan they prepare a first day of school script. As the days progress the teacher stays flexible and has a contingency plan, a Plan B, available should the need arise. But Plan B only works if there is a Plan A.

Many Students Come From Inconsistent Home Environments

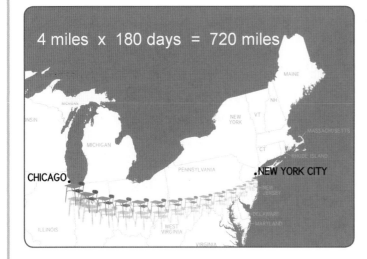

Each day in the United States over 1.5 million kids come to school from a homeless situation.[2]

Each day over 9,000 kids are reported to a public agency as having been abused or neglected.[3]

Each day more than 160,000 students refuse to come to school for fear of being bullied.[4]

Each day 7,000 students drop out of high school.[5] Their empty desks form a line four miles long. Four miles x 180 school days = 720 miles, forming a row of empty desks that would stretch from Chicago to New York City.

[2]StandUp For Kids, www.standupforkids.org.
[3]Child Welfare Information, www.childwelfare.gov.
[4]National Association of School Psychologists, www.nasponline.org.
[5]Alliance for Excellent Education, www.all4ed.org.

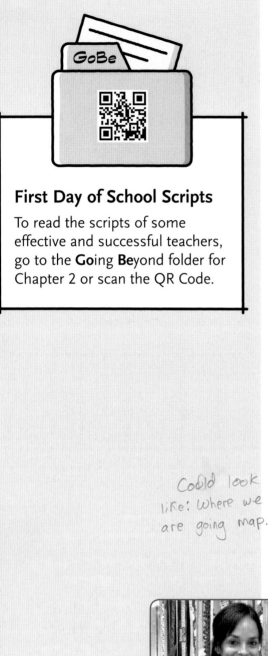

First Day of School Scripts

To read the scripts of some effective and successful teachers, go to the **Go**ing **Be**yond folder for Chapter 2 or scan the QR Code.

Could look like: Where we are going map.

Diana Greenhouse

Script for the First Day of School

Effective teachers have a script ready for the first day of school. As you prepare your room and yourself for this significant day, make preparations for the students who will spend their first day with you. They will arrive with equal amounts of anticipation and anxiety. You can lessen their anxiety and heighten their anticipation (and ease your own nerves at the same time!) with a well-organized and welcoming room.

Your first day of school script will show them that you know what you are doing and what you want to achieve.

Melissa Boone of Texas had a script when she began her first year of teaching in an elementary school. She detailed what she would wear, where she would stand, what she would say, how the room would be arranged, and what the students would do. She was ready. She made her students ready for the year ahead. Today, she is a successful teacher-leader.

John Schmidt was so ready and successful from the beginning that the Homewood-Flossmoor High School district in Illinois began using him as a demonstration teacher in the district's new teacher induction program—after teaching for just two years!

The major reason for having a script or plan is that student achievement is best when students understand what they are to learn. They will perform better when they know what the teacher expects of them. The best strategy to use to improve achievement and prevent problems is being prepared, because being unprepared has consequences.

If you do not structure the classroom, your students will structure the classroom for you.

Diana Greenhouse, a teacher in Texas, says, "What an incredible first year of teaching this has been. When I look back at all I accomplished, it takes my breath away. My students learned and I loved every minute of teaching.

"And it all started with that very first minute of the first day. I started the school year with a PowerPoint presentation of my classroom management plan."

Kazim Cicek

Classroom Management Plans

Diana Greenhouse's and Kazim Cicek's PowerPoint classroom management plans are in the **Go**ing **Be**yond folder for Chapter 2 or scan the QR Code.

Kazim Cicek says he spent his first three years in the teaching profession being a warrior. The students fought him and he fought them. Then, four days before the start of his fourth year—one that he did not want to start—he heard Harry Wong at a summer meeting and had a "light bulb moment." Over a long weekend, he created a PowerPoint presentation of his classroom management plan.

At the end of his fourth year he said, "The wish I wished my students was also given to me. I, too, had a wonderful year."

Today, he is a very happy and successful teacher-leader.

teachers.net

The work of Diana Greenhouse and Kazim Cicek first appeared on the teachers.net website. Since June 2000, we have contributed 150 articles as a monthly column featured in the Gazette hosted on the website.

We have highlighted examples from teachers who have shared their successful implementations of **THE First Days of School: How to Be an Effective Teacher**. The profiles encompass elementary, high school, and special education teachers, fine arts instructors and librarians, and cover a range of subjects including English, science, and technology. College professors have also been featured. There is even a teacher's first-day-of-school script in Spanish.

A cumulative, short summary of all past columns can be found in the June/July 2015 column. Don't hesitate to beg, borrow, and steal from these teachers! Use their ideas to create your own successful classroom.

**Access all of these past columns at
www.iWong2Learn.com.**

This teacher is ready on the first day of school.

Student achievement at the end of the school year
is directly and conclusively related to
the degree to which the teacher implements
classroom procedures
from the beginning of the school year.

There is overwhelming evidence that the first two to three weeks of the school year are critical in determining how well students achieve for the remainder of the year.

You must have everything ready and organized when school begins. **Your success and that of your students throughout the entire school year will be determined by what you do on the first days of school.**

To learn how to successfully implement classroom procedures, see Chapter 15 and Chapter 16.

The Four Stages of Teaching

According to Kevin Ryan of Boston University, there are four stages to teaching.[6] Yet many teachers never progress beyond the second—the Survival stage. The purpose of *THE First Days of School: How to Be an Effective Teacher* is to get you out of stage two and on to the third stage, Mastery, so that you can make an Impact on the lives of your students.

The Four Stages of Teaching

Fantasy ➤ Survival ➤ Mastery ➤ **Impact**

Stage 1: Fantasy. Many neophyte teachers have the naive belief or Fantasy that to be a successful teacher, all they need to do is relate to their students and be their friend. They rarely talk about standards, assessment, or student achievement. Entertaining students with activities is their concept of teaching.

> *Nobody can go back and start a new beginning, but anyone can start today and make a new ending.*
>
> Marie Robinson

[6] Kevin Ryan, *The Induction of New Teachers* (Bloomington, IN: Phi Delta Kappa Educational Foundation, 1986).

Stage 2: Survival. Teachers in the Survival stage have not developed instructional skills as explained in Unit C. They spend their time looking for busywork for students to do, such as completing worksheets, watching videos, and doing seatwork—anything to keep their students quiet. Student learning and achievement are not their goals; they teach because it's a job. The paycheck is their goal. They survive from day to day.

Stage 3: Mastery. Teachers who know how to achieve student success employ effective classroom management and lesson mastery practices. These teachers know how to manage their classrooms with procedures. They teach for Mastery with objectives and assessments, and they have high expectations for their students. Student learning is their mission and student achievement is their goal.

Stage 4: Impact. Effective teachers make a difference in the lives of their students. These are the teachers students return to years later and thank for affecting their lives. A student learns best when the teacher has made an appreciable Impact on the student's life. When a teacher reaches this stage, they have gone beyond Mastery; they have arrived as a teacher.

When you reach the Impact stage, you can then revisit the Fantasy stage and fulfill your dream of making a difference in the lives of your students. You'll also become a teacher-leader, leading and coaching other teachers. You'll live a happier life with a sense of pride and accomplishment, knowing that you are contributing to the profession, the noblest of all professions.

Effective Teachers Impact Lives

E fficient and effective teachers have greater influence and impact on students' lives. You were hired to impact lives. You were hired not so much to teach third grade, or history, or physical education, as to influence lives. Touch the life of a student, and you will have a student who not only wants and strives to learn history, physical education, even science and math, but will also turn cartwheels to please and impress you with their success.

School

School is a powerful place. Students go to school to learn, work, and produce—just like in an adult workplace. School is where students acquire and develop knowledge, skills, and values that will make them productive citizens and help them realize their fullest potential as human beings.

66

The highest stake of all is our ability to help children realize their full potential.

Samuel J. Meisels

99

The Effective Teacher IS the difference.

The beginning of the school year is a critical moment in time.

What you do in the first days of school will determine your success in affecting the lives of your students during the rest of the school year.

What you do in the first days of school will determine your success or failure as a teacher for the rest of the school year.

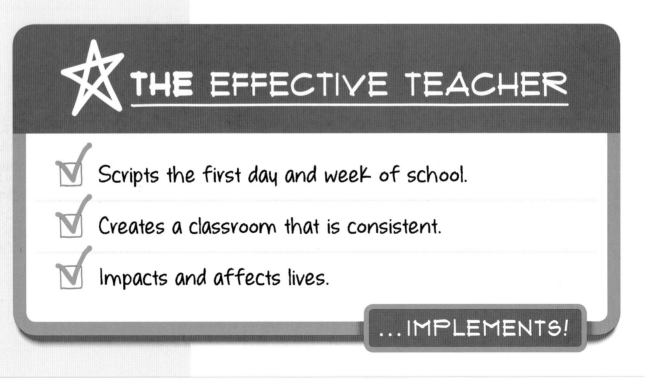

★ THE EFFECTIVE TEACHER

☑ Scripts the first day and week of school.

☑ Creates a classroom that is consistent.

☑ Impacts and affects lives.

...IMPLEMENTS!

Planning for Success

The first year of teaching can be successful for a new teacher. But first the bad news. <u>Sixteen percent</u> of new teachers will not make it beyond their first year of teaching, and <u>fifty percent</u> will not make it beyond their fifth year. Now the good news.

We teach you to plan so that you can plan to teach.

Those with a plan, and who know how to manage a classroom (Unit C) and how to teach for lesson mastery (Unit D) will have a successful and satisfying life as a teacher.

As it says on the cover of this book: **We teach you to plan so that you can plan to teach.** The importance of this statement and the impact it will have on your success cannot be overstated. Planning is critical for a successful start to anything undertaken—in the classroom or in life.

You Will Be Expected to Perform Immediately

When you are a first-year teacher, you are an equal with all the other teachers. You will have the same students they teach; you will teach from the same curriculum; you will have the same administrators; you will have the same duties and responsibilities. Unlike the business world where you start "at the bottom," and work your way up, in education you are on an equal basis with every other teacher in the school on the first day, and every day, of the school year.

You will be immediately expected to perform your full complement of duties while learning them at the same time. You will manage somehow, but you will manage better if your district puts you through an induction program. The most important thing to recognize is that becoming an effective teacher is a never-ending learning process.

Education is not a product; it is a never-ending process. This book provides some insight, ideas, and choices about how to start your first days of school. Note the word, "choices." The quality of the choices you make today will dictate the quality of your opportunities tomorrow. (See page 291.)

☆ THE KEY IDEA

Effective teachers continue to learn and make choices based upon that knowledge.

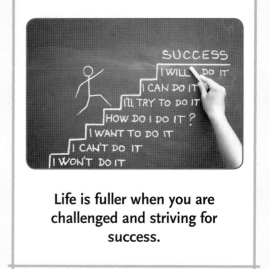

Life is fuller when you are challenged and striving for success.

Don't Be a Pal

Our heart goes out to all the neophyte teachers who want to know their students and be their friend. Be friendly, caring, loving, and sensitive, but do NOT be their friend. They have enough friends of their own.

Students of today need you to be an adult role model they can look up to with admiration and pride. If you become a student's friend, the student will start asking you for favors, as people do of friends. And if a favor is not granted, the student becomes incensed: "I thought you were my friend. I hate you!"

It is better to be a paragon than a pal. ✎

Jessica Ferguson shows the classroom management plan she uses as an eighth-grade language arts teacher in Fort Smith, Arkansas.

The Three Myths That Stifle New Teacher Success

1. **I need a week to get to know my students.**
   The truth: They need to know who you are on day one.

2. **Learning must be fun.**
   The truth: Learning results from lesson targets and objectives.

3. **Students will learn from the technology.**
   The truth: Teachers teach, not the technology.

She Started With a Plan

Jessica Ferguson, after graduating with a teaching degree from Arkansas Tech University, went to her first job interview. She walked in carrying a folder she had made with her classroom management plan. When asked what her strength was, she replied, "Classroom management. Here is a copy of my plan if you would like to review it. I will be happy to answer any questions."

She nailed the interview. The director of human resources called her six hours later to offer her a job. Why? She had a plan, and was hired after her first job interview.

When the first day of school rolled around after what seemed like an eternity, Jessica says, "I reacted just as any first-year teacher would have. I nervously entered the classroom, tried to calm my shaking nerves, and took a brief moment to gaze at my very own classroom. However, I was not nervous for very long.

"I had a plan, and I knew exactly how to implement that plan. The very first day of school, I took time during every class period to set my procedures and rules in place. In fact, I took time the entire first week of school to review the classroom procedures with my students. My students knew exactly what I expected of them. There were no guessing games or hidden surprises for my students. They knew to enter the room quietly and immediately begin bellwork. They knew to throw away their trash at the end of the period. They even knew to wait until I said the magic words, 'Have a good day,' to dismiss the class.

"**Because I immediately implemented my procedures, I quickly gained the respect of my students.** Having procedures set in place relieves the pressure off of me as the teacher. When a student forgets a procedure, all I have to ask is, 'And what is the procedure, please?' There is no hassle, no confusion and, most importantly, there is no arguing. It only takes but a moment to redirect the student.

"**With procedures in place, it is possible for even a first-year teacher to become immediately successful.**"

> Every one of us is both a student and a teacher.
> We are at our best when we
> teach ourselves what we need to learn.

Almost everything we do begins with small steps, such as starting with training wheels on a bicycle, swimming in three feet of water, or practicing at a driving range or putting green. We call this "setting the stage," an idiom for creating the conditions and acquiring the skills needed for achieving competency and mastery.

The first days of school are when the stage is set for the rest of the year. If the first days are carefully planned and successfully implemented, they allow you to accomplish what you envision. As Stephen R. Covey says in his book, *The 7 Habits of Highly Effective People*, "Begin with the end in mind."

This book, **THE First Days of School**, and its companion, **THE Classroom Management Book**, will help you create the plan you need.

She Succeeded With a Plan

When Sarah Jondahl came into teaching, she had a skill set in a classroom **management binder complete with most everything she needed to start successfully.** The binder was compiled as an assignment in her classroom management class at Western Kentucky University. Well over a decade later, she is an even more effective and successful teacher.

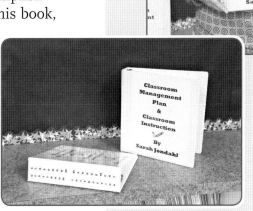

Sarah Jondahl's original classroom management binder has now grown to two binders.

It is Sarah's binders that are the inspiration behind the creation of *THE Classroom Management Book*.

How Colleges Can Help You

Lena Nuccio teaches the classroom management class at the University of New Orleans, where *THE First Days of School* is the required textbook. The required assignment is to create a classroom management plan binder using the principles in the book.

Lena prides herself on making sure that everything her students do in class is something practical they can implement in their classrooms. Students leave her course with a classroom management plan that they can use immediately.

Lena Nuccio requires her students to create Classroom Management Plan Binders to prepare for life in the classroom.

The First Year of Teaching Is the Most Crucial

New teachers feel
isolated,
vulnerable, and
deeply concerned with how
   they will be perceived, yet they are
hesitant to ask for help.

They are hired,
given a key,
told which room is theirs, and
left to their own devices.

They are given the most difficult assignments.
They feel anxious.
They feel inadequate.
They are given little support.
They need someone to give them hope,
   someone to tell them that the initial hardship will eventually end.

How Principals Can Help You

Karen Whitney

Karen Whitney was principal of a challenging school in South Dakota. Yet teachers found it a pleasure to work there, just as students enjoyed coming to school. This was because she and the staff created a school environment that was consistent. Students who come from chaotic and inconsistent homes need and crave a school that is safe, organized, predictable, and productive.

Karen taught all of her teachers, including every new teacher, how to make each day of the year flow consistently, from the first day of school onwards. Her school-wide classroom management plan is detailed in Chapter 16.

Karen also taught teachers how to create an instructional plan with consistent lesson objectives. This is detailed in Chapter 21.

Just think how much easier teaching would be for a new teacher, and every teacher, when students each day experience a well-managed plan and everyone knows what to do. That is when teaching is a pleasure and learning flourishes.

The District Can Help You

Attention: **If you are a new teacher looking for a teaching job, you need to ask if the district has an induction program.** This entails more than simply giving you a mentor. Districts with comprehensive induction programs care that you succeed. Please do not be so foolish as to think that you can succeed on your own without help.

In teaching, entry into the profession can be sudden. In some schools, new teachers are merely given a key to a room and told to go teach. They are left to

- figure it out themselves,
- do it themselves, and
- keep it to themselves.

No Chaos and No Conflict

Tammy Meyer teaches at a school that can be challenging. One day, she hosted a pre-service teacher. He was told to observe and become involved in everything in the classroom.

The next time he came to visit, she asked him, "So, what do you think of this business of teaching?" He said, "It wasn't what I expected. When I was in middle school, there was chaos and conflict every day. I didn't see any of that here."

Tammy said, "That's because we have procedures, and everyone knows what to do, when to do it, and how to do things for learning." It was the perfect learning experience for a pre-service teacher.

Ten Questions to Ask

When you interview for a job, there are ten questions you need to ask. These can be found in the **Go**ing **Be**yond folder for Chapter 3 or scan the QR Code.

Ten Questions to Ask

What will really prepare you for teaching in your district is an organized, new teacher induction program. Induction is a structured, multi-year program that will train and support you as you become an effective teacher. To learn more about induction, read many of the articles at www.iWong2Learn.com. Also, read our book, *New Teacher Induction: How to Train, Support, and Retain New Teachers.*[1]

Do not sign a contract until you ask if the district has a new teacher induction program. Effective districts want to help their teachers succeed. They offer induction programs that begin before the first day of school and may extend for several years thereafter. Induction is more than orientation, mentoring, or evaluation. It's the training a district gives to bring out the teacher you are meant to be.

The Flowing Wells Unified School District in Tucson, Arizona, is one of the best school districts in the United States. They have produced more teacher-of-the-year nominees and winners than any other district in Arizona. **This is because they have an induction program that trains every new teacher and administrator for three to eight years in how to become an expert teacher.**

Flowing Wells Institute for Teacher Renewal & Growth

fo•cus (fō′ kəs) *noun.* 1. Close attention. 2. State of maximum clarity.

verb. 1. To concentrate attention. 2. To adjust one's vision.

A page from the Flowing Wells program shows the inductees that their time will be spent on very targeted instruction.

Students do not learn from programs, technology, or ideologies. **Students learn from how well teachers teach. Thus, the emphasis of the Flowing Wells professional learning program is on instruction.** The Flowing Wells induction program begins with three days devoted to effective instructional practices.

The only way to improve student learning is to improve teacher instructional practice. Good instruction is fifteen to twenty times more powerful than family background, income, race, gender, and other explanatory variables.[2]

[1]Annette Breaux and Harry K. Wong, *New Teacher Induction: How to Train, Support, and Retain New Teachers* (Mountain View, CA: Harry K. Wong Publications, 2003).

[2]Theodore Hershberg, "Value-Added Assessment and Systemic Reform: A Response to the Challenges of Human Capital Development," *Phi Delta Kappan*, vol. 87, no. 4 (December 2005): 276–283.

The fourth day of the induction week is focused on classroom management, but the new teachers are not simply taught about the principles of classroom management. They are asked to read the chapters on procedures in *THE First Days of School*, and then they are taken to visit demonstration classrooms to observe how master teachers teach procedures on their first day.

Wow!

This is coordinated in advance by hiring four or five master teachers (from varied grade levels and content areas) who are asked to get their classrooms ready early. Then they actually simulate a first day of school, with the new teachers acting as their "students." The master teachers then debrief and explain how the first day of school and every day thereafter should be organized.

This demonstration is especially powerful because it helps new teachers understand how to create the organizational procedures for their own first day of school.

During the three- to eight-year induction process, all new teachers are part of a lifelong professional learning program with more than thirty different courses offered, all with follow-up observation and coaching.

See Chapter 23 for more information on Flowing Wells and how they are creating very effective teachers.

Learning Is Ongoing

Our induction program helped me have a very successful first year. Thanks to my administrator, the staff developer, and the book **THE First Days of School***, my days have been very exciting and worthwhile. I have continued to use the tools provided in the induction program and the book to help me achieve success with my students each new year.*

Jaime Diaz
Tucson, Arizona

Some school districts have model classrooms that are prepared before the first day of school. Induction program teachers visit these classrooms to experience how a classroom can be organized for the start of school.

If your district and school do not have an induction program, work with your colleagues or find an instructional coach to help you create a classroom management plan of your own.

Every Business Trains

Have you ever wondered why seemingly problem students do so well when they work at a local store or fast-food restaurant? It's because they have sophisticated training programs to prepare workers before they face the public.

In the business world, new employees receive comprehensive training from day one, allowing them to gradually gain knowledge, experience, and responsibility. Go behind the scenes at any place of business and you will see workers reviewing training videos, reading instruction manuals, getting hands-on training, and learning various aspects of their jobs. **Effective districts and schools have training or comprehensive induction programs for all newly hired teachers.**

Training is standard for most professions.

The only reform effort that clearly resulted in student achievement gains had clear instructional expectations, supported by extensive professional development, over a period of several years.[3]

C. T. Cross and D. W. Rigden

GoBe

The Moberly Induction Program

Effective school districts have a culture where they consistently and continuously invest in teacher effectiveness. Read how a small, rural school district does this in the **Go**ing **Be**yond folder for Chapter 3 or scan the QR Code.

[3]C. T. Cross and D. W. Rigden, "Improving teacher quality," *American School Board Journal*, vol. 189, no. 4 (April 2002): 24–27.

Your Colleagues Can Help You

So, what do you do if your university did not have a classroom management class, your district does not have an induction program, and your principal says, "Oh, you'll figure it out"?

There is one more major resource for you to use to create your classroom management plan: your colleagues.

The biggest secret to teaching success is to Beg, Borrow, and Steal.

It's not really stealing. It's really research and learning. There are many effective teachers at your school. Walk into their classrooms and look around. If you see something that you think might help you, say, "Gimme, gimme, gimme." Most veteran teachers will be happy to share and help.

In schools, we are part of a community of equals, not a community of experts or competitors. We share common goals and aspirations, the most important being student learning. Don't be afraid to ask and learn. If you want positive results for yourself and your students, know that your colleagues are your best resource.

There are no pat answers in education, no simple solutions, no quick fixes, no sure model, no foolproof methods. Teachers who become effective do so because they make teaching a profession and not a job. **They continue to learn, and from their fund of knowledge, they make choices for their classrooms and for their professional life.**

Your first day of teaching will be an exciting, anticipated event, but very daunting at the same time. **You can succeed if you learn how to be effective on the first days of school.**

And after the efforts on the first days of school, you will have the rest of the school year and the rest of your professional years ahead to truly enjoy life as a happy, successful, and exciting teacher.

Inside every great teacher there is an even better one waiting to come out.

Some districts have positive learning communities where new teachers fit in seamlessly.

Don't be afraid to learn.
Knowledge is weightless, a treasure you can always carry easily.

dreams don't WORK unless you do

Dreams

Hold fast to dreams
For if dreams die
Life is a broken-winged bird
That cannot fly.

Hold fast to dreams
For when dreams go
Life is a barren field
Frozen with snow.[4]

Langston Hughes

[4]Langston Hughes, *The Collected Poems of Langston Hughes*, ed. Arnold Rampersad (New York: Alfred A. Knopf, 2004).

★ THE EFFECTIVE TEACHER

☑ Has a goal of teaching for effectiveness.

☑ Participates and contributes in an induction program.

☑ Goes to professional meetings to learn.

☑ Works cooperatively and learns from colleagues.

...IMPLEMENTS!

The Importance of Effective Teachers

The single largest factor in improving the educational outcome of a student is the effectiveness of that student's teacher. Knowing this, this statement seems obvious: **The best way to close the student achievement gap is to close the teacher effectiveness gap.**

The greatest asset of a school is its people.

The education researcher and theorist John Goodlad analyzed forty years of educational innovations while he was at UCLA. He could not find a single innovation that substantially increased student achievement. **He discovered that the only factor that substantially increases student achievement is the effectiveness of a dedicated teacher.**

Hundreds of studies and decades of research have confirmed Goodlad's findings. An effective teacher working with an effective principal can create a school culture that promotes student learning and achievement. **We have known for decades that teacher effectiveness is directly proportional to student success.** Then why isn't it the driving force in decision making by all levels of policy makers? What's the problem?

THE KEY IDEA

The single greatest effect on student achievement is the effectiveness of the teacher.

An effective teacher is the most reliable means for increasing student achievement.

No Focus on Student Learning

Michael Fullan, Ontario Institute for Studies in Education, found that "Education in the United States has fallen from first to twenty-seventh place because they delve into 'ad hoc' programs."[1]

Linda Darling-Hammond, Stanford University, says, "In the United States, we pour energy into a potpourri of innovations and then change course every few years."[2]

Marc S. Tucker, Harvard University, determined that, "The United States constantly makes program and structural changes with no focus on student learning."[3]

The quality of a school cannot exceed the quality of its teachers. Closing the achievement gap will never be realized as long as educators keep flitting from one piecemeal change to another with no focus on student learning.

Only teachers and their <u>instructional practices</u> will improve student learning.

Good teachers, effective teachers, matter much more than particular curriculum materials, pedagogical approaches, or programs.

---

[1] Michael Fullan, *Change Leader: Learning to Do What Matters Most* (San Francisco, CA: Jossey-Bass, A Wiley Imprint, 2011).

[2] Linda Darling-Hammond, "What we can learn from Finland's successful school reform," *NEA Today* (October/November 2010).

[3] Marc S. Tucker, ed., *Surpassing Shanghai: An Agenda for American Education Built on the World's Leading Systems* (Cambridge, MA: Harvard Education Press, 2011).

Instead of training teachers to become more effective, school leaders and policy makers have spent the past seventy-five years and billions of dollars jumping from one program, fad, or ideology to another, hoping that a magic, silver bullet to improve student learning and achievement will suddenly appear.

People Are the Greatest Asset

An asset is a valuable and useful thing, person, or quality. Businesses know that their greatest assets are their employees and they spend more than sixty billion dollars each year training them to make them more and more valuable to a company.

The greatest asset of a school is its people.

Well-trained, dedicated administrators, teachers, librarians, nurses, counselors, and all the other non-certified people are a school's greatest asset.

We know that the effective teacher trumps all other educational resources when it comes to student achievement. What the teacher knows and can do is the most significant factor in student achievement. **The more effective the teacher, the more successful the students.**

> Close the teacher gap and
> you close the achievement gap.

Effective teachers build lessons so students can experience success.

How to Close the Achievement Gap

The achievement gap facing poor and minority students is not due to poverty or family conditions, but to systematic differences in teacher effectiveness. A student who is taught by an ineffective teacher for two years in a row can never recover the learning lost during those years. As a teacher's effectiveness increases, the first students to benefit from this improvement are those from lower-achieving groups.

These are some observations on the importance of effective teaching.

- Good teachers improve student achievement, earnings, and quality of life.[4]

- The most effective teachers produce as much as six times the learning gains as the least effective teachers.[5] (See Teacher Quality and Growth graph.)

- Teacher expertise accounts for more difference in student performance—40 percent—than any other factor.[6]

- Students who have several effective teachers in a row make dramatic achievement gains, while those who have even two ineffective teachers in a row lose significant ground.[7]

- Differences in teacher quality account for more than 90 percent of the variation in student achievement.[8]

- The single greatest effect on student achievement is not race, not poverty—it is the effectiveness of the teacher.[9]

- As teacher effectiveness increases, lower-achieving students are the first to benefit.[10]

The ineffective teacher affects little, if any, growth in students. **The effective teacher**, even in an ineffective school, produces improved student learning and increased student achievement.

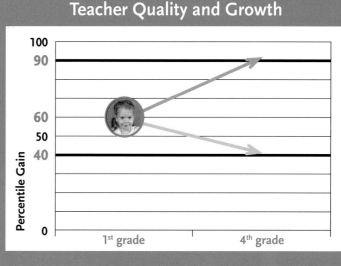

Teacher Quality and Growth

[4] Rachel Sheffield, "Harvard Study: Good Teachers Improve Student Achievement, Earnings, Quality of Life," *Heartlander Magazine* (January 28, 2012).

[5] B. Rowan, R. Correnti, and R. Miller, "What Large-Scale Survey Research Tells Us About Teacher Effects on Student Achievement," *Teachers College Record*, vol. 104, no. 8 (2002): 1525–1567.

[6] National Commission on Teaching and America's Future, prepared by Linda Darling-Hammond, *Doing What Matters Most: Investing in Quality Teaching* (NACTAF, Washington, DC, November 1997): 8.

[7] Joetta Sack, "Class Size, Teacher Quality Take Center Stage at Hearing," *Education Week*, vol. 18, no. 34 (May 5, 1999): 22.

[8] National Commission on Teaching and America's Future, *Doing What Matters Most: Investing in Quality Teaching*: 9.

[9] June C. Rivers and William L. Sanders, "Teacher Quality and Equity in Educational Opportunity: Findings and Policy Implications" (presented at the Hoover/PRI Teacher Quality Conference, Stanford University, May 12, 2000).

[10] William L. Sanders and June C. Rivers, "Cumulative and Residual Effects of Teachers on Future Academic Achievement" (University of Tennessee Value-Added Research and Assessment Center, November 1996): 7.

School and Teacher Effectiveness Impact on Learning on Student at 50th Percentile	
School and Teacher	**Percentile After Two Years**
Ineffective school and Ineffective teacher	3rd
Effective school and Ineffective teacher	37th
Average school and Average teacher	50th
Ineffective school and Effective teacher	63rd
Effective school and Average teacher	78th
Effective school and Effective teacher	96th

The international evidence tells us that the most effective policy in raising standards is the rather boring long-term one of raising the quality of teaching and learning.[13]

Adrian Perry
University of Sheffield,
United Kingdom

[11] Robert Marzano, *What Works in Schools* (Arlington, VA: Association for Supervision and Curriculum Development, 2003).

[12] Kenneth Leithwood, Karen Seashore Louis, Stephen Anderson, and Kyla Wahlstrom, *How Leadership Influences Student Learning* (Center for Applied Research and Educational Improvement, University of Minnesota; Ontario Institute for Studies in Education, University of Toronto; The Wallace Foundation, September 2004).

[13] Adrian Perry, Christian Amadeo, Mick Fletcher, and Elizabeth Walker, "Instinct or Reason: How education policy is made and how we might make it better" (UK: CfBT Education Trust Perspective Report, 2010).

Imagine your child is at the 50th percentile and you place your child in one of the following situations. After two years, Robert Marzano's research[11] says this:

- If the student has an **ineffective teacher** in an **ineffective school**, student achievement **will drop** from the 50th percentile to the 3rd percentile.

- If the student has an **ineffective teacher** in an **effective school, student achievement will still drop** to the 37th percentile.

- However, if your child has an **effective teacher** in an **ineffective school**, student achievement will rise to the 63rd percentile.

It's the Teacher

It bears repeating. It's the teacher. It's the teacher. It's the teacher. Hall of Fame football coach Joe Gibbs says to this point, "You win with people." Translated for schools, "You win with teachers." Programs, ideologies, or structural changes do not increase student achievement. **An effective teacher increases student achievement.**

It's the Principal

Extensive research and observation have shown that principal leadership is second only to classroom instruction among all school-related factors that contribute to student learning.

Researchers from the Universities of Minnesota and Toronto conducted a large-scale study of school leadership in 2004 and found that there are virtually no documented instances of troubled schools being turned around without intervention by an effective leader.[12]

If a school leader is constantly trying new programs or has not established a stable culture with clear priorities, teachers won't know what to do and the teaching experience can be frustratingly restrictive. Whereas in a school with a culture that consistently emphasizes student learning and achievement, **teachers are able to be innovative planners, exceptional classroom managers, adept critical thinkers, and competent problem-solvers.**

Individual teachers may be able to manage change in their own classrooms, but effective, school-wide reform is impossible without effective principals.

The secret to the success of a school is CONSISTENCY.

When teachers know the principal is consistent, people on the instructional teams experience tremendous freedom and trust to excel.

Every Profession Has a SKILL SET

Every profession requires specialized skills, referred to as a **SKILL SET.** Doctors, cabinet makers, movie animators, and school bus drivers possess distinctive skill sets. Effective administrators and schools of education teach their teachers the skill set needed to achieve student learning and success. Ineffective administrators and schools of education run around looking for programs or ideologies that will supersede what teachers are potentially capable of doing.

The purpose of this book is to provide you with a skill set to manage a classroom and teach lessons successfully.

Effective teachers and principals plan to create consistency by creating a skill set in three areas:

1. **They practice positive expectations.** Because students know what to do (the procedures) and what to learn (the objectives), it is easy to reinforce positive expectations and drive students to greater potential. **The students "know how to SUCCEED."** This is Unit B.

2. **They manage with procedures. There is a set of schoolwide procedures that governs how the school is run.** This is why the hallways are clear; the students are at work; and people are happily collaborating and contributing. **The students "know what to DO."** This is Unit C.

3. **They use a common lesson plan format.** With consistent lesson format from room to room, students know what to achieve and how to improve their learning. **The students "know what to LEARN."** This is Unit D.

Success in a profession requires executing the specific skill set of the profession at an effective level.

More can be done to improve education by improving the effectiveness of teachers than by any other single factor.[14]

Wright, Horn, and Sanders

[14] S. Paul Wright, Sandra P. Horn, and William L. Sanders, "Teacher and Classroom Context Effects on Student Achievement: Implications for Teacher Evaluation," *Journal of Personnel Evaluation in Education*, vol. 11 (1997): 57–67.

Successful Teachers Come in All Subjects and Grade Levels

Effective teaching practices work in all classrooms, from K–16. There is nothing in *THE First Days of School* about how to teach a certain subject. The teachers in these examples have adapted the book's techniques and principles and put them into practice in their classrooms to become very effective teachers.

Robin Barlak: Preschool Special Education Teacher. Robin adapts procedures so her students can experience success. She makes learning enjoyable for teachers, classroom assistants, therapists, students, and parents.

Kristen Wiss: Kindergarten Teacher. Kristen teaches procedures until all students know what to do. She uses posters to remind them of the steps and then teaches how to be responsible for following through. She can have four groups doing different things all at once, and every student knows what to do.

Katie Weber: Elementary School Teacher. Katie stands at the door and welcomes her students each morning. They can choose a hug, a handshake, or a high-five slap. While Katie is greeting students, they know the procedures for getting ready for the day and they start them without Katie's presence in the room.

Sarah Jondahl: Elementary School Teacher. Sarah began teaching on her first day of school with a classroom management plan binder. It has grown to two binders. She's organized for student success. Students love her and so do parents.

Tiffany Landrum: Elementary School Teacher. Tiffany lists the learning objectives of the day on the board and reviews them at the start of class. The expectations for learning are set before the lessons begin so students can focus on what they need to do to succeed.

Cristina Bianchi: Middle School Teacher. Cristina taught and then left for maternity leave. When she returned, she simply had the class practice some of the procedures to reestablish them, and the class sailed along as if she had never been away. She credits her success to spending time building a solid classroom foundation with an organized structure.

Jeff Gulle: Middle and High School Teacher. Jeff has an agenda posted before the students enter the classroom. By looking at the agenda, students know the objectives of the lesson, the flow of the instructional activities, and how to get started with learning before the lesson begins.

Alicia Blankenship: High School ESL Teacher. Alicia tapes a chart of recurring procedures students need to be successful in the classroom on their desks. She teaches multiple periods each day, and using this technique saves her valuable instructional time. Anyone who assists in the classroom can readily see the charts and know procedures and expectations.

Chelonnda Seroyer: High School English Teacher. Chelonnda was successful the moment her first student walked into her very first classroom. She had an assignment ready and posted for her students, and her students got to work.

Karen Rogers: High School Science Teacher. Karen shows her procedures with a PowerPoint presentation. She uses scoring guides so her students and their parents know what needs to be done to achieve.

Noah Roseman: High School Spanish Teacher. Noah has an agenda written out on the chalkboard to guide his students through the progression of learning. Even though it is written in Spanish, his students all know what to do.

Elecia Lathon: College Instructor. Elecia's mother was a teacher and told her there was no elevator to success, one had to take the stairs. All students in her Classroom Management class are required to create a plan—the stairs to their success.

Stories of Successful Teachers

The complete story for each of these teachers can be found in the **Go**ing **Be**yond folder for Chapter 4 or scan the QR Code.

Thus, the effective teacher in an effective school will have two things:

1. A set of organized procedures
2. A consistent lesson plan format

How Students Learn Best

The Grattan Institute,[15] an Australian think tank, studied four of the world's five top performing school systems. These schools were in Hong Kong, Shanghai, Korea, and Singapore. It found these facts to be true:

- **They DO NOT rely on special facilities, advanced technology, high levels of financing, or new curricula.**

- **They DO rely on teacher groups that continuously conduct research on how to produce lessons that result in higher levels of learning.**

Researchers found that processes are in place where teachers continually meet to develop effective lessons. Students learn from the lessons that teachers develop, and the best lessons are developed by teachers who create, dissect, assess, and evaluate a lesson as a group. The group watches the lesson being taught and, in the debriefing, the group discusses the lesson, not the teacher.

The teachers and students in the top performing schools are no better than the teachers and students in the United States or anywhere else. The difference is that American educators jump from program to program, new technologies, fad to fad, government initiative to initiative. **Students learn from lessons; they do not learn from programs, technology, and fads.**

In top performing schools, the teachers simply focus on continually improving lessons. They call this creative procedure "lesson research" or "lesson study," and it is described in Chapter 23.

Teachers Want Solutions

Programs do not produce achievement; teachers produce student achievement. Money is much better spent training and developing teachers than in buying one

> *To improve student learning, do not change the school structure. Change the instructional practice to focus on learning.*[16]
>
> Richard Elmore
> Harvard Graduate School of Education

[15] B. Jensen, A. Hunter, J. Sonnemann, and T. Burns, *Catching up: Learning from the best school systems in East Asia* (Melbourne, AU: Grattan Institute, Report no. 2012–13, February 2012).

[16] Richard F. Elmore, "Why Restructuring Alone Won't Improve Teaching," *Educational Leadership*, vol. 49, no. 7 (April 1992): 44–48.

Teaching Is Most Important

Teaching is the most important school-based factor influencing student performance.[17]

program after another. Educational leaders know that what matters is whether schools can offer their neediest students good teachers trained in effective strategies to teach strong academic knowledge and skills.

The effective teacher is a creative teacher, one who can think, reflect, and implement. **Effective teachers steal from the best and learn from the rest.** They look at the resources available to them and reorganize those resources to work towards a goal.

Teachers do not want programs; they want solutions.

At a Fraction of the Cost

Learning must be the preeminent focus of a school and every practice in a school must be focused on its impact on student learning. A district's priority should be to create schools with a cadre of effective teachers, who, in turn, know how to research and create lessons that are more effective.

This is the major difference between successful and unsuccessful schools:

- **Unsuccessful schools stress programs.** They spend millions of dollars adopting programs and bandwagon fads in constant pursuit of the quick fix.

- **Successful schools stress effective practices.** They wisely invest in their teachers and the effectiveness of their teachers. They don't teach programs; they teach effective teaching practices to their teachers.

At a fraction of the cost, the student achievement gap can be closed by spending money on training and developing teachers rather than adopting one program or fad after another.

**Again, close the teacher gap
and you close the achievement gap.**

---

[17] S. Rivkin, E. Hanushek, and J. Kain, "Teachers, Schools, and Academic Achievement," *Econometrica*, vol. 73, no. 2 (2005): 417–458.

That Noble Title *Teacher*

As we begin each new school year, let us remember the fine nuances and the distinguishing essence of that proud word Teacher.

Let us be reminded of the tools you have at your command, because of your talents, your traits, and your training . . . and because you chose to become a Teacher.

Teacher—you are a poet, as you weave with your colorful magic language a passion for your subject. You create a vast and grand mosaic of curiosities to imagine, secrets to unfold, connections only to begin the cycle of learning.

Teacher—you are a physicist, as you bring magic, logic, reason, and wonder to the properties, changes, and interactions of our universe.

Teacher—you are a maestro, a master of composing, as you conduct and orchestrate individuals' thoughts and actions from discordant cacophony into harmonic resonance.

Teacher—you are an architect, as you provide each student a solid foundation, but always with a vision of the magnificent structure that is about to emerge.

Teacher—you are a gymnast, as you encourage the contortions and gyrations of thoughts and the flexing and strengthening of ideas.

Teacher—you are a diplomat and the ambassador of tact and sensitivity, as you facilitate productive, positive interactions among the multiplicity of personalities and cultures, beliefs, and ideals.

Teacher—you are a philosopher, as your actions and ethics convey meaning and hope to young people who look to you for guidance and example. As you prepare for your first day and each day, when your students enter and you encounter their attitudes, ranging from eager, enthusiastic anticipation to uncomfortable, uncertain apathy, recall the powers you have within . . . from poet to philosopher . . . and present yourself to those students as a person worthy of the noble title . . . Teacher.

Trish Marcuzzo
Omaha Public Schools

This essay is available as a color poster at
www.EffectiveTeaching.com.

⭐ THE EFFECTIVE TEACHER

☑ Focuses on effective practices that improve student achievement.

☑ Is an innovative planner who knows how to research and create effective lessons.

☑ Works collaboratively as an adept critical thinker and competent problem-solver.

☑ Is the epitome of the greatest asset of a school.

...IMPLEMENTS!

The Research Process

Research is a process of critical thinking, experimentation, and problem solving. It is the ability to analyze, examine, and question in order to find the best processes and procedures in any endeavor. Research is simply the use of the human mind to search for and seek answers, or as some would say, to find the "truth."

Many teachers know what to do and how to do it, but effective teachers know WHY it is being done.

Research is what a person does to find answers. The reason for research is to discover why things happen and how they can be improved. **Thus, people who know what to do and people who know how to do it will always be working for those who know why it is being done.**

Steps in the Research Process

Problem: What do I want to know?

Prediction: What do I think is the right answer?

Procedure: How will I solve the problem?

Data: What will I look for?

Conclusion: What do the results tell me?

Effective teachers use research to improve their effectiveness.

When you change a recipe, you are doing research.

Why It May Be Dangerous to Teach as You Were Taught

There is overwhelming research on how to improve student learning and achievement (page 45). Unfortunately and erroneously, many teachers do not ask why they are teaching in the manner they are teaching.

Far too many teachers teach as their academic college professors taught them, sitting in a lecture hall, thinking that's the way to teach. No education professor, administrator, staff developer, or teacher at a workshop has ever said that the model of teaching presented in the box is the way to teach. Yet, many teachers think this is teaching.

> ### This Model of Teaching Has NO Research to Support It
>
> - **Assign chapters to read.**
> - **Answer the questions at the back of the chapter or on the worksheet.**
> - **Deliver a lecture and have students take notes.**
> - **Show a video or do an activity.**
> - **Construct a test based on a number of points.**
> - **Control the distribution of grades.**

Regrettably, many teachers also succumb to teaching according to the latest program, fad, or political agenda. They jump from one program or fad to another, never asking for the why or research evidence of its effectiveness. These programs and fads change with every new political and educational administration.

In 1991, Ron Ferguson at the Harvard Graduate School of Education stated, "A large scale study found that every additional dollar spent on raising teacher quality will net a greater gain in student achievement gains than (in chasing after) any other use of school resources."[1]

In 1998, after spending $500 million in research, the Annenberg Foundation reported:

> **The only factor that positively impacted student achievement was when money was invested in providing teachers with sustained opportunities to improve their classroom skills.**[2]

Programs and ideologies do not produce student achievement. Teachers produce student achievement. Teaching is a profession, and like all professions, its

Chasing After the Silver Bullet

For well over seventy-five years, American education has spent billions of dollars chasing after one program, scheme, or fad. To see this list, go to the **Go**ing **Be**yond folder for Chapter 5 or scan the QR Code.

---

[1] Ronald F. Ferguson, "Paying for Public Education: New Evidence on How and Why Money Matters," *Harvard Journal of Legislation* 28 (Summer 1991): 465–98.

[2] *The Annenberg Challenge: Lessons and Reflections on Public School Reform* (Annenberg Foundation, March 2002): 39–41.

Why Educational Research Applies to Every Teacher

John P. Rickards from the University of Connecticut discovered two things:[3]

1. The most ineffective place to print questions is at the end of a textbook chapter.

2. It is ineffective to give a student all the questions for an assignment at one time, and then ask the student to answer all the questions and to turn them in all at one time.

steal.

Rickards found that if you want a student to achieve high-level comprehension, you should intersperse the questions throughout the text or the assignment. You do this to constantly assess the learning success of the students.

You know that this is true from having taken reading comprehension tests. Reading comprehension tests are not written with pages of text, followed by a long list of questions. They constantly go back and forth, a paragraph or two of text followed by a few questions.

Put another way, no doctor asks questions when the patient is dead or unconscious. A doctor intersperses questions during the treatment of a patient, constantly assessing the health of the patient.

Likewise, the effective teacher does not ask all the questions at the end of the discussion, class period, video, chapter, lecture, or meeting.

The effective teacher who wants high-level comprehension intersperses questions throughout all class activities. This is what the research tells us.

Why Do Effective Teachers Scatter Questions During a Video?

Educational research tells you why.

Bob Wallace, a middle school teacher in New Jersey, reported the following as a result of his research with his students.

He divided his students into three groups and did the following:

Group 1: He showed the students a video and gave them a test.

Group 2: He briefed the group on the video to be shown and then showed the same video shown to Group 1 and gave the same test.

Group 3: He briefed Group 3 exactly as he had Group 2 and then showed the same video. However, during the video, he stopped the show frequently. During each stop, he asked questions and held class discussion. He then gave the same test he had given to Groups 1 and 2.

Guess which of the three groups scored the highest on the test? Group 3, of course.

She Stopped the Video Frequently

Stacey Allred taught a video-guided workshop on **THE First Days of School**. She used "Aha" pages to reflect on the video. To see her work confirming the research findings on questioning, go to the **Go**ing **Be**yond folder for Chapter 5 or scan the QR Code.

---

[3] John P. Rickards, "Stimulating High-Level Comprehension by Interspersing Questions in Text Passages," *Educational Technology*, vol. 16, no. 11 (November 1976): 13.

members must continuously learn new knowledge and skills. A dedicated, professional teacher will still be "learning to do it better" the day she or he retires.

- Ineffective teachers look for programs that will teach for them or talk more about the gimmicks and games they find to "keep the kids quiet."

- Effective teachers talk more about the research they constantly conduct to improve the achievement of their students. (See Chapter 21.)

The teachers who see themselves as learners are best able to lead a shift toward a culture of learning in the school. **It's teachers who research and analyze, and share their insights and discoveries with their colleagues, who improve student learning and achievement.**

How Students Achieve

We know how to improve student achievement and there is overwhelming research that tells us how.

John Hattie

The most significant research on student learning and achievement has been done by John Hattie, formerly at the University of Auckland in New Zealand and now at the University of Melbourne in Australia. He is the author of *Visible Learning: A Synthesis of Over 800 Meta-Analyses Relating to Achievement*. His work of over twenty years, and still continuing, involved looking at achievement results from 1,200 meta-analyses, 65,000 studies, and 250 million students.[4]

He found that among the many strategies or techniques a teacher uses, some are more effective than others. He identified effective teaching practices and ranked them from what works best to what works least. He gave each practice an "effect size," meaning how great the effect is on learning that is visible.

What doesn't work includes class size, retention, school type, and in his words, "misguided focus on national testing."

VISIBLE LEARNING:
A SYNTHESIS OF OVER
800 META-ANALYSES
IN EDUCATION

JOHN HATTIE

---

[4]John Hattie, *Visible Learning: A Synthesis of Over 800 Meta-Analyses Relating to Achievement*, (New York: Routledge, 2009).

⌐ The major effect that does work is "feedback."
Effective educators know it as "checking for
understanding" and then reteaching until the
student learns the objective of the lesson. ⌐

Hattie said, "Students should be able to visibly see the
intention of each lesson (objectives) and how to know
(rubric) if they were successful." Student success comes
from feedback, but a teacher can only give feedback if a
lesson has a set of objectives and a rubric to form the basis
for feedback. This concept is explained in Chapter 19.

These are some of the research findings in *Visible Learning*:

- Simply tell students what they will be learning
  (objectives) before the lesson begins and student
  achievement can be raised as much as 27 percent.

  Remember this

- Additionally, provide students with specific feedback
  (rubric) about their progress and achievement can be
  raised as much as 37 percent.

> When you acknowledge and
> accept that, as a teacher,
> you make a difference,
> you dignify yourself
> and the teaching profession.

Tell the students what they are going to learn and how
you will access their learning, to help them succeed.

Effective teachers do what research
discovers is most effective.

Effective teachers use proven,
research-based practices.

Why would you do otherwise?

The Four Beliefs of an Effective Teacher

1. It is the teacher who makes the difference in the classroom.

2. By far the most important factor in school learning is the ability of the teacher.

3. There is an extensive body of research and knowledge about teaching that must be known by the teacher.

4. The teacher must be a decision maker able to translate the research and body of knowledge about teaching into increased student learning.

After Madeline Hunter

Research on Improving Student Achievement[5]

Aligned time on task:
Students who are actively focused on educational goals do best in mastering the subject matter.

> Research findings: More than one hundred and thirty studies have supported that the lesson objectives, learning activities, assessment rubrics, and tests must be correlated and emphasized. When this is done, students will be engaged in their learning. (To see how this is implemented, refer to Chapter 18 and Chapter 19.)

Learning community:
People in small research groups can support and increase one another's learning.

> Research findings: New teachers, and all teachers, need access to good leadership and good colleagues. Peer learning among small groups of teachers is the most powerful predictor of improved student achievement over time. (To see how learning teams are implemented, consult Chapter 21.)

Professional development:
Professional development is the only strategy school districts have to strengthen the effectiveness of their teachers and principals. Professional development is also the only way teachers and principals can learn so that they are able to improve their effectiveness.

> Research findings: The only reform effort that clearly resulted in student achievement gains had clear instructional expectations, supported by extensive professional development, over a period of several years. (To see an example of an exemplary professional development program, see Chapter 23.)

Wait time:
Pausing after asking a question in the classroom results in an increase in achievement.

> Research findings: Students are usually given less than one second to respond to a question. Following a question, particularly a high-order question, increasing wait time to three to seven seconds results in students responding with more thoughtful answers and an increase in achievement.

Improving achievement is no great mystery; nor is it an impossible task. The major principles of effective teaching are in the *Handbook of Research on Improving Student Achievement*. The research for the handbook was sponsored by twenty-nine leading education organizations serving three million members. You'll learn how to apply this research in Unit C and Unit D.

Gordon Cawelti (ed.)

---

[5] Gordon Cawelti, ed., *Handbook of Research on Improving Student Achievement* (Bethesda, MD: Editorial Projects in Education, 2004).

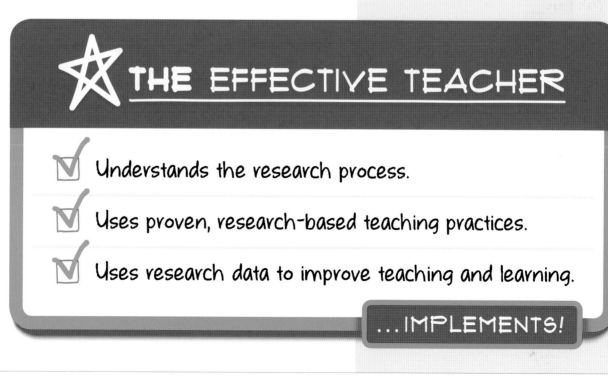

⭐ THE EFFECTIVE TEACHER

☑ Understands the research process.

☑ Uses proven, research-based teaching practices.

☑ Uses research data to improve teaching and learning.

...IMPLEMENTS!

Unit

First Characteristic—Positive Expectations

The effective teacher has positive expectations for student success.

Chapters

People Want to Succeed

All living things have a life force that urges them to survive. Their instincts drive them to seek food and shelter and escape predators. People are different inasmuch as they also have a drive to succeed.

The expectations you have of your students significantly influence what they are capable of achieving in class and in life.

They strive to excel and realize their potential. You can accomplish anything in your classroom if you set high expectations both for yourself and for your students.

**The dreams that shape our lives
flow from the attitudes and expectations
we nurture every day.**

As described in Chapter 2, there are four stages of teaching—Fantasy, Survival, Mastery, and Impact. Some teachers are SURVIVORS who do little or nothing to nurture their lives. They have minimal or negative expectations. Those teachers who strive for MASTERY in order to achieve IMPACT, however, nurture their lives and the lives of those around them with a constructive attitude and positive expectations. They are confident they can become effective teachers and that their students will thrive.

☆ THE KEY IDEA

Student success is limited only by the expectations teachers have of them.

Effective teachers believe that all students have potential.

> **The greatest discovery of my generation is that a human being can alter his life by altering his attitude of mind.**
>
> William James

> *All the wonders you seek are within yourself.*
>
> Sir Thomas Brown

GoBe

Teacher Expectations and Student Achievement

To understand more on how TESA can influence student achievement go to the **Go**ing **Be**yond folder for Chapter 6 or scan the QR Code.

[1] Jennifer Alvidrez and Rhona S. Weinstein, "Early teacher perceptions and later student academic achievement," *Journal of Educational Psychology*, vol. 91, no. 4 (December 1999): 731–746.

From Ulrich Boser, Megan Wilhelm, and Robert Hanna, *The Power of the Pygmalion Effect: Teachers Expectations Strongly Predict College Completion.* Washington, DC: Center for American Progress (October 2014).

Positive and Negative Expectations

An EXPECTATION is what you expect or believe will or will not happen. If you have positive expectations, you have an optimistic attitude—you believe you can achieve good things and good things will happen. If you have a pessimistic attitude, you have negative expectations—you believe bad things, or nothing, will happen.

Years of research and practical classroom experience clearly show that students do better when more is expected of them and their teachers have positive expectations. This has been proven in classroom after classroom and the results can be quite significant. It starts from the moment a student steps into a school. It may sound unlikely, but it has been proven that a teacher's expectation of a preschooler's ability was a robust predictor of that student's high school GPA.[1]

Teachers who have positive expectations for themselves have positive expectations for their students.

The Two Kinds of Expectations

- Positive or high expectations
- Negative or low expectations

Teacher Expectations and Student Achievement

Good and Brophy, whose research on the three characteristics of effective teachers are the central three units of **THE First Days of School: *How to Be an Effective Teacher***, also did research on "expectation theory." This theory was used by the Los Angeles County Office of Education to develop the Teacher Expectations and Student Achievement program (TESA) over forty years ago. The program is so good that it has stood the test of time and is even more appropriate today.

The name of the program says it all—what teachers expect will result in student achievement. The program does not require technology and costs no money to implement.

Negative Expectations

If you have the pessimistic belief that whoever you teach or whatever you do will not work out or will fail, you are constantly looking for justification, proof, and demonstration of why you have failed.

Examples of Negative Expectations

- "You don't understand the culture where I teach."

- "What's wrong with these kids? They just don't want to learn."

- "They can't read; they can't spell; they can't sit still; they can't behave; they can't remember anything."

- "Professional development meetings are boring and useless; this is why I sit in back and expect nothing useful."

Result of Negative Expectations

The odds are that what you expect will not happen, won't happen because you will expend energy to ensure it doesn't happen. You will predispose yourself to failure for yourself and for those around you, particularly your students.

Positive Expectations

If you have the optimistic belief that whoever you teach or whatever you do will result in progress, success, or achievement, you are constantly alert and aware of opportunities to help you and your students succeed.

Examples of Positive Expectations

- "What we achieve comes from how we work together."

- "I believe that every child can learn and will achieve to his or her fullest potential."

- "I strive for mastery and am proud that I am an effective teacher."

- "I am always learning, and that is why I enjoy going to workshops, accessing the Internet, and working collaboratively in a professional learning community."

Results of Positive Expectations

The odds are that what you expect and want to happen will happen because you expend energy to make it happen. You will predispose yourself to success for yourself and for those around you, particularly your students.

**It takes just as much energy to achieve positive results
as it does to ensure negative results.
Why waste your time and energy assuming failure
when the same amount of time and energy
can help you and your students succeed?**

*Positive
Outlook*

These are some things teachers unconsciously do:

- Ask more complex questions of higher achieving students than lower achieving students.

- Give less wait time to girls and students perceived to be lower achieving than to boys and students perceived to be higher achieving.

- Call on higher achieving students more often than lower achieving students. A study found that, within an allocated time period, teachers may interact with some students as few as five times and with others as often as a hundred and twenty times.

- Seemingly provide help to lower achieving students, but in actuality provide help more often to higher achieving students because they themselves seek it. High-achieving students tend to ask more questions and receive more praise than low-achieving students. When high-achieving students gave correct answers they were praised 12 percent of the time, whereas low-achieving students who gave correct answers were only praised 6 percent of the time. They received criticism, however, for wrong answers 18 percent of the time, while high-achieving students were only criticized 6 percent of the time.[2]

- Spend 25 percent less time listening to lower achieving students than to higher achieving students.

- Allow lower achieving students to sit in the back of the classroom where they can be ignored.

The premise of TESA is that by applying positive teacher-student interaction, academic achievement can be raised.

Students Know What Teachers Expect

Students are extremely sensitive to the way teachers behave toward them. Teachers may typically act more concerned and vigilant toward lower-achieving students by helping them with their work and explaining how to correct mistakes. But at the same time they may also be conveying a less positive attitude by being condescending (even hostile), giving less praise and warm support, and not taking time to listen to what's happening in these students' lives.

feeling seen!

Expectations

Give your students more than they expect.

And you will get back more than you ever expected.

Student success is limited only by the expectations teachers have of them.

---

[2]Thomas L. Good and Jere E. Brophy, "Behavioral Expression of Teacher Attitudes," *Journal of Educational Psychology*, vol. 63, no. 6 (December 1972): 617–624.

In a study led by Rhona Weinstein, it was found that even young students in first grade can accurately and consistently describe the expectations a teacher has of them by their teacher's facial expressions, body language or posture, or even through a light touch (although that cannot be done nowadays).[3]

As a teacher, who you are, what you do, and what you say will greatly influence the young people who will be the productive citizens of tomorrow's world. The expectations you have of your students will greatly influence what they achieve in your class and in their lives.

There is nothing more gratifying than knowing that you have the power to make a difference in the lives of your students. However, you must ensure that the impact you make on their lives is a positive one.

Classic Research on Teacher Expectations

The classic research on teacher expectations was done in the 1960s by Robert Rosenthal of Harvard University and Lenore Jacobson of the South San Francisco school district.[4] They fed erroneous information to a group of South San Francisco elementary school teachers and watched the teachers make the results come true.

To begin the experiment, teachers were led to believe that students at Oak School had been given the Harvard Test of Inflected Acquisition, a test that did not actually exist, in the spring of the preceding year. When school resumed that fall, the researchers and administrators informed teachers they were going to be rewarded for their teaching excellence by taking part in an important experiment.

The teachers were told that the test had identified a group of students, 20 percent of the student body, who would be "spurters" or "bloomers." The researchers said that it was expected that these special students were going to be capable of greater intellectual growth than their peers and that they, being excellent teachers, were going to achieve great results with them.

The teachers believed that the distinction of being a spurter or bloomer student was based on the pretest scores. In reality, the names of the students had been selected

She Was the Turning Point in My Life

Teaching is a journey of the heart. To read how a teacher turned a student's life around with positive expectations, go to the **Go**ing **Be**yond folder for Chapter 6 or scan the QR Code.

[3] Rhona S. Weinstein, H. H. Marshall, L. Sharp, and M. Botkin, "Pygmalion and the Student: Age and Classroom Differences in Children's Awareness of Teacher Expectations," *Child Development*, vol. 58, no. 4 (August 1987): 1079–1093.

[4] Robert Rosenthal and Lenore Jacobson, *Pygmalion in the Classroom: Teacher Expectations and Pupils' Intellectual Development* (New York: Holt, Rinehart and Winston, 1968).

Set the Bar High

Teachers who set and communicate high expectations to all their students obtain greater academic performance from those students than teachers who set low expectations. Students tend to learn as little—or as much—as their teachers expect.[5]

GoBe

Dedicated to My Parents and Teachers

The two most important groups of people, as far as young people are concerned, are parents and teachers. Find Harry Wong's tribute to these groups in his life in the **Go**ing **Be**yond folder for Chapter 6 or scan the QR Code.

---

[5] Department of Education, *What Works: Research About Teaching and Learning* (Washington, DC: Office of Educational Research and Improvement (ED), March 1986): 47.

completely at random. The teachers were told that based on their teaching excellence, they would be given the names of these special students, but on two conditions:

1. They were not to tell the students that they were special.

2. They were not to tell the parents that their children were special.

The researchers and administrators again emphasized that the expectation was that the teachers would do extremely well with these special students.

Eight months later, all Oak Park students were given an actual IQ test and a comparison was made between the designated spurter or bloomer students and all the others. The results showed a significant gain in intellectual growth for the 20 percent who had been designated as special in the primary grades, but no significant gains in the intermediate grades.

The researchers and administrators gathered the teachers, showed them the growth results of their students, and congratulated them on their spectacular success. The teachers were pleased but not surprised. They said that since the students were special, they were very fast learners.

Then the researchers and administrators revealed the truth. They informed teachers that the group of so-called spurters or bloomers had been picked at random, that no selections had been based on actual IQ or aptitude.

The teachers then decided that the results that had been achieved must have been a result of their teaching excellence. Once again, the researchers and administrators revealed that all teachers had been involved in the experiment. No teachers had been selected on the basis of being better than any others.

This was a perfectly designed experiment. There was only one experimental variable—**EXPECTATIONS**.

- ■ The expectations of the administrators toward the teachers were stated explicitly. They said that they were special teachers, and that 20 percent of students were special students who showed potential for intellectual growth. The expectation was that the special teachers would do extremely well with the group of special students.

- The expectations of the teachers toward the students were unspoken and conveyed implicitly. Because the teachers believed they had some very special students in their care, this influenced how they taught and what they expected of these students, as conveyed by their body language, personalities, and attitudes.

The researchers concluded that the results strongly suggested that students who are expected by their teachers to gain intellectually do in fact show greater intellectual gains after one year than do students of whom such gains are not expected.

Following this classic research experiment, many additional studies have been done. Some have been able to replicate the findings, while others have not. Regardless, educators and parents are keenly convinced that teacher expectations have the power to affect student outcomes.

The Complete Teacher

Several centuries ago Izaak Walton wrote *The Compleat Angler*. To this day, every person who enjoys fishing can learn how to be a better or more complete angler by reading this book. The advice is timeless and still as relevant as it ever was.

For those teachers who want to improve their effectiveness in the classroom, there are innumerable books, websites, workshops, and programs available to them that are just as timeless and relevant.

Yet, there is always a group of teachers who are content to stagnate in the SURVIVAL stage. They sit in the back row of a professional meeting doing something other than trying to be a complete teacher; they close the classroom door so that no one can see the minimal work being done by both themselves and their students; and they complain and rationalize that all faults, deficiencies, and problems lie with the school administration and the students they have to contend with.

FLOWING WELLS HIGH SCHOOL KEYS TO SUCCESS

Whether you think you can or think you can't— you are right.

Henry Ford

All our dreams can come true—if we have the courage to pursue them.

Walt Disney

No legacy is so rich as honesty.

William Shakespeare

I do the very best I know how, the very best I can, and I mean to keep on doing so until the end.

Abraham Lincoln

In the middle of difficulty lies opportunity.

Albert Einstein

Success is the maximum utilization of the ability that you have.

Zig Ziglar

The most successful schools have expectations that everyone will succeed.

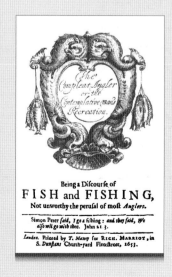

The Compleat Angler or the Contemplative man's Recreation.

Being a Discourse of
FISH and FISHING,
Not unworthy the perusal of most *Anglers*.

Simon Peter said, I go a fishing : and they said, We also will go with thee. John 21 3.

London. Printed by T. Maxey for Rich. Marriot, in S. Dunstans Church-yard Fleetstreet, 1653.

The great tragedy is that other teachers see this behavior and mimic it like a group of Pine processionary moth caterpillars, blindly following one another with negative attitudes and expectations that lead to self-defeating behaviors that soon permeate and downgrade the entire school culture.

These attitudes are all too easily transferred to the classroom where students can sense them and then teachers wonder why their students are misbehaving and not mastering their lessons.

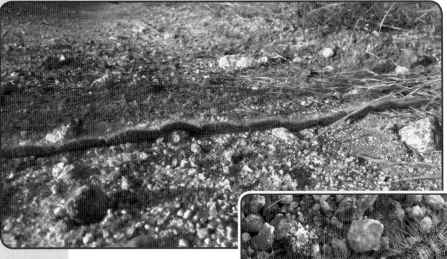

Nose to end, Pine processionary moth caterpillars follow one another.

> I see each child as having something special about them that nobody else has. I might be the only person in their life who sees that gift in them, and I feel that it is my responsibility to show it to them.
>
> Pam Almond
> Raleigh, North Carolina

There are also many examples of positive expectations. Just as negativity promotes negativity, positivity promotes positivity.

Positive expectations are inspirational. They are a great source of motivation and energy. They encourage teachers and students alike to do their very best, be their very best, and even to exceed expectations.

Melissa Dunbar of Kerrville, Texas, wrote a poem that she reads to her students on the first day of school and then posts as a reminder:

I believe in you.
No matter what you've done, I believe in you.
No matter what's happened to you, I believe in you.
No matter what people say, I believe in you.
No matter if you're rich or poor, I believe in you.
No matter your age or size, I believe in you.
No matter where you live, I believe in you.
No matter your position or lack of one, I believe in you.
No matter, no matter, no matter, I believe in you.

Students measure their success by the time invested in them and the expectations teachers have of them. Like everyone everywhere, students are responsive to those who are interested in them and they will strive to please those who believe in them.

Those teachers who have gone beyond Survival, either because they have taken the initiative to improve their own effectiveness or because the school district has a program to help them become more effective, have made a choice, and life is about making choices. The choice is this:

You can exist and survive, or
You can strive for Mastery and make an Impact on the lives of your students and on your own.

It's very simple:

If you think you can't, you won't.
If you think you can, you will.

As teachers, we have the satisfaction and privilege of helping students realize their dreams and potential. As effective teachers, our mission is to give students the skills, knowledge, and attitudes necessary to being happy, fulfilled, and successful in life. And what better way to impart these important skills, knowledge, and attitudes than to have them ourselves and model them for our students.

People with positive belief systems have high expectations, and their high expectations of others will have positive results in their personal and professional lives.

> **My teacher thought I was smarter than I was—so I was.**
>
> Six-year-old

> *Children are like wet cement. Whatever falls on them makes an impression.*
>
> Haim Ginott

How Do You Count?

What counts is not the number of hours you put in, but how much you put into those hours.

Some people go through life adding years to their life.

Others go through life adding life to their years.

From the moment students enter your classroom, let them know you believe in them and that you expect them to succeed in your classroom and in life.

☆ THE EFFECTIVE TEACHER

☑ Has a statement of positive expectations ready for the first day of school.

☑ Creates a classroom climate that communicates positive expectations.

☑ Models positive behavior and attitudes to all students and colleagues.

...IMPLEMENTS!

Invitational Education

Cindy Wong, a teacher in San Jose, California, sent an invitation for Back-to-School Night home with each of her students. **The parents of twenty-five out of thirty students came to school that night! How did she do it?**

> **Effective teachers have the power and the ability to invite students and colleagues to learn together.**

☆ THE KEY IDEA

An intentionally inviting teacher in an inviting classroom gives students a sense of purpose and importance.

On the day of Back-to-School night, she had her students make a gold-foil origami crane and copy a letter explaining the significance of the gift. They left this on their desks, along with a personal note for their parents. The students couldn't wait to tell their parents about the "special surprise" waiting for them in the classroom. Some parents said that their children insisted they go just to get their presents! This resulted in twenty-five out of thirty students being represented at Back-to-School Night.

Dear Parents,

Welcome to your child's classroom! What happens in this classroom will affect your child's future. Your child's time here will be well spent. He or she may even come home exhausted from all the thinking done during the day. But I will make every minute count. We have a fantastic group of children in this class. I am looking forward to a terrific year ahead. With your help, we can make it happen.

Sincerely,

Mrs. Wong

Dear Mom,

Thank you for caring about me and taking the time to come and learn about my class. We have been learning about a young girl named Sadako who bravely fought leukemia. She believed in good-luck signs. The crane was one sign, a symbol of peace and dreams come true. Here is a crane I made especially for you. With it, I wish you love, peace, and everlasting happiness. I love you!

Love, Emilio

At Back-to-School night, Cindy Wong asked each parent to write a response to his or her child's note and leave it on the desk. The students couldn't wait to come to school the next day to see what their parents had written. What a way to create an inviting classroom!

> No one has yet fully realized
> the wealth of sympathy, kindness,
> and generosity hidden
> in the soul of a child.
> The effort of every true educator
> should be to unlock that treasure.
>
> Emma Goldman

Why Was I Not Invited?

It upsets me to this day. When I was in junior high school, I had straight A's and was in the honor class. One day, the teacher went around the class and gave invitations to several students, but not to me. They were asked to join the National Honor Society. To this day, I am still puzzled, confused, and disappointed that I was not invited.

Rosemary Tripi Wong

The Basis of Being Inviting

Invitational education creates, sustains, and enhances truly welcoming learning environments. The approach is based on trust, respect, optimism, intentionality, and care to facilitate better learning outcomes and increased personal growth.

When people, places, policies, procedures, and programs (the 5 P's of invitational education) deliberately work together, they create a learning environment that helps everyone realize their fullest potential.

> **The basis of being inviting is being intentional.**

Being intentional means doing something with intention, with purpose, and by design. Effective teachers know what they are doing, such as intentionally mastering the three characteristics of effective teaching.

The effective teacher is deliberately inviting. We all like to be invited to go shopping, to go to a party, to join a group. And we all have the common courtesy to greet people at the door, to exchange pleasantries when introduced to others, and to offer food or drink to a visitor. These are all obvious, expected, and practiced. These same concepts should be practiced in the classroom.

Walk around and see if your classroom is inviting. What first impression does it make on a student or visitor?

- Is the door clearly marked?
- Are welcome and information signs posted?
- Are signs written clearly and concisely?
- Is the first assignment clear and understandable?
- Are there clues that show you care for young people?

The effective teacher is committed to regarding all students as able, valuable, responsible, and possessing untapped potential in all worthwhile areas of human endeavor.

The person who is asked or complimented is INVITED. The person who is not asked or complimented is DISINVITED. This concept was formulated by William W. Purkey and is known as invitational education.[1]

Knowing students leads to their success.

> *Until I was thirteen,
> I thought my name was Shut Up.*
>
> Joe Namath

Success Is Easy

Theresa Borges from American High School in Miami says, "Success is easy. Pay attention to the students. Like a detective, listen to what they have to say.

- I notice and compliment a new haircut and new shirt, and especially a right answer.

- I analyze handwriting for original work; I offer lunchtime tutoring.

- I call back parents by the end of the same day. I never get a second request from a parent for contact or a phone call.

- I visit students in the hospital, go to funerals (unfortunately), and give awards to students who achieve perfect scores on tests.

- I put stickers on perfect papers, even in Algebra 2.

- I read about our athletes in the paper, and go to games that I can attend.

- I know what video games they like and what music they listen to.

"Of course, knowing your curriculum is vital, but taking the time to know your students leads to success."

*Makes me think of:
– going to student activities*

[1] William W. Purkey and John Novak, *Inviting School Success: A Self-Concept Approach to Teaching, Learning, and Democratic Practice* (Belmont, CA: Wadsworth, 1996).
William W. Purkey and Betty L. Siegel, *Becoming an Invitational Leader: A New Approach to Professional and Personal Success* (Boca Raton, FL: Humanix Books, 2013).

Are You Inviting or Disinviting?

Inviting Verbal Comments

"Good morning."
"Congratulations."
"I appreciate your help."
"Tell me about it."

Disinviting Verbal Comments

"It won't work."
"I don't care what you do."
"You can't do that."
"Because I said so, that's why."

Inviting Personal Behaviors

Smiling and making eye contact
Listening attentively
Holding the door open
Thumbs up or high five

Disinviting Personal Behaviors

Looking at your watch
Sneering; being distracted
Letting the door shut behind you
Dismissive gestures

Inviting Physical Environment

Fresh paint and pictures
Living plants
Clean floors
Comfortable furniture

Disinviting Physical Environment

Dark corridors; stark classrooms
No plants
Leftover food, dust, and litter
Beat-up or uncomfortable furniture

Inviting Thoughts (Self-Talk)

"Making mistakes is all right."
"I've misplaced my keys."
"I could learn to do that."
"Sometimes I have to think
    what to say."

Disinviting Thoughts (Self-Talk)

"Why am I so stupid?"
"I've lost my keys again."
"I never could do that."
"I never know what to say; I'm so
    slow to catch on."

You Are a Significant Person

Invitational education states that all individuals have significant people in their lives. These include teachers, leaders, mentors, colleagues, bosses, parents, relatives, coaches, administrators, spouses, and close friends. Each is significant in different ways.

Your students are influenced more by the depth of your conviction than by the height of your intelligence. It is a matter of changing students, not to your way of thinking, but to your way of feeling.

> **Students can refuse words,
> but they won't refuse an invitational attitude.**

Give your students more than they expect, and you will get back more than you ever expected.

> **The invitational messages extended by
> the significant people in a person's life have
> the power to influence the life of that person.**

Effective teachers have the power and the ability to invite students and colleagues to learn together each day and in every class. Attentiveness, expectancy, attitude, enthusiasm, and evaluation are the qualities that determine whether a teacher is being inviting or disinviting. These characteristics significantly influence a student's self-concept and increase or decrease the probability of student learning and achievement.

> **"You are important to me as a person."
> This is the message that we all need to convey
> to our students and our colleagues every day.**

Every teacher, every professor, every educator ought to spend time in a kindergarten or first-grade class each year, just to look at and feel the excitement that's there. Very young students get excited about everything in the world.

> ❝
> ### If Only the Finest Birds in the Forest Dared Sing, How Quiet the Forest Would Be
>
> *If only the best readers dared read, how ignorant our country would be.*
> *If only the best singers dared sing, how sad our country would be.*
> *If only the best athletes engaged in sports, how weak our country would be.*
> *If only the best lovers made love, where would you and I be?*
>
> *I would be tired!*
>
> William W. Purkey
> ❞

You Are Special to Me

Wayne Hill of Mesa, Arizona, has a way of demonstrating to his students that they are significant people.

On the first day of class, before introduction of the class, I greet the students by holding up a $20 bill and ask who would like the $20. Obviously many hands go up. I crumble the bill and again ask the same questions and hands go up. I throw the bill onto the floor, stomp and smash the bill into the floor. I hold it up and again ask the same question. All hands go up.

I ask the students why they still want the $20 after I have crushed, stomped, and smashed it. Their response is always, "Because it is still worth $20; it has not lost its value."

I explain to the students that sometimes in life we feel like we have been stepped on and made to feel dirty. But never forget that someone at home or someone here at school cares about you. I tell them, "You are special to me. Don't ever forget."

When I discuss the dismissal procedure for the class, I explain that I dismiss the class, not the bell. I dismiss the class only after all students are seated and quiet. I simply say, "Don't ever forget." The class responds, "We are special."

They leave the class and often I hear the kids repeating as they walk out the door, "We are special." When they see me on the campus, they shout out to me, "Hello, Mr. Hill. We are special."

All the world's their stage, and there is nothing they cannot do, even though some cannot read, write, or count. Yet they are ready and willing to do anything their teacher asks them to do.

Then look at their teachers. They know that their charges cannot read, write, count, or even speak correctly. Some of these students do not even know how to eat properly, use the bathroom, or hang up their jackets without help. Yet these teachers do not complain that they have a bunch of low achievers. Instead, their demeanor and their classrooms sparkle with an invitational attitude toward learning.

Welcome Them to School

Just as you go on a vacation with high expectations, students come to school with high expectations. They come to get an education, meet friends, participate, have fun, study, and learn. Their entire day revolves around school and their friends. It is an exciting time in their lives. **Welcome them to school, each and every day.**

⭐Organize a First Day of School Celebration⭐

I ♥(heart) this idea

- Stand at the bus stop and welcome students on The First Day of School. Wave and smile like it's Aunt Jessie whom you have not seen in fourteen years and she's just disembarked from the plane.

- Stand at the front entrances of the school. Have at least one greeter at every entrance so that no one will fail to receive a warm, friendly welcome.

- Bring out the school band to play at the curb or near the entrance.

- If you don't have a band, have a group of students and teachers assembled to wave with welcoming smiles.

- Hang up a computer-generated banner welcoming students to school.

- Distribute a school newspaper extolling the virtues of the school and the wonderful school spirit of the teachers and the students.

- Have guides in the hall. Hang up directional signs to help students find their classrooms.

At Hull Middle School in Duluth, Georgia, Principal Denise Showell (right) and Counselor Rosemary Aschoff (left) roll out the red carpet to greet their students.

- Have your name and room number clearly visible on the classroom door along with your personal greeting of welcome.

- Let the first message spoken over the public address system be one of welcome and positive expectations for the school year.

Read Chapter 12 on greeting students. Greeting is the perfect start for each day and each class period.

> 66
> *Schools should be built better and kept up better than banks because there's more wealth in them.*
>
> Martin Haberman
> 99

We must **TEACH** and **SHOW** our students these beliefs:

- **School is where we are responsible for one another.**
- **School is where we gain knowledge.**
- **School is where we give and receive love.**
- **School is where we become successful.**

School is not a place; school is a concept. School is not a place where students are forced to listen to lectures, stare at tablet and computer screens, fill in worksheets, leaf through dull textbooks, and endure hours of frustration and boredom in drab, dirty classrooms and corridors.

School is a concept wherein students are welcome to learn, achieve, and enhance the quality of their lives without fear of intimidation or harm, guided by hospitable, caring people in a clean and orderly environment.

Every student needs to feel welcomed on the first day and every day of the school year.

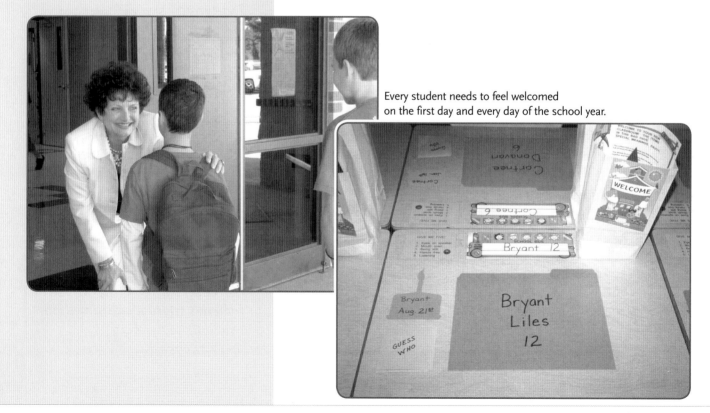

The Four Levels of Invitational Education

There are four levels of invitations that can be issued to students. The level of invitation will determine your effectiveness as a teacher.

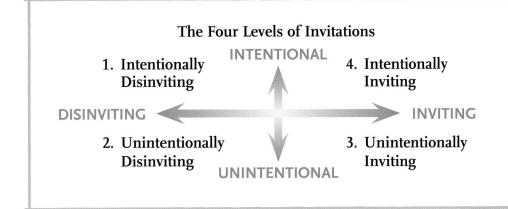

The Four Levels of Invitations

INTENTIONAL

1. Intentionally Disinviting

4. Intentionally Inviting

DISINVITING ←————————→ INVITING

2. Unintentionally Disinviting

3. Unintentionally Inviting

UNINTENTIONAL

1. Intentionally Disinviting. This is the bottom level at which a few curmudgeonly teachers operate. They deliberately demean, discourage, defeat, and dissuade students. They use expressions like these:

> "Why do you bother coming to school?"
> "I've only given one A in the 16 years that I've been teaching."
> "You will never amount to anything."

And they never smile.

2. Unintentionally Disinviting. Some teachers are oblivious to the fact that they are negative people. They feel that they are well meaning but are seen by others as chauvinistic, condescending, racist, sexist, patronizing, or thoughtless. They make comments like these:

> "What if they do not want to learn?"
> "If you don't want to learn, that's your problem."
> "These people just don't have the capacity to do any better."
> "I was hired to teach history, not to do these other things."

And they keep their arms folded when interacting with students.

Everyone Is a VIP

Oklahoma City principal Sharon Creager keeps a "VIP book" in her office with this inscription on the inside cover:

> **"Congratulations to these Very Important Pupils, who have distinguished themselves in various ways. These are the stars of our future."**

Teachers send students to the office to have their names entered in the VIP book. The book is on permanent display in the hall and has never been vandalized. Each morning, the new VIP names are read out during morning announcements.

3. Unintentionally Inviting. These are the "natural-born teachers." Such teachers are generally well liked and effective, but they are unaware of why they are effective. They are usually affable, and this characteristic often hides the fact that their students may not be learning to their fullest potential. These teachers are sincere, try very hard, and we generally like to have them as friends. They offer remarks like these:

> "Aren't you sweet!"
> "Charge! Let's go, team!"
> "That's neat."
> "Just try harder."

And they bubble with excitement.

4. Intentionally Inviting. Intentionally inviting teachers have a professional attitude, work diligently and consistently, and strive to be more effective teachers. They have a sound philosophy of education and can analyze the process of student learning. Most importantly, they are purposely and explicitly invitational. They know what it means to be invitational, and they work at it. They say things like this:

> "Good morning. Have a great day."
> "Let me help you with these lesson objectives."
> "Follow this rubric and I will help you make progress."
> "Would you like to help me?"

They also use the proper emotion at the appropriate time.

When you intentionally apply the power of POSITIVE EXPECTATIONS and INVITATIONAL EDUCATION, you become a very powerful and effective teacher.

Students Will Succeed

Coming to school every day can seem like a hopeless task for some students unless they can succeed at what they do. Students will succeed when they believe that the teacher believes in them; when they realize that the teacher views them as people who have the potential to succeed; and when they know the teacher is providing instruction that works in their best interest (Unit D).

You're Invited

Read more information on invitational education in the **Go**ing **Be**yond folder for Chapter 7 or scan the QR Code.

In spite of our attempts to invent teacher-proof materials and even in spite of our attempts to create "relevant new curricula," one simple fact makes most of this ambition quite unnecessary. It is as follows:

> *When a child perceives a teacher to be an authentic, warm, and curious person, the child learns. When the child does not perceive the teacher as such a person, he has difficulty learning, or does not learn what is being taught.*

Increasing the act of teaching has not really made much difference, for there is always the simple fact that teaching is the art of being human and of communicating that humanness to others.[2]

Neil Postman and Charles Weingartner

> **Human potential, though not always apparent, is there waiting to be discovered and invited forth.**
>
> William W. Purkey

How to add. adapt for k?

Web of Life Activity

Have the students stand in a circle. Using a large ball of yarn, begin by holding the end of the yarn and naming someone across the circle. Say something kind about that student like, "Juan plays fair," and then toss the ball to him or her while holding on to the piece of yarn.

He or she says another student's name, makes a positive comment about him or her, and tosses the ball of yarn holding on to another section of yarn.

The ball continues to be tossed around the circle weaving a "web" until it is totally unrolled, creating a "web of life."

The teacher or leader then comments that everyone is important, belongs, and has something to contribute to the group. This activity invites students to create a sense of cohesiveness, and gives them a feeling of acceptance and significance.

Days at school can be depressing experiences for some students unless there is an invitational message that gives them a sense of purpose and importance.

[2]Neil Postman and Charles Weingartner. *The School Book: For people who want to know what all the hollering is about* (New York: Delacorte Press, 1973).

I have come to a frightening conclusion.

I am the decisive element in the classroom.

It is my personal approach that creates the climate.

It is my daily mood that makes the weather.

As a teacher I possess tremendous power to make a child's life miserable or joyous.

I can be a tool of torture or an instrument of inspiration.

I can humiliate or humor, hurt or heal.

In all situations it is my response that decides whether a crisis will be escalated or de-escalated, and a child humanized or dehumanized.[3]

Haim G. Ginott

[3] Haim G. Ginott, *Teacher and Child: A Book for Parents and Teachers* (Macmillan, 1972).

☆ THE EFFECTIVE TEACHER

☑ Has an intentionally inviting personality.

☑ Creates an inviting classroom environment.

☑ Works at being intentionally inviting.

☑ Maintains an inviting attitude.

...IMPLEMENTS!

You Are Treated as You Are Dressed

Job interviewers tell us they make an initial judgment on an interviewee within twenty seconds. Salespeople are instructed that they have just seven seconds to make an impression.

> You do not get a second chance to make a first impression.

Effective teachers know that the clothes they are wearing and the smile that decorates their face are the first things students notice when they are greeted at the classroom door.

Students tend to imitate the behavior and appearance they see in the classroom. **When teachers dress as the professional educators they are, they gain respect and set a positive example for their students. They are dressed for success.**

> As you are dressed,
> so shall you be perceived;
> and as you are perceived,
> so shall you be treated.

Always dress better than your students. If you do not care about yourself, why should students care about you?

The effective teacher dresses to model success.

⭐ **THE KEY IDEA**

The effective teacher dresses professionally to model success.

Dress to Be Effective

This chapter is not about dress code or dress policy. This chapter is about the impression you make on students and the influence you can have on their success in a way that is not directly related to your teaching methods, lesson plans, or classroom organization.

This chapter addresses the fact that the way you dress will have an impact on your effectiveness as a teacher, and your effectiveness will determine the success of your students.

Teacher Statistics

When we look at some facts about teachers in the United States, they reveal an educated, highly competent group of professional people who are actively engaged in society at large.

These facts have been sourced from the National Education Association, American Federation of Teachers, Market Data Retrieval, National Center for Education Statistics, Institute of Education Sciences, U.S. Department of Labor, and *Scholastic Teacher*.

- Number of full-time teachers: 3.5 million[1]

- Average annual salary: $56,643[2]

- 43 percent held a Masters in Education in 2011, and an additional 12 percent held a Masters in other areas[3]

- Heavy users of premium or platinum credit cards

- Avid readers who read publications such as *Gourmet* and *National Geographic*

- 75.9 percent are married, and 92 percent of their spouses are employed either full or part time

- 58 percent own a home

[1] *Digest of Education Statistics*, 2013, U.S. Department of Education, Institute of Education Sciences, National Center for Education Statistics (NCES 2015-011, May 2015): Introduction and Chapter 2.

[2] *Digest of Education Statistics*, 2013.

[3] C. Emily Feistritzer, *Profile of Teachers in the U.S. 2011* (Washington, DC: National Center for Education Information, 2011).

It's common sense. People react to and treat other people by the way they dress and groom themselves. A salesperson sees two shoppers approaching, one appropriately dressed and the other inappropriately dressed. You know very well who will get immediate and better service.

How much credibility would a bank have if the teller who processes your account was dressed in jeans and wore a T-shirt emblazoned with the slogan "Poverty Sucks"?

Make no mistake—we judge others by their dress, and they judge us, too. It may not be fair. It may not be right. But people tend to respond and react to other people by the way they have chosen to present themselves. In an ideal world, it would be wonderful to be accepted for our inner strengths and qualities alone, not for our external appearance. In the real world, however, our all-too-visible selves are under constant scrutiny. We all make judgments. We look at someone and make judgments and assumptions about status, income, occupation, and even attitude and character.

> It is not what IS.
> It is what is PERCEIVED that prevails.

You Are a Walking, Talking Advertisement

It may be shallow or superficial for people to be so affected by external appearances. But this is the way societies are all over the world and saying that things should be different will not change the way they are. You are much better off making the way you dress work for you than having it work against you. **You do not get a second chance to make a first impression.**

We are walking, talking advertisements of who we are and what we aspire to be. It is not only the clothes we wear and the way we groom ourselves. Our actions, attitudes, words, and general demeanor all make very public statements. **We are walking, talking advertisements of who we believe we are as professional educators.**

When you walk into class late, you have just made a statement. When you walk into class late with a can of soda or a cup of coffee in your hand and a scowl on your face, you are making a statement.

When you walk into class early, when you're standing at the door with a smile and an extended hand of welcome, the assignments are posted, the room and materials are ready, and there is a positive classroom atmosphere—you are making a statement.

When you allow teasing in class, you are making a statement. When you refuse to tolerate teasing in class, you are making a statement. **The statements that you make influence how the students will behave and what they will achieve in class. How students behave and what they achieve will determine your success as a teacher.**

> *Give an elementary student three days, and the student will mirror you. Give a high school student ten days, and the student will mirror you.*
>
> Charles Galloway

**Every time you act,
you validate who you are.**

Teachers Are Professional Educators

Students see their parents go to work each day, dressed in business attire or institutional uniforms. Their jobs usually require that they look professional. Then students come to school and observe the inappropriate, casual attire of some teachers. The statistics show that teachers are middle-class intellectuals with college degrees, highly competent people with teaching credentials. But as a group, they often disregard the fact that they will be judged by the way they present themselves.

This is why the teaching profession has a difficult time gaining respect and credibility. This is also why some teachers have difficulty impressing and influencing students —and if teachers cannot impress students, no teaching or learning will take place. These teachers leave school at the end of the day frustrated over their own inadequacies.

Make no mistake about reality. **When you select your clothes each day, you are making a statement about yourself to the world.**

What Is Appropriate?
People expect other people to behave appropriately, use appropriate language, and to have appropriate manners. Doing what is **appropriate** is doing what is proper or correct in the circumstances or situation.

Teachers have a responsibility to encourage learning, and learning begins by gaining and maintaining the respect of students. Your respect begins with your appearance.

Appropriate and Professional

One of the reasons we have schools is for students to learn what is appropriate. Young people learn what is appropriate in the society they live in by watching and imitating their adult role models.

In the classroom, it is your appearance, your language, and your behavior that your students will accept as appropriate. By the end of the first or second week of the school year, the entire class will have absorbed signals from you as to how they should behave for the rest of the school year.

The most important message you can send and establish in your classroom is that you are a professional educator and your mission is to ensure that your students succeed. So the key is looking professional, not attractive or interesting. **The advantage of looking professional is that it protects you from self-destructing in the first few seconds, before your students make any hasty judgments about you.**

The effective teacher is a professional educator who dresses appropriately to model success. The important word is appropriately. We often see signs like this one:

> ## Could Not Believe What I Saw
>
> *After Christmas vacation, one of my students left some pictures of the class holiday party on my desk. I took a look at myself and I could not believe how I looked. I looked like I didn't care about myself.*
>
> *The next day I came to school more appropriately dressed, and they all noticed and commented on how nice I looked. I was so happy and they made me feel so good.*
>
> *I now spend more time caring about who I am. The students care about me. I am proud of who I am. And they are also so much better behaved now as a result of who I represent.*
>
> Fifth-grade teacher

New and young teachers may need guidance in what is appropriate. It is imperative that there exists a school or district induction program coupled with a coaching program staffed by dedicated, effective, teachers. Experienced, professional educators are the best role models. They know what leads to success for themselves, their students, and the school. Teachers new to the profession will follow their lead.

Professional attire imparts the status you need from the start.

> *Hold yourself responsible for a higher standard than anybody else expects of you. Never excuse yourself.*
>
> Henry Ward Beecher

Successful teachers dress for success.

Dress for Respect

You can be sure that students notice and are affected by how their teachers are dressed, in the same way they notice the appropriateness of their own and each other's ways of dressing. Clothing may not make a person, but it can most certainly be a contributing factor in unmaking a person. Our appearance affects how we are perceived and received in definite ways, whether we like it or not.

Understand that the clothing a teacher wears has nothing to do with whether students like that teacher. But clothing definitely has an effect on students' respect for a teacher, and respect is what the teacher must have if learning is to take place. **Research reveals that a teacher's appearance affects the work, attitude, and discipline of students.**

Even as a Substitute Teacher

My daughter, who just started a school counselor's job in a Phoenix school, agrees with me that we can win the kids over with our appearance. "I dress very nicely as a substitute teacher. The kids hold the door for me. One on each side! That's pretty scary and wonderful that they are influenced so easily by appearance."

As shared with Harry Wong

Worth the Time

Yes, ties take time to tie and sometimes get uncomfortable. However, a tie tells everyone you meet, "I respect you, my job, and myself, and I'm willing to take the time to show it."

As a professional educator, you should be dressed to achieve four main effects:

1. Respect
2. Credibility
3. Acceptance
4. Authority

When you have achieved these effects, they will be assets you can use when relating to students, peers, administrators, parents, and the community. If you have these assets, you have a much greater chance of being an effective teacher who can influence students to learn and succeed.

Every profession has its appropriate attire.

" Celebrate the Children

We had an evening program to celebrate the work of the children and the parents came appropriately dressed, not formal or glamorous, just nicely appropriate.

I looked around the room and saw T-shirts and workout clothes—on some of the teachers. I was so ashamed.

A teacher
(who asked to remain anonymous)

"

If you are professionally and appropriately dressed, students will comment when you look nice, and if something is out of place, they will tell you because they know that you are a person who cares about yourself. But if you consistently come to school inappropriately dressed, they will not say a word because they surmise that if you do not care about yourself, they need not care about you. **Dress appropriately because it is very important to know that students care about you.**

When students care about you, they will respect you, learn from you, and buy from you. As a professional educator, you are selling your students knowledge and success for the future.

What's Out

Tennis shoes are for sports and exercise.
Sweatshirts and yoga gear are for the gym.
T-shirts and see-through apparel are casual and carefree.
Low-cut, baggy pants, and torn clothing look casual and sloppy.
Flip-flops and beachwear are for vacations and lounging.
Trendy clothes do not establish authority and should be left to students.
Blue jeans are for after school and weekends.
Excessive jewelry is distracting and excessive fragrance can cause irritation or allergic reactions.

What's In

Bright colors are appropriate and enjoyed by elementary students.
Soft, muted tones are recommended for secondary school.
Men will always look professional with a tie and collared shirt, vest, sweater, or bow tie.
A simple, modest dress or skirt, pants, and blouse are appropriate for women.
Clean clothes convey good hygiene.
Pressed clothes tell people you care.
Neat, cleanly tailored clothes establish confidence.

GoBe

Dressing for Success

"Your personal appearance can give you the job you want." Read how in the **Go**ing **Be**yond folder for Chapter 8 or scan the QR Code.

You Dress Where You Want to Be

DeRutha Richardson, a Career Education teacher at Muskogee High School in Oklahoma, decided to conduct a class project about perceptions and professional image.

On the first day of the project, she came to class dressed in the most negative manner she could conjure up. She wore an old ill-fitting jacket over a long, fishtail dress and tennis shoes with flannel socks over her stockings. She slicked her hair back, wore no makeup, and even faked a missing-tooth effect.

She was amazed at what happened in the classroom.

She lost all control of the class, could not get the students' attention, and endured fifteen minutes of pure chaos. She had to leave the classroom and return dressed in a professional manner before she could restore order in the classroom.

Her students, who soon will be entering the job force, experienced firsthand the importance of appropriate dress for any occasion. Dress is the silent language that will make or break them in their professional careers.[4]

---

[4]DeRutha Richardson, "Projecting Professional Images . . . Through the Eyes of Photo Lenses," March 2007. wwwuk.kodak.com/global/en/consumer/education/lessonPlans/lessonPlan018.shtml.

Preparing Students for the World

It is universally agreed that one major function of schools is to prepare young people for tomorrow's world. Yes, the world, not a particular city, state, or country. We live in a competitive, global economy where people work for companies that are international in scope. It is likely that many of your students will work for a company that will have offices all over the world.

> **If you want to succeed in the world, you must think globally.**

Have you ever noticed that school secretaries almost always come to school better dressed than a lot of the teachers? School secretaries convey their competence by dressing appropriately.

Experts tell us that young people get their values from their friends. That's true to the extent that there is a values vacuum to be filled. It is imperative that parents and teachers get there first. If we are to prepare students for the future, we need to instill the values, attitudes, and outlook they will need to participate constructively and successfully in the complex global economy.

You may feel that you lack an international perspective. If you feel that you need to increase your knowledge and awareness, take some time to do some research. Go to a major airport and watch passengers arriving and departing on national and international airlines. Observe the way they dress, their mannerisms, their interactions, how they greet and bid each other farewell. There will be many similarities among people, but there will also be cultural and national differences. Learn how the world operates.

Then go to the business district of a large city and observe people walking by—the executives, storeowners, salespeople, and support service people. These are people leading busy, professional lives. Notice their clothes, shoes, hairstyles, and accessories. Observe their attitudes, the way they react in different situations, and how they interact with others.

Having observed the world, after you are dressed and ready to walk out the door in the morning, look at yourself in the mirror. Think of your students, all of whom look to you as a model in how to succeed in today's world. Ask yourself the following three questions:

1. Would a real estate agency hire you dressed as you are?

2. Would a restaurant allow you to hand food to a customer dressed as you are?

3. Would you have confidence sending your beloved child, grandchild, godchild, niece, or nephew to school to be taught by a teacher dressed as you are?

Believe it or not, even criminals have a clear sense of the nonverbal messages people give out by their attitude and appearance. In an eye-opening experiment, groups of convicted muggers were shown videos of people walking along the street. Overwhelmingly, the muggers picked people who walked slowly, people with stooped shoulders, people who looked helpless, disheveled, and downtrodden. They rejected people who walked erect, purposefully, and confidently. These latter people conveyed the message that they were in control of their lives.

The way you present yourself announces to the world whether you care or do not care about yourself and others. Everyone you encounter can read this message. As a teacher, which of these two statements do you want to make?

1. I am a member of a group of underpaid, untidy, uninspired, and unappreciated people.

2. I am member of a group of proud, dedicated, responsible, and appreciated professionals.

Whichever message it is, that is the one conveyed to your students, to parents, to school administrators, and to your colleagues, most of whom find the very casual dress of many fellow teachers totally unacceptable.

> **You Will All Succeed**
>
> When our daughter took our granddaughter to her first day of kindergarten in Japan, she walked in casually dressed, as we might do in the United States, thinking she would drop the child off and go home. Well, not at all.
>
> First, she discovered that all of the other parents were dressed up in their finest for a full day of ceremonies in celebration of the first day of school. They were in the room with the children, and there were speakers on the platform with a big banner that said, "Welcome to Kindergarten. You Will All Succeed."[5]
>
> Ernest L. Boyer

[5] Ernest L. Boyer, "On Parents, School, and the Workplace," *Kappa Delta Pi Record*, vol. 25, no. 1 (Fall 1988): 8.

21st Century Skills

Schools are bombarded with the mantra of 21st century skills—creativity, critical thinking, problem solving, decision-making, communication, and collaboration. These are the skills people need today and in the future to be responsible citizens, to have satisfying and successful careers, and for personal and social fulfillment.

But one critical skill is missing from this list—how to dress for responsibility and success in a global society and economy.

Experts in sales, management, and leadership training will all tell you the same thing. The way you appear and the way you behave conveys a message to the world that reveals who you are and what you expect of life. When you dress like a professional educator, you are helping your students prepare for a future in the competitive, global economy.

You have every right to expect the most from your career, your life, and from the lives of your students. The realization of your expectations can begin with the simple matter of how you dress.

☆ THE EFFECTIVE TEACHER

☑ Comes to work dressed like a professional.

☑ Demonstrates appropriate attitudes and behavior.

☑ Is a successful role model for students.

☑ Is informed by global perspectives.

...IMPLEMENTS!

HOW TO CREATE A CULTURE OF COURTESY AND COOPERATION

Students of Today

It's a sad fact that many people are starved for attention, including some of the students in your classroom. Many teachers are the last bastion for helping students in all aspects of their lives.

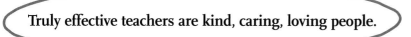

Truly effective teachers are kind, caring, loving people.

Here are some statistics that reveal many of today's social problems, such as inadequate parenting, alienation, and isolation.

- The average child receives an estimated twelve minutes of quality, personal, focused, undivided attention each day from his or her parents.

- By the time they are eighteen, most American children have spent more time in front of the television or mobile phone than they have with friends or parents.

- The average adolescent spends more than three hours alone every day.

- Loneliness is the number one problem of the elderly, many of whom are afraid to venture out of their homes or apartments.

In 1987, the Carnegie Foundation surveyed 22,000 teachers and produced the results in a report called *The Condition of Teaching: They Cannot Do the Job Alone.*

- 90 percent said that a lack of parental support was a problem at their schools.

- 89 percent said that there were abused or neglected students at their schools.

- 69 percent stated that poor health was a problem for their students.

- 68 percent reported that some students were undernourished.

- 100 percent described their students as "emotionally needy and starved for attention and affection."

★ **THE KEY IDEA**

The heart of education is the education of the heart.

The depth of your heart determines the height of your dreams.

These are sobering statistics. Teachers can feel overwhelmed and helpless about the magnitude of what needs to be done. But these facts highlight the potential schools have to address some of these problems. School is not only where students learn knowledge and skills, it is also where they interact with adults other than their parents, have a social life, and make friends. It is where they learn how to share and conduct themselves appropriately and politely in society.

Most importantly, these statistics highlight the essential role individual teachers play in students' lives. **The attention, care, and inspiration an effective teacher can offer a student is invaluable.** An effective teacher is a significant role model who can do much to improve the lives of students and influence them for the better for the rest of their lives.

Connections, not Relationships

It is important to clarify the difference between having relationships with your students, a word used all too frequently in education, and making positive connections with them. Teachers should not attempt to fill emotional inadequacies in students' lives and enter into relationships based on friendship. Students do not want a teacher-student relationship. The term itself is co-equal and you can imagine how dangerous and inappropriate this type of relationship can be. It will undermine and defeat what you can achieve as an effective teacher.

Also many of our students—and the number grows each school year—come from cultures where they are taught to respect, honor, and look up to adults, in particular teachers and parents. These students do not want or understand connecting with teachers through friendly relationships.

> **If you want respect, cooperation, and engagement, cultivate connections, not relationships.**

Students thrive best in a classroom where the teacher creates moments of CONNECTION in the context and confines of a well-managed classroom. Connections are easily made by having one meaningful interaction with

We'll Stand Behind You

She was scared to give a report. Read how the class supported a nervous student in the **Go**ing **Be**yond folder for Chapter 9 or scan the QR Code.

every student at least once a day or class period during the normal flow of activities. The simplest way to make connections is to greet students at the door with a smile.

The most effective way to make connections with students is to have a well-managed classroom where students are on task, allowing you to spend one-on-one time with them.

Procedure is a term used throughout this book. There are procedures used to manage a classroom. There are procedures used in the instructional program. **There are also procedures used to enhance the quality of teaching so that it opens hearts and minds.**

Five Significant Concepts

There are five significant concepts of behavior that can help people achieve whatever they want in life. Effective teachers use them in the classroom to create a culture of courtesy and cooperation. They use them to make meaningful connections and enhance positive expectations. These concepts are addressing students by name, saying "please" and "thank you," smiling, and showing care and warmth.

> **The effective teacher creates a culture of courtesy and cooperation.**

**The Five Significant Concepts
That Create Courtesy and Cooperation**

1. Name
2. Please
3. Thank You
4. Smile
5. Love

Address Each Student by Name

Effective salespeople employ a very simple but valuable technique. They find out your name, introduce themselves to you to make a connection, and then use your

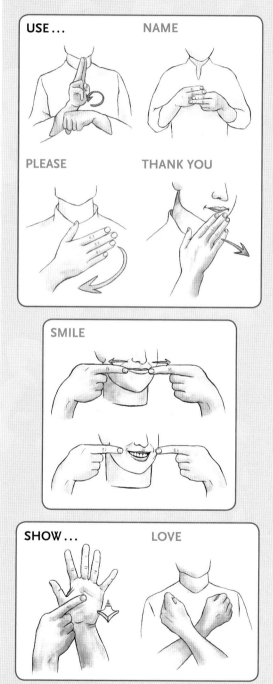

The Five Significant Concepts

USE... NAME

PLEASE THANK YOU

SMILE

SHOW... LOVE

Use sign language to communicate nonverbally. Watch the DVD, *You Have Changed My Life*, as William Martinez tells his story in word, song, and sign language.

Name tags help in getting to know your students faster and facilitate students getting to know each other.

proper name every seven to ten sentences when they speak to you. Why? **When you address someone by name, you are treating that person with dignity and respect.**

Your name is very important. It identifies and dignifies you. Other people in the world may have the same name as yours, but as far as you are concerned, you are the only person in the world with your name. It is a name that you can easily hear called above the din of a crowd. And when you hear your name, you pay attention. Salespeople know this when they use your name. You pay attention. You pay attention because you are important!

When you address a student, use the student's name. Effective teachers use names, especially when they want a student to do something or behave in a certain way.

Use a student's name in a friendly, respectful manner. Never address a student in an angry or condescending tone. This is a put-down of a person's identity and dignity.

Pronounce the student's name correctly. Spell a student's name correctly. A person's name is precious and personal. It is that person's property. It is imperative that students hear the correct pronunciation of their names. Failure to do so will tell all students that they do not have to respect each other's names and as a result, can tease, bully, and make fun of each other's names.

When you use a person's name, you are saying to that person, "I know who you are. You are important. You are important enough for me to identify you by name."

When you use a person's name, you are saying, "I care enough to know who you are."

Say "Please," Please

Cultured, polite people can be identified by their manners. The heart of courtesy is respect for people.

Courtesy and respect convey a message that says, "I am paying attention to you." The neglect of courtesy leads to the collapse of community, and this can be seen in ineffective schools and classrooms where people demean one another.

People who neglect to say "please," even when speaking to children, are teaching impressionable young people that it is

No matter the language, please is a sign of courtesy and respect.

all right to bark orders and to run roughshod over the dignity of others. The young people may not react or respond, but they resent the lack of courtesy implicit in such treatment.

When you fail to say "please" to a student and couch your request as an order, you are slowly chipping away at that person's freedom and dignity, and many of your students come to school having been yelled at all day and night, with none of their freedom and dignity intact.

When you say, "Would you please get me a bottle of glue?" it is in fact shorthand for saying, "If you please—if it gives you pleasure—get me a bottle of glue." You are asking the student not only to help but also to feel kindly toward you.

"Please" is an acknowledgment of that kindness. When you say "please," you are in effect saying, "I respect you and your kindness and your worth as a human being."

Kindness begins with the word "please."

- Cultured, polite, and well-mannered people automatically use the word "please." They have learned appropriate behavior.

- Repetitive use of the word "please" is important if a student is to learn to use the word "please" in life.

- "Please" is usually used when you ask someone to do something for you. Thus the most effective way to use "please" is to precede the word with the person's name, as in "Trevor, *please* . . ."

- Consider adding the word "please" to instructions on your worksheets, assignments, and other papers that you distribute in class.

Repetition Is the Key

For a child to learn something new, you need to repeat it an average of eight times.

For a child to unlearn an old behavior and replace it with a new behavior, you need to repeat the new behavior an average of twenty-eight times.

Twenty of those times are used to eliminate the old behavior, and eight of the times are used to learn the new behavior.

After Madeline Hunter

I Really Appreciate What You Did, "Thank You"

You really cannot use "please" without using "thank you." The two just go together. Not using the two together would be like having a knife without a fork, a belt without a buckle, a letter without an envelope. When you say "thank you," you are acknowledging that someone did something kindly for **YOU** and not because you ordered **THEM** to do it.

"Thank you" says to others that you appreciate their effort and kindness. If you have positive expectations that students will work hard and learn to be kind, then saying "thank you" is your way of acknowledging they have been courteous and diligent and that you appreciate what they have done for you.

- "Thank you" is the perfect transition; it paves the way to the next request, lesson, or task in class. It makes whatever you want done next much easier.

- The most effective way to use "thank you" is to use it with the person's name, "I truly appreciate what you did. *Thank you,* Jane" or "Jane, I truly appreciate what you did. *Thank you.*"

- Consider adding the words "thank you" to instructions on your worksheets, assignments, and other papers that you distribute in class.

You know you've done a good job of teaching when your student says, "*Thank you* for teaching me to say 'Thank you.'"

Please, No "No Problem." Thank You!

The worst response to "thank you" is "no problem." This implies that the task was a problem. A more appropriate response to "thank you" is "my pleasure," indicating that the task was done with pleasure and not because it was a problem.

:·MORNING ROUTINE:·

1. Remove jacket or coat. Hang it up in your locker.
2. Empty Knapsack or bag.
3. Put runners or inside shoes on.
4. Walk into the classroom quietly.
5. Have 2 sharpened pencils and necessary books ready.
6. Hand in all completed homework.
7. Begin BELLWORK assignment on your own.
8. Read the agenda for the day.
   Have a great day! Thank-you! ☺ Mrs. Jay

"Please" and "thank you" are used in these teachers' classrooms.

Today
Leaf Classification
Analyze & Demo

Friday. May 4

Bellwork
1. Write objective in planner.
2. Complete leaf ID worksheet.

Agenda   Thank
1. Bellwork   You!
2. Classification
   - Worksheet
   - Quiz
3. Clean up & dismiss

Science Investigation   Page 237
                                       Questions 1, 2, 8, and 10

1. Please review data from
   test performed yesterday.   Period 2
2. Organize findings in a   Page 237
   pie chart.   Questions 1, 2, 8, and 10
3. Write a 3 sentence
   summary.   Period 4
4. Assign someone to present   Project due
   findings to class.
5. Please rehearse!   Period 5
          thank you   Page 237
                                    Questions 1, 2, 8, and 10

A Smile, the Frosting on a Cake

Many teachers ask, "How do I motivate my students? How do I get them engaged? How do I get them to cooperate?" The answer is very simple—a smile is all it takes. A smile is the key that unlocks the heart of learning. What is more motivational than a smile? What is more invitational than a smile? What is more effective to get a student engaged than a smile? A smile sets the stage for a caring classroom and kindles the desire to learn. A smile is free and easy to give.

An effective smile comes from a nurturing teacher in a consistent, predictable classroom.

Gift your students a smile they will carry with them the rest of their lives. There is a truism to the phrase we have heard so often, "People care when they know you care about them."

If you truly want to achieve maximum effectiveness when you use a person's name and say "please" and "thank you," SMILE. It requires no effort and is even easier than frowning—smiling uses far fewer muscles than frowning and hence is less tiring to do. But like using "please" and "thank you," smiling is a behavioral trait that must be learned.

A smile is the frosting on a cake, a high-five when a job has been done well, or enthusiastic words of praise that say "I am REALLY proud of you." It's the little *lagniappe* that sets you apart.

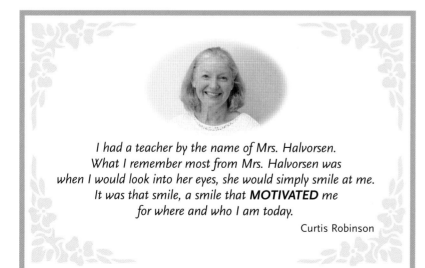

*I had a teacher by the name of Mrs. Halvorsen.
What I remember most from Mrs. Halvorsen was
when I would look into her eyes, she would simply smile at me.
It was that smile, a smile that **MOTIVATED** me
for where and who I am today.*

Curtis Robinson

"
Our Business

Ours is not the business of producing doctors, or lawyers, or teachers, or nurses, or scientists, or policemen, or salespeople, or factory workers—or higher test scores.

Ours is the business of producing smiles on young faces, happiness in young hearts, and dreams in young minds.

The rest will take care of itself.

Dan Seufert

"

> **A smile is a light to tell people that your heart is connected with theirs.**
>
> Lynn Birdsong

A smile communicates three things:

1. You are a person who knows the ultimate in hospitality and graciousness.

2. You have that little extra bit of polish or panache that marks you as a cultured person.

3. You feel good about yourself and want others to feel good about themselves, too.

A smile is the universal language of understanding, peace, and harmony. If, indeed, we want the next generation to have a world of peace and understanding, we need to teach its sign—a smile.

A smile is the most effective way to create a positive atmosphere, to disarm an angry person, and to convey the message "Do not be afraid of me; I am here to help you."

- There is no need for a great big smile; a controlled, slight, disarming smile is all you need.

- Accompany the smile with the name of the person.

- As you smile and speak, use momentary pauses. This is called timing. Every performer knows that the key to delivering a speech, telling a joke, or giving a performance is timing. Timing creates the pregnant, expectant pause before an important, emotional statement or punch line.

Love what you teach, and be loving to those you teach.

Technique for Smiling, Speaking, and Pausing

Step 1. SMILE. Smile as you approach the student, even if your first impulse is to behave harshly toward the student.

Step 2. FEEDBACK. Observe the reaction to your smile. Are you receiving a smile in return, or at least a signal that the student is relaxing and receptive to your approach?

Step 3. PAUSE. (Timing, timing.)

Step 4. NAME. Say "Wayne" with a slight smile.

Step 5. PAUSE.

Step 6. PLEASE. Add "please," followed by your request. Do this in a calm, firm voice, accompanied by a slight, nonthreatening smile.

Step 7. PAUSE.

Step 8. THANK YOU. End with "Thank you, Wayne" and a slight smile.

Example

(Smile. Pause) *Wayne, please stop talking to Amanda and get to work on your assignment.* (Pause) *Thank you, Wayne.* (Slight smile.)

Practice this in a mirror, over and over again.

Loving and Capable

Only two things are necessary for a happy and successful life—being loving and being capable. Effective teachers never stop looking for ways of being more capable.

Truly effective teachers are not only capable, they are also kind, caring, and loving. Years later, when students remember their most significant and inspirational teachers, the ones they will remember most are the ones who really cared about them.

Effective teachers know they cannot get a student to learn unless that student knows the teacher cares.

Notes in a Lunch Box

Every day, along with the frosted cupcake, Kimberley jotted down a few words of loving encouragement on a note that she placed in her son Kenny's lunch bag. And every afternoon, Kenny returned his lunch bag with her note inside.

Kimberley often wondered if he even read the notes. One day, Kenny returned his lunch bag without the note. Out of curiosity, his mother asked, "Honey, where's your note?"

Kenny looked at her, not sure if he had done something wrong. "I gave it to Tim," he said. "His mother doesn't give him notes and I, well . . . I thought he could use mine."

"You did?" Kimberley questioned.

"Yeah. His mother is really sick and he's so sad right now," Kenny explained. "Maybe you can write a note for him tomorrow or maybe I can give him the one you wrote last Thursday. That was a good one."

> *Love is life...*
> *And if you miss love,*
> *you miss life.*
>
> Leo Buscaglia

The effective teacher offers both a product and a service.

Ineffective teachers think all they have to do is offer a product, as in "I was hired to teach history" or "I was hired to teach third grade."

Effective teachers offer more than a product; they offer a service, too. Effective teachers not only help students learn, they enhance the quality of their lives. They treat students with the same courtesy and respect they expect for themselves. This service increases their effectiveness, and the effectiveness and potential of their students.

The sincerest form of service requires no money, no training, no special clothes, and no college degrees. **The sincerest form of service comes from listening, caring, and loving.**

There Will Never Be a Shortage of Love

Love is the reason for teaching.
It costs nothing, yet it is the most precious thing
    one can possess.
The more we give, the more it is returned.
It heals and protects,
    soothes and strengthens.
Love has other names, such as
    forgiveness . . .
    tolerance . . .
    mercy . . .
    encouragement . . .
    aid . . .
    sympathy . . .
    affection . . .
    friendliness . . .
    and cheer.
No matter how much love we give to others,
    more rushes in to take its place.
It is, really, "the gift that keeps on giving."
Give love in abundance—
    every day.

Love is the reason for teaching.
It is the most effective and inspirational
quality a teacher can possess.

You don't need to tell your students that you love them, but you can certainly express it through kind words and actions. If you choose to be a significant and effective person in a student's life, you must demonstrate your care and love both implicitly through your body language and explicitly through what you say.

When significant people use loving words and actions, they exponentially increase the likelihood of eliciting positive behaviors from others.

Thank you for being a loving, inspirational, and positive role model for your students.

Teachers Do It All

There are no commercial programs, no websites, and no books on teaching love as a unit. The source is within us—each and every one of us. It is our words, attitudes and behavior that teach love and when love is taught, it is reflected throughout the classroom.

Truly effective teachers teach from the head AND the heart.

Effective teaching has very little to do with programs and structural changes. Programs do not teach students. Changing class size does not teach students. Teachers teach students.

- Programs do not make apathetic teachers into caring ones.

- Programs do not turn ineffective teachers into effective teachers.

- Programs do not understand that half the class does not speak English.

- Programs do not give a student a warm smile or a word of praise.

- Programs do not say "thank you" or "please."

- Programs do not believe in students.

Teachers do all this and more.

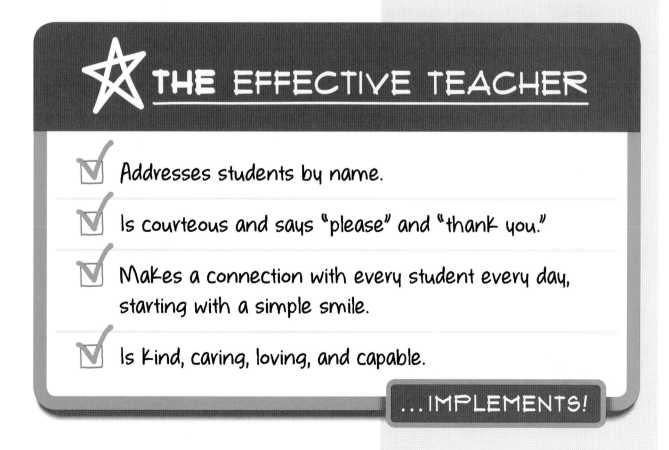

☆ THE EFFECTIVE TEACHER

☑ Addresses students by name.

☑ Is courteous and says "please" and "thank you."

☑ Makes a connection with every student every day, starting with a simple smile.

☑ Is kind, caring, loving, and capable.

...IMPLEMENTS!

Unit

Second Characteristic—Classroom Management

The effective teacher is an extremely good classroom manager.

Planning for Student Success

The success of your students is greatly dependent on your ability to convey and implement a Classroom Management Plan. If you do not have a plan, students will plan the year for you, and then you are in serious trouble.

> Classroom management refers to what teachers do to organize students, space, time, and materials so that learning takes place.

Begin the year with a clear, compelling plan of how you want to organize your classroom, how you expect students to participate, and what you will accomplish together. Then explain this plan to your students. Make them part of your plan. Students want to know your plan, just as they want to know what they are to do to achieve and succeed. Truly, students want to please their teachers. They want teachers to guide them to success.

Research has identified THE single most important factor influencing student success is classroom management. Three researchers reviewed eleven thousand studies spanning a period of fifty years on factors that govern student learning. They concluded that there are twenty-eight significant factors and placed them in rank order. At the very top of the list is classroom management.[1]

The least important factor influencing student success is the demographics of the student body. In other words, at the end of the list are race, skin color, gender, national and religious background, the financial status of the family, and the neighborhood in which students live.

Once and for all, let's stop using student demographics as an excuse for lack of achievement. Classroom management, not demographics, determines success.

THE KEY IDEA

The effective teacher has a well-managed classroom where students learn in a task-based environment.

Effective teachers have a plan and share the plan with their students.

Twenty-Eight Factors Governing Student Learning

1. Classroom management
2. Instructional/learning process
3. Parental and home support

↓

28. District demographics

[1] Margaret Wang, Geneva Haertel, and Herbert Walberg, "What Helps Students Learn?" *Educational Leadership*, vol. 51, no. 4 (December 1993/January 1994): 74–79.

Review Chapter 2: "How to Succeed on the First Day of School"

How you manage your classroom determines how well your students will learn.

- Classroom management skills are of primary importance in determining teaching success.[2,3]

- The most significant factor governing student learning is classroom management.[2,3]

- Effective classroom management practices must begin on the first day of school.[4]

THE First Days of School: How to Be an Effective Teacher is based on the following research findings:

Effective teachers have three characteristics:[5]

1. They have classroom management skills.
2. They teach for lesson mastery.
3. They practice positive expectations.

**It is the teacher—
what the teacher knows and can do—
that makes the difference in the classroom.**

What Is Classroom Management?

The first thing to clarify is that classroom management **is NOT discipline.** You manage a store; you don't discipline a store. You manage a team; you don't discipline a team. If you go to Amazon.com and do a topic search for books on "management," over nine hundred thousand titles will come up. Using the "Look Inside" utility to examine some of the content, you will see that not a single book on management talks about disciplining employees.

**It is only in education where management
is confused with discipline.**

Management and discipline are NOT synonymous terms. But discipline is how many educators define and view classroom management—not as procedures for learning, but as rules and regulations. This is not to say that discipline is not important. Discipline is behavior management, and that can be found in Chapter 17.

---

[2]Edmund T. Emmer and Carolyn M. Evertson, *Classroom Management for Middle and High School Teachers*, 9th ed. (Boston, MA: Pearson Education, 2012).

[3]Carolyn M. Evertson and Edmund T. Emmer, *Classroom Management for Elementary Teachers*, 9th ed. (Boston, MA: Pearson Education, 2012).

[4]Douglas Brooks, "The First Day of School," *Educational Leadership*, vol. 42, no. 8 (May 1985): 76–79.

[5]Thomas Good and Jere Brophy, *Looking in Classrooms* (Needham Heights, MA: Allyn & Bacon, 2007): 313–314.

Management is what managers do. They have the capacity to produce an effect by transforming resources into function and results. Teachers who organize, structure and coordinate classroom events to maximize time for teacher instruction and student learning are much more effective than teachers who believe that classroom management has to do with forcing students into compliance.

- **Discipline is behavior management**, and teachers who want discipline are mandating COMPLIANCE from students.

- **Classroom management is organization with procedures**, and effective teachers teach RESPONSIBILITY to classroom procedures.

It is the principal who makes the difference in the school.

Management is the organization and coordination of work, people, resources, and technology to achieve a well-defined set of objectives, without wasting materials, time, or energy. **Classroom management consists of the practices and procedures a teacher uses to create and maintain an environment in which instruction and learning can take place most effectively.** Learning is the result of good management.

Effective teachers manage a classroom. Creating a well-managed classroom with established procedures is the essential priority during the first two weeks of school. With effective classroom management, students know what to do to learn and succeed.

It is the teacher who makes the difference in the classroom.

- Classroom management is a means of organizing, structuring, and planning events to maximize student learning and get things DONE in the classroom.

- Effective classroom management ensures student engagement and creates a productive working atmosphere.

The effective teacher knows that a student's potential can only be realized when the work environment is organized

THE Classroom Management Book

Over one hundred fifty educators share their wisdom, techniques, and plans in **THE** book that specializes in classroom management.

Get Your Act Together

There's an idiom, "Get your act together." This reprimanding phrase is used when there is confusion, disorganization, and incoherence.

The purpose of Unit C is to show you how to get your act together—how to get organized; develop a clear, orderly plan of action; structure activities so they are done effectively; and achieve results.

---

[6]Jere E. Brophy and Carolyn M. Evertson, *Learning from Teaching: A Developmental Perspective* (Needham Heights, MA: Allyn & Bacon, 1976).

and structured. A student's self-confidence must also be nurtured and self-discipline instilled. **Under the guidance of an effective teacher, learning takes place because classroom management is the foundation for all student achievement.**

The purpose of classroom management is to organize the classroom so students know what to do to learn and succeed.

Classroom management is based on procedures. Procedures are used to create a management plan that achieves learning goals. Procedures are the tasks students must do to increase their chances of learning. Procedures are the foundation upon which successful teaching takes place. Procedures set students up for achievement. Well-established and well-rehearsed procedures simplify the challenges of succeeding in school and create a positive, constructive learning environment.

A procedure is a routine that students do repeatedly without any prompting or supervision. Watch students in a well-managed classroom. They act responsibly because they know the procedures and routines that structure the class and keep it organized. They are working; they are producing; they are learning and achieving.

And *you*, the teacher, can go home each day with a satisfied smile on your face! A well-established management plan organizes and structures events so that students are able to successfully accomplish what they need to DO in the classroom.

Self-Assess Your Classroom Management Effectiveness

Brophy and Evertson say, "Almost all surveys of teacher effectiveness report that classroom management skills are of primary importance in determining teaching success, whether it is measured by student learning or by ratings. Thus, management skills are crucial and fundamental. **A teacher who is grossly inadequate in classroom management skills is probably not going to accomplish much.**"[6]

Use the Managing Classroom Procedures Rubric to help yourself make progress in becoming a highly effective classroom manager.

Managing Classroom Procedures Rubric			
Highly Effective	Very Effective	Partially Effective	Ineffective
Instructional time is maximized because classroom procedures are well-established and students are responsible for carrying out procedures on their own initiative.	A minimum of instructional time is wasted because procedures are implemented with occasional prompting from the teacher.	Some instructional time is wasted because the teacher must often remind and reteach what procedures are to be followed.	Much instructional time is wasted as there are no procedures in place and the teacher must constantly stop instruction to repeatedly tell students what to do.

Characteristics of a Well-Managed Classroom

A well-managed classroom has a set of procedures and routines (chapters 15 and 16) that structure the classroom so a teacher can achieve two results:

1. Fostering student involvement and cooperation in all classroom activities

2. Establishing a productive working environment

Classroom management refers to the procedures and routines that ensure the many activities taking place in the classroom—reading, taking notes, participating in group work, taking part in class discussions, participating in games, and producing materials—run smoothly without stress or disruption. An effective teacher has every student involved and cooperating in all of these activities.

Unit C will help you accomplish the goals of fostering student involvement and establishing a productive working atmosphere so you can be a very effective teacher. In a well-managed classroom, the environment is conducive to learning. Students are working; they are paying attention; they are cooperative and respectful of each other; they exhibit self-discipline; and they remain on task. All materials are ready and organized; the furniture is arranged for productive work; and, a calm and positive atmosphere prevails.

> *Management is the art of getting things done through people.*
>
> Mary Parker Follett

GoBe

Teacher Behaviors

Read what the research says are the six behaviors of good classroom managers. Find them in the **Go**ing **Be**yond folder for Chapter 10 or scan the QR Code.

This classroom is arranged for productive work.

This classroom has a positive atmosphere.

These students are on task.

These students are cooperative and respectful of one another.

The Characteristics of a Well-Managed Classroom[7,8]

1. Students are deeply engaged with their work, especially with academic, teacher-led instruction.

2. Students know what is expected of them and are generally successful.

3. There is relatively little wasted time, confusion, or disruption.

4. The atmosphere of the classroom is work-oriented, but relaxed and pleasant.

The Mother of Classroom Management

The "mother of classroom management" is Carolyn Evertson. She is a professor at Peabody College, Vanderbilt University. She has written more than one hundred book chapters, journal articles, monographs, and reports, and has been cited over a thousand times. She and her colleagues have written *Classroom Management for Elementary Teachers* and *Classroom Management for Middle and High School Teachers*, currently in their ninth editions.

These books have been out since the early 1980s and talk about organization. **Yet, the profession still incorrectly talks about classroom management as discipline.**

Too many teachers do not teach. They do activities. And when problems arise, they discipline. Many classrooms are unmanaged. And when classrooms are not managed, little learning is accomplished.

A well-managed classroom is task-oriented. Students know what is expected of them and how to succeed. Extensive research confirms that most students will make better achievement gains in a well-managed classroom.

A well-managed classroom has a predictable environment. Both teacher and students know what to do and what is expected of them. When you manage the classroom environment, you should be able to close your eyes and envision learning taking place and WHY it is taking place.

---

[7]Emmer and Evertson, *Classroom Management for Middle and High School Teachers*, 9th ed.
[8]Evertson and Emmer, *Classroom Management for Elementary Teachers*, 9th ed.

Techniques to Help You Implement the Four Characteristics of a Well-Managed Classroom

Characteristics	Effective Teacher	Ineffective Teacher
1. High level of student engagement with work	Teacher has students on task and working cooperatively to achieve what needs to be done. (See page 180.)	Teacher is working.
2. Clear student expectations	Teacher is clear about the learning objectives of every assignment. (See page 225.) Teacher tells students the learning objectives that tests are based upon. (See page 268.)	Teacher says, "Read Chapter 3 and I'll give you a test." Teacher has not been clear about expectations and objectives and students don't know how to focus their studying.
3. Little wasted time, confusion, or disruption	Teacher has well-rehearsed procedures and routines in place. (See page 168.) Teacher starts class immediately. (See page 130.) Teacher has assignments posted. (See page 132.)	Teacher makes up rules and disciplines according to his or her mood. Teacher takes roll and dallies so the day's schedule is disrupted. Objectives are unclear and students repeatedly ask for assignments.
4. Work-oriented, but relaxed and pleasant atmosphere	Teacher has invested time in practicing procedures so that they become routines. (See page 148.) Teacher knows how to bring class to attention. (See page 155.) Teacher knows how to praise the deed and encourage the student. (See page 152.)	Teacher tells but does not rehearse procedures. Teacher yells and flicks light switch to get attention. Teacher uses generalized praise or none at all.

> *Power comes when you make life predictable for people.*
>
> Howard H. Stevenson

It is the teacher's responsibility to manage a classroom and ensure that a task-oriented and predictable environment has been established.

They Get It Right

People expect procedures for everything they do in life: going to the movies, waiting in lines, in the workplace, etc. Teaching children the procedures they need to follow in class gives them life skills and makes teaching less stressful.

When procedures are in place, the teacher can focus on teaching. Students know automatically what needs to be done. They know when and how to do it, because you have taught them until they get it right.

Marie Coppolaro
Queensland, Australia

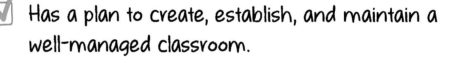

THE EFFECTIVE TEACHER

☑ Has a plan to create, establish, and maintain a well-managed classroom.

☑ Can explain the difference between classroom management and discipline.

☑ Has students working responsibly on task.

☑ Maximizes instructional time with little confusion, wasted time, or disruption.

...IMPLEMENTS!

Plan and Plan Even More

The most important word in classroom management is the "P" word. Plan, plan, and plan some more. Effective teachers plan, and then plan some more. Over-planning is a good thing!

> Plan, plan, and plan some more.
> There's no such thing as too much planning.

The better you prepare a Classroom Management Plan, the greater the benefits you will transfer to students, especially those who need support.

Some if not many of your students come from chaotic home environments where life is a struggle. They did not ask to be born into the situation they are in; it is what it is.

Effective teachers spend time organizing and structuring their classrooms to provide students with the stability and consistency they need to have a chance at success.

- A work-oriented environment is what you want to establish during the first week of school.

- The first week of school should stress large group organization and student procedures.

- Spend the first week of school on classroom management.

You increase the chance of student successes and decrease the chance of disruptions if the classroom is ready before students arrive. Then, during the first week of school, the emphasis should be entirely on implementing your Classroom Management Plan.

An effective teacher creates an environment that facilitates teacher instruction and student learning.

THE KEY IDEA

Plan and prepare your classroom to maximize learning and minimize misbehavior.

Your Effectiveness Is Determined Before You Leave Home

You need to prepare yourself, professionally and personally, before you leave home and as you enter the classroom every day.

What you will accomplish during a working day is determined before you start the day.

- Half of what you will accomplish in a day is determined before you leave for work.

- Three-quarters of what you will accomplish in a day is determined before you enter the school door.

What you will accomplish during a working day is directly related to planning and preparation.

The Stairs to Success

Elecia Lathon teaches the classroom management class at Louisiana State University in Baton Rouge. Elecia uses an analogy and some of her mother's wisdom to explain why her students need to take the stairs to success.

Elecia Lathon and her student, Megan Toujouse, proudly displaying her classroom management plan.

"Many years ago my mom, also an educator, said to me, 'If you fail to plan, you're planning to fail because there are no elevators to success; you have to take the stairs.'"

"This didn't mean anything to me until I began teaching. I had a plan, but my plan was to make a difference. However, I soon realized I had no real plan or steps for making this happen. This is why every student in my classroom management course creates a classroom management plan, one in which we take the stairs. Those stairs are known to my students as labs. The labs consist of students developing their philosophy of education, creating classroom layouts, rules, consequences, procedures, assessments, communicating with parents, components of an effective lesson plan, and the final management plan.

"We build the management plan step-by-step, piece-by-piece throughout the semester and students leave with something they can take on job interviews, share with colleagues, and use for many, many years as a classroom teacher."

Megan Toujouse was one of Elecia's students. She claims that the classroom management course was possibly the most important education class she took throughout her academic career.

"When I went for my job interview, my principal told me that my classroom management plan was a good snapshot of what she could expect from me.

"I was hired at my first interview.

"I've used my classroom management portfolio during my first two years of teaching more times than I can count."

> ❝
> *You attack the day with an enthusiasm unknown to mankind.*
>
> Family-instilled mantra
> Jim Harbaugh
> ❞

A Successful Restaurant Is Ready

The table is ready. The table is set and waiting when you arrive at your reservation time.

The dining room is ready. The ambiance is conducive to a pleasant dining experience.

The staff is ready. You can expect excellent food and good service because the staff is trained and rehearsed and has high expectations that you will enjoy your dinner.

An Effective Teacher Is Ready

The work is ready. Desks, books, papers, assignments, and materials are ready when the bell rings.

The room is ready. The classroom is clean and arranged to create a pleasant, safe, work-oriented atmosphere.

The teacher is ready. The teacher has a warm attitude and positive expectations that all students will succeed.

Karen Rogers is a high school teacher in Kansas. She tells everyone that her classroom has to be well managed because otherwise, she says, "I will be chasing after the kids all year long."

She continues, "I love the first days and weeks of school. When adults walk into my classroom, they are amazed that my students all know what to do, when to do it, and how to do it."

Karen has a Classroom Management Plan that creates a predictable and consistent classroom, and with consistency she earns her students' trust.

Trust comes from the security of consistency.

Be Ready

Prepare your classroom and have it ready for your **students every day of the school year from the first day to the last.** This is obvious and essential. When you have a dinner party, you prepare so you are ready when your guests arrive.

Successful restaurants are ready to welcome you when you arrive for your meal.

Karen Rogers and her Classroom Management Plan.

Most Important Words

The three most important words for any worthy endeavor are **preparation, preparation, preparation.**

The three most important words for an effective teacher are **preparation, preparation, preparation.**

When your team plays, they have trained and are ready to compete. When you walk into a restaurant, an office, or a store, you expect it to be ready—for YOU. You become frustrated and annoyed if things aren't ready.

In the "real" world outside the classroom, you would probably be fired if you were not ready. If a client calls and you aren't ready, you probably lose the sale; if you aren't ready for an interview, you probably won't be hired. Students must learn to prepare and be ready if they want to succeed in the real world when they leave school. It is part of our job as educators to teach readiness by modeling readiness in our work, in our class environment, and in ourselves. Teachers who are not organized and prepared send a loud message that they are not ready to teach.

Your classroom conveys a message. What do you want your students to expect?

> **Readiness determines teacher effectiveness.**

A messy, disorganized, or barren classroom sends a negative message. It indicates to students that you don't care for them or for yourself. A clean, well-organized, attractive classroom sends a positive message. It tells students that you respect them enough to provide a calm, pleasant working environment. When students feel respected, they return the respect. **Invite your students to enter a classroom where you are prepared and that you have prepared for their benefit.**

> **All battles are won or lost before they are fought.**
>
> Sun Tzu

Preparing Your Classroom

These are some suggestions for how to proceed with preparing your classroom. They, like most suggestions in this book, are generalized and conceptual. Apply and adapt them to your grade level and situation.

Before you move any furniture or put anything on the classroom walls, consider these guidelines.

- Don't overcrowd and over clutter. Limit the amount of furniture and technology equipment. Students love to touch and fiddle with things. It's time-consuming and difficult to keep everything clean and some pieces of equipment can also pose safety hazards.

- Don't over-arrange and over-decorate. Your room should be neat and pleasant, but don't spend time making it the ultimate showcase you want by Back-to-School Night. Some bare, clean bulletin boards, shelves, and plant containers look inviting, ready to be gradually filled as the year progresses.

- Don't spend time having the learning center or classroom resource center complete. You don't need a learning center on the first day of school. Wait a week or so until students are familiar and comfortable with classroom procedures, routines, and rules before you allow them to work at the learning center.

- Do learn the regulations regarding fires, earthquakes, tornadoes, hurricanes, and other natural disasters, as well as lockdown situations, and ensure that the classroom is organized and ready for such emergencies.

- Do make sure that all of your windows close, your doors lock, and your all of the lights in the room function.

Prepare Floor Spaces

- Count the number of desks and chairs needed. Arrange to have damaged furniture replaced and sufficient furniture brought in. Ask for needed items well ahead of time.

Prepare the classroom for learning.

Before You Do Anything Else

Begin with cleanliness. Cleanliness is . . . effective!

Research proves that a school's and classroom's cleanliness, orderliness, and character influences the student's behavior and the ability of a teacher to teach.[1]

Gather a collection of cleaning supplies—liquids, sponges, mops, and rags. Dust. Clean. Scrub. Polish. Imagine royalty is coming. Who's more important and deserving than your students?

[1]J. A. Lackney, "Teachers as Placemakers: Investigating Teachers' Use of the Physical Environment in Instructional Design" (Madison: University of Wisconsin, College of Engineering, School Design Research Studio, 1996).

The classroom should be arranged so that nothing gets in the way of learning.

Students Who Face the Board Learn More

Seating arrangement impacts student learning and student health. Read more about this in the **Go**ing **Be**yond folder for Chapter 11 or scan the QR Code.

- Don't be hostile if things don't happen as efficiently as you want them to, especially if your requests are made at the last minute. Administrators and custodians are truly helpful people and want quality education for students as much as you do. Get to know them, and you'll discover that they are competent, cooperative, compassionate, and helpful. They are not the ogres the negative teachers want you to believe they are. They will assist you with your needs.

- Even if you plan to have a different classroom arrangement during the school year, it is wise to begin the year with desks facing the teacher. Desks do not have to be in traditional rows, but chairs should face forward so that all eyes are focused on you at the start of the school year. This minimizes distractions, allows you to monitor behavior more readily, and helps you become familiar with the students in your class.

- Keep high-traffic areas clear. Keep clear access to storage areas, bookcases, cabinets, and doors. Don't put desks, chairs, or tables in front of doors, water fountains, sinks, pencil sharpeners, or your desk. Allow enough clearance to move up and down and around the last seat in the row.

- Plan areas for students' belongings. Provide space to hang jackets and for their various things like binders, backpacks, books, lunch bags, umbrellas, shoes, show-and-tell items, lost-and-found items, sporting equipment, musical instruments, and projects.

- Have a strategic location ready for students who may need to be isolated from the rest of the class.

Prepare Work Areas

- Think of how you will divide your classroom into distinct areas. There needs to be private areas versus group work areas; work areas versus neat areas; and teacher areas versus student areas.

- Arrange work areas and desks so that you can easily see and monitor all students and areas no matter where you are in the classroom. Make sure that you have enough chairs for the work areas.

- Arrange the space so that students can easily see you, as well as frequently used whiteboards, bulletin boards, screens, demonstration areas, and displays.

- Be sure that you have all necessary materials for your work areas, such as books, laboratory supplies, media, activity cards, tools, and instruments.

- Test any electrical or mechanical equipment to make sure it works before you use it.

- Use tote trays, boxes, coffee cans, plastic containers, or whatever to store the materials students will need. Arrange your room so that these are readily accessible to all students.

Label containers so everyone can find anything.

Prepare Wall Spaces

The most effective classes are those where students are self-disciplined, self-motivated, and take responsibility for learning. Teach your students to consult the classroom display boards for the agenda, assignments, and information on what to do and how to do it. (See Chapter 14.)

- Have a consistent place for listing the day's agenda, opening assignments, and homework. Display the feature topic, theme, chapter, or skill for the day or the current unit.

- Display your classroom rules in a prominent place. You can relocate it after the first week. (See Chapter 17.)

- Post procedures, duties, calendar, clock, emergency information, maps, schedules, menus, charts, decorations, birthdays, and student work.

- Post a large example of the proper heading or style for papers to be done in class. Post examples of tests students will take, assignments they will turn in, and papers they will write.

- Cover one or more bulletin boards with colored paper and trim, and leave them bare and undecorated. The purpose of these boards is to display student work.

Four Basic Rules of Organization

1. **Separate school from personal matters.** The students are priority. Avoid personal matters at school.

2. **Clear your desktop.** Use labeled vertical files to keep your desktop clear of paper files.

3. **Organize incoming and outgoing papers.** Designate two places: one for students' incoming papers and another for outgoing ones.

4. **Consolidate, consolidate, consolidate.** To minimize searching and fumbling around, use small boxes, clear plastic containers, magazine files, and desk organizers to consolidate and store things.

Left-brain people have files.
Right-brain people have piles.
Scatter-brain people have piles of files!

Prepare Bookcases

- Do not place bookcases or display walls where they obstruct any lines of vision.

- Rotate materials on the shelves, and leave out only those items you are willing to allow students to handle.

- Do not place books or other loose materials near an exit where they can easily disappear or where they may obscure emergency information.

Prepare Teacher Areas

Maximize your proximity to students, and to frequently used materials and equipment. Time is lost, and disruptions more probable, when it requires too many steps for teachers and students to reach each other, gather materials, or use classroom equipment.

The closer you are to your students, the more you will minimize classroom behavior problems and maximize cooperation. When the teacher is physically close to students and can get to them quickly, their on-task behavior increases. When the teacher is far from students and cannot get to them quickly, the more likely they are to stop working and disrupt others. **Maximize your proximity to minimize your problems.**

> **Discipline problems are directly proportional to the teacher's distance from students.**

- Place the teacher's desk, filing cabinet, and other equipment so they do not interfere with the flow of traffic. Do not create a barrier between yourself and your students. Place your desk so that you can move quickly to a student to assist, reinforce, or discipline.

- Place the teacher's desk so that you can easily monitor the classroom while at your desk or working with individual students.

The closer the teacher is to the students, the less likely behavior problems will occur in the classroom.

- Place the teacher's desk away from the door so that no one can take things from your desk and quickly walk out.

- If you choose to have everything on and in your desk treated as personal property, make this clear when you teach classroom procedures.

Prepare Teaching Materials

- Have a letter ready listing the materials you want students to bring from home. Have a place and a procedure ready to store these materials.

- Have a method ready for matching students to a desk. You could have name cards ready on each desk, or use a document camera, interactive whiteboard, or PowerPoint slide to display desk arrangement with students' names.

- Have your basic materials ready for the first week of school. These include books, papers, pencils, rulers, glue, chalk, felt pens, stapler, tape, clipboard, crayons, felt-tip markers, construction paper, instruments, calculators, supplies, manipulatives, playground equipment, and computer software. Buy a bell or a timer if you wish to use either as a signal.

- Find and organize containers for your materials. Use copy paper boxes, crates, coffee cans, milk cartons, and shoeboxes to store materials. Label your containers, and place in each an inventory card listing everything that should be in the container.

- Store seldom-used materials out of the way, but be sure they are inventoried and ready for immediate use.

- Place electronic media near outlets and where the students will not trip over the wires. Have an extension cord and an adapter plug handy.

- Organize and file your masters, lesson plans, and computer memory sticks. Do likewise with your extra worksheets so they are immediately ready for any students who were absent or who need extra help.

When to Prepare so You Are Prepared

You don't train your football team on game day. You don't drill a well when you are thirsty.

And you don't discuss procedures during an emergency. It's too late then. Prepare so you are prepared when there is an emergency.

Organize yourself for easy access when needed.

A Prepared Teacher Is an Effective Teacher

Teachers who are ready maximize student learning and minimize student misbehavior. Plan ahead and organize yourself so that you know exactly what you are going to accomplish and how you will accomplish it every day of the school year. When you have planned and prepared, you will be ready, willing, and able to teach with a confident smile, supporting and inspiring your students to achieve and succeed.

Finally, Prepare Yourself

rganization is the key to effectiveness. Make a place for everything and put everything in its place.

- Keep your briefcase, tote, handbag, keys, and other valuables in a safe location.

- Have emergency materials handy, such as tissues, rags, hand sanitizer, paper towels, soap, first-aid kit, and extra lunch money. Store these for you to use and distribute, not for students to help themselves.

- Obtain a teacher's guide for each textbook you will be using. Obtain a manual for each piece of technology equipment you will use in your class.

- Obtain a supply of the forms that are used for daily school routines, such as attendance, tardy slips, hall passes, and referrals. Put them where you can access them immediately.

THE EFFECTIVE TEACHER

- ☑ Is ready with a Classroom Management Plan.

- ☑ Prepares the classroom so it is clean, safe, organized, and consistent.

- ☑ Plans and prepares the classroom to be a work-oriented environment.

- ☑ Maximizes proximity to students to minimize behavior problems.

...IMPLEMENTS!

Seven Things Students Worry About

Everyone knows that the first day of school is a very stressful day for students. They are anxious and unsure about everything, very afraid of making mistakes and appearing foolish. **Everything possible should be done to welcome students so that they know where to go and how to get there on time.**

> The way you introduce yourself and greet students on the first day of school can determine how much you will achieve together for the rest of the school year.

⭐ **THE KEY IDEA**

Students learn best when they are welcomed into a safe, organized, and consistent classroom.

Douglas Brooks discovered that there are seven things that students worry about on the first day of school, beginning with, "Am I in the right room?"[1] **Finding the correct room on the first day of school can be one of the most frightening experiences for students.** There is nothing more embarrassing than discovering that they are in the wrong room—fifteen minutes after class has begun.

Before and On the First Day of School

There is much that you can do even before the first day of school to establish ties with students' homes, parents, or guardians. Simply making contact, introducing yourself, and communicating essential information can alleviate a great deal of anxiety and uncertainty about the first day of school.

Then, on the first day itself, greet students at the classroom door with warmth and enthusiasm. Make them feel welcome. Make them feel at home. For many students, the classroom is the best home they have. It is where they receive appropriate attention, it is where there are people who believe in them, it is where they are expected to achieve and succeed.

WHERE AM I SUPPOSED TO SIT?

WHO IS MY TEACHER AS A PERSON?

AM I IN THE RIGHT ROOM?

WHAT ARE THE RULES OF THIS CLASSROOM?

WHAT WILL I BE DOING THIS YEAR?

HOW WILL I BE GRADED?

WILL MY TEACHER TREAT ME FAIRLY?

These are the seven things students worry about on the first day of school.

---

[1] Douglas Brooks, "The First Day of School," *Educational Leadership*, vol. 42, no. 8 (May 1985): 76–78.

66

Dear Dr. Wong,

When I came home from your in-service meeting, I asked my 13-year-old son the following question: "What's the most frightening thing about the first day of school?"

After thinking for a moment, he said, "Two things—having the teacher mispronounce your name and walking into the wrong classroom."

Classroom teacher
Garland, Texas

99

Communication with Parents or Guardians

How to communicate quickly with parents or guardians can be found in the **Go**ing **Be**yond folder for Chapter 12 or scan the QR Code

Am I in the right room?

Mrs. Newnam
Fifth Grade
Gifted and Talented
Storer Elementary
Welcome!!!
Get ready for a fantastic school year!

Enter if you have a great attitude, a super work ethic, and a love for learning!

Many teachers like Samara Newnam of Muncie, Indiana, answer the seven things students worry about and want to know on the first day of school with a PowerPoint presentation of seven slides. Samara begins with letting students know they are in the right room.

Before School Begins

Here are some techniques used by effective teachers with students, parents or guardians before the school year begins. They are reassuring, inspire confidence, and ensure that all channels of communication are open. Apply and adapt the examples to your situation.

1. **Send a letter home to parents or guardians BEFORE school begins.**

   - Tell parents or guardians that you are looking forward to having their child in your class.

   - Ask them to put the dates of the school's open house in their calendar, and explain why it is important for them to attend. You will be explaining homework, grading, discipline, and classroom procedures.

   - Include information on what materials you want students to have ready for school.

2. **Send a letter home to each student BEFORE school begins.**

   - Connect with your students before school starts. Send a postcard of welcome. Email the family.

   - Tell the students who you are.

   - Invite them to call or email you if they have questions.

   - Help them prepare by listing the materials they should have with them. They will be ready if you are ready. Do not surprise your students.

   - Tell them *your* expectations, not theirs.

Dear Brooke,
   I'm glad you're in my class this year! I'll see you on TUESDAY in ROOM 25.
   Please bring this card with you. It will be your admission ticket to class.
   Your first assignment will be on your desk.
   You will be seated in ROW __E__ NUMBER __2__.
   See you soon!
               Sincerely,
               Miss Abbott

"LET US DARE TO READ, THINK, SPEAK AND..."
John Adams, 1765
poweroftheletter...

Brooke Fox
6810 Pine Street
Portage, MI
      49002

Welcome!

Shared by Val Abbott,
Portage Public Schools,
Michigan

GoBe

Home Visitations

They were treated like celebrities when they visited the homes. Read why in the **Go**ing **Be**yond folder for Chapter 12 or scan the QR Code.

3. **Visit the home of each student BEFORE school begins (check to be sure that this is an appropriate thing to do).**

- Introduce yourself.
- Bring with you the letters just described.
- Share with parents or guardians how they can help.

Begin Each Day with a Greeting

Greet each student individually and warmly each day **and each class period.** Welcome them into the classroom. The greeting is a brief moment between teacher and student, but it is a meaningful moment. Your student has your full attention and it gives you the opportunity to assess how they are. The greeting shows them that you care and that you consider each one of them special. It is a positive interaction that creates a caring and constructive atmosphere that spreads throughout the classroom.

Here is a successful technique used by many effective teachers for greeting students on the first day of school.

Step 1. Post the following information on the wall next to the classroom door where students can see it and compare it to the correct information on their registration forms.

- Your name
- Room number
- Section or period, if appropriate
- Grade level or subject
- An appropriate welcome or greeting

Stand at the door on the first day and each and every day thereafter with a giant smile on your face, hand extended in an invitational pose, to welcome students into the classroom.

The Teacher Believes in Me

It all starts with a phone call. That is how a great year begins for me. In August I call each and every student to say that I cannot wait to see his or her smiling face on the first day of school. Yes, it is a time commitment, but it is priceless. Many students are so anxious to tell me about their summer—one even asked if he could bring his bike to school on the first day because he just learned how to ride and wanted to show me! Some students are shy and quiet on the phone; however, their parents assure me that the phone call was excitedly shared with friends, neighbors, and grandparents.

When I call my students' homes before the school year starts, it's to talk to the children. I only identify myself on the phone and ask to speak to the child. If a parent has a quick question, I'll answer it; but if it's a bigger concern, I ask to meet or talk later. This primary phone call is all about the children.

This one commitment, of contacting all my students, really sets the tone for a great year. I even call my last year's fourth graders to wish them luck in middle school. One parent told me that this phone call was the turning point for her daughter who was so nervous about going to middle school. This student said, "If Mrs. Rush believes in me, then I know I can do it."

Peggy Campbell-Rush
Gladstone, New Jersey

This is no different from finding flight information at an airport, a doctor's name on the office door, or information about times and prices at a movie theater. Displaying essential information is an effective and cordial way to start a new school year.

Step 2. Stand at the classroom door. Greet everyone with a smile, hand extended ready to shake hands, and an expression that lets students know you can't wait to meet them. **Stand at the classroom door with a big smile and a ready handshake—every day.** Exchanging greetings is common courtesy in society no matter where we are or what we are doing: visiting, doing business, shopping, traveling, eating at a restaurant. It should not be any different at school. It may be that you're the only teacher greeting students in this way. Does that make you wrong and the others right? Of course not! It makes you more effective at what you do.

Step 3. As students stand in front of you, wondering if you are the right teacher and if this is the correct classroom, welcome them to a new school year and tell them the following information:

- Your name
- Room number
- Section or period, if appropriate
- Grade level or subject
- Anything else appropriate, such as seating assignment

Step 4. Check each student's registration card, and if the student is in the wrong place or is lost, help the student or find a guide who will.

Step 5. After you greet each student, the student should enter the classroom and be able see the same information that was on the wall outside the classroom written or posted in the classroom:

- Your name
- Room number
- Section or period, if appropriate
- Grade level or subject
- An appropriate welcome or greeting

Because students are exposed to the same information three times, it is highly unlikely that any of them will find themselves in the wrong place on the first day of school. Their anxiety and any tendency to be confrontational are reduced. They will feel welcomed, at ease, and a little more confident.

The Research Behind Greeting

Allan Allday, in the department of special education at the University of Kentucky, did two research studies based on the greeting technique he read about in ***THE First Days of School***. He specifically investigated:

- Effects of teacher greeting on student on-task behavior[2]

- Effects of teacher greeting to increase speed to on-task engagement[3]

In the classroom where the teacher greeted the students at the door, there was an increase in student engagement of 32 percent. That is, they worked on their assignment and did not misbehave. In the second study, students got on task faster when they were greeted at the door, in comparison to the control class that was not greeted.

Start of Day greeting!

Help your students find your room by posting information outside the door as well as inside the classroom.

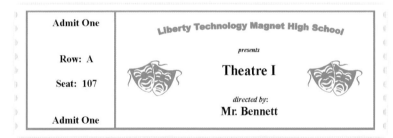

Chris Bennett, a theater arts teacher in Tennessee, gives his students a theater ticket when he greets them at the door of the auditorium, which is their classroom.

Examples of Effective Greeting

Here are examples of two schools that employ the greeting technique effectively so that discipline is not a factor, bullying does not exist and, more importantly, students are on task and doing their classroom work. It all begins at the door.

---

[2] R. Allan Allday and Kerri Pakurar, "Effects of Teacher Greetings on Student On-task Behavior," *Journal of Applied Behavior Analysis*, vol. 40, no. 2 (Summer 2007): 317–320.

[3] R. Allan Allday, Miranda Bush, Nicole Ticknor, and Lindsay Walker, "Using Teacher Greetings to Increase Speed to Task Engagement," *Journal of Applied Behavior Analysis*, vol. 40, no. 2 (Summer 2011): 393–396.

The students at SISCL are greeted each day by the teacher and a classmate.

A greeting may the only positive interaction a student has all day.

It me

As the students enter through the doors of the Staten Island School of Civic Leadership (SISCL), also known as Public School (PS) 861, they find a teacher and a student greeter waiting for them.

The teacher and student greeter model the procedure, shaking hands and saying "Good Morning" to each other. They then greet the other students.

This routine is used every day with a new student greeter rotating each week. It is carried on each school year, so students develop a sense of structure within a consistent environment.

> **Structure, mixed with care and love, is what every child needs in his or her life.**
>
> **Structure, mixed with care and love, is what every student needs in the classroom.**

Brockton High School in Brockton, Massachusetts, has 4,200 students, the largest high school in Massachusetts and one of the largest in the nation. It has nine buildings and is the size of an aircraft carrier, yet students feel comfortable at this high school because they are greeted each morning as if they are entering someone's home, a safe and welcoming place.

Susan Szachowicz, former principal, together with teacher, Charles Russell, greeted students each morning as they came through one of the four entrances to the school. She did this every day for years and her school developed into a nationally recognized school with a culture of care and consistency that conveys the message that every student has a right to succeed. A positive atmosphere permeates Brockton High School.

Greeting students establishes a sense of belonging. Recognizing students tells them, "I'm glad you're here." What a powerful message to send to students each day. The tone for the school day is set the moment the students see you. It can be one of "I am too busy to deal with you," or it can say "Happy to see you. Let's get on with learning!"

Entering the Classroom

After greeting students at the classroom door, effective teachers, when possible, have the classroom ready with students' names or numbers on their desks. This is highly cherished by those students who do not have a place to call "home" at home.

Put a personal letter on each desk and attach another sheet of paper, already addressed to you, to encourage responses from those students who would like to write back to their teacher. Put a coded number on the back in case a student sends a troubling, unsigned message seeking help.

Listen to your students during the first days of school. Be observant. The impressions you have and the connections you make will help guide your teaching, benefiting individuals and the class atmosphere as a whole.

Your Important First Words

On the first day of school, there are two major things you want to state at the outset: your name and your expectations. It's in your best interest not only to tell the class your name, but to pronounce it clearly so they will call you by the name you want.

Students want to know who you are as a person, and if you will treat each of them as a person. It is important that you dispel any fears they may have about being in your class. The best way to do this is to smile, exude caring, and communicate positive expectations.

Being an effective teacher has to do with DOING. Demonstrate that you are effective by doing things that show how you constantly strive toward improved performance.

- Have your script or plan ready for the first day of school.
- Proudly and positively introduce yourself and the classroom to the students.
- Explain how the class is organized for their success.

The students now know what the classroom expectations are. They have an immediate assurance that you are organized for what matters most: **their success!**

How NOT to Start the First Day of School

The ineffective teacher suddenly enters the classroom just as the bell rings. The teacher's name and the room number are nowhere to be found. The teacher never mentions his or her name, the room number, the class, the grade level, or the period. The teacher regards the class with an icy stare.

Or, if the teacher is in the classroom when students walk in, he or she stands behind the desk, glaring, inspecting everyone with a look that says, "You're infringing on my space."

The teacher announces that he or she will call the roll. The teacher also announces that as the roll is called, the seating assignments will be changed so that everyone is seated in alphabetical order. A collective groan arises. (See "Succeeding with Your First Request," page 127.)

The teacher reads out the name of the first student. He or she then points to the student sitting in the first chair and demands, "Up." That student rolls his or her eyes, shuffles forward, and leans against the wall.

The teacher then points to the first student on the roll and says, "You, sit there."

As each student is dislodged from his or her chair, they lounge along the wall.

The students are all looking at each other, shaking their heads. "Who is this disorganized person?" they think. "Our teacher? It's going to be a long year!"

A Reputation of Love

Jone Couzins teaches in Ohio. On the last day of the school year she asks her seventh-grade classes to write letters of advice to the next year's seventh graders.

On the first day of the new year, she distributes the letters to the incoming seventh graders. They are among the most anxious students in the building on the first day.

She tells them the letters are meant to help them adjust to life at the school. After reading the letters, their assignment is to answer the letter they received and compare their own experiences during the first week of school to the experiences and advice from the present eighth grader.

Of all the comments made by the new students, the one that surfaced most often was, "I know that I'm going to like Mrs. Couzins's class because she said she loves kids."

One Teacher's Welcome

Welcome. Welcome to another school year.

My name is Mr. Wong. There it is on the board. It is spelled W-O-N-G and is pronounced "Wong." I would like to be addressed as Mr. Wong, please. Thank you. I am looking forward to being your teacher this year. Relax.

I am a veteran teacher with over thirty years' experience. Outside of class, I go to workshops, conferences, professional meetings, college classes, and seminars. I also read the professional journals and work together with my fellow teachers in professional learning communities. I keep up-to-date in my teaching skills. Most importantly, I love to teach! I enjoy teaching, and I am proud to be a teacher. So you can relax. You are in good hands this year with me.

You are going to have one of the greatest educational experiences of your life. This classroom will be well organized, and you will feel well cared for while you are in it. We will not only study [subject], but I will also share with you some life skills and secrets that we call procedures that will help you succeed in the years ahead. I can assure you that if you should run into me at the mall twenty-five years from now, you will say, "You were right, Mr. Wong. That was the most memorable, exciting, and fascinating class I ever had."

So welcome!

How to Speak to the Class *Aimed at me!*

Learn to speak clearly and effectively. Students will gauge their confidence in you by how you say what you want to say. Stand up when you address the class. Speak in short, clear sentences or phrases. Students have a way of turning off when they listen to long, complex sentences. Your purpose is to establish sureness and understanding, not to impress or overwhelm with your intelligence.

Learn to use volume effectively. The most effective teachers have a firm but gentle voice. Learn to "speak loudly" with your tone, not your volume. When you speak softly, the class listens carefully. You modulate the noise level of the class by the loudness of your voice. And on those rare occasions when you may need to raise your voice, you will have twice as much impact.

Learn to use nonverbal language effectively. A nod, a smile, a stare, a frown, a raised eyebrow, or a gesture is often all that is needed to communicate approval or disapproval, and it does not even disturb the class at work. Body language can speak volumes. Use it to manage the classroom and minimize disruptions.

Learn to communicate control effectively. Your manner and voice should be gentle and calm. Smile generously, but be firm. Your voice should communicate that you are not the least bit flustered or angry by what is happening. You are simply in control of yourself and every student in the classroom. Students know what you expect from them, and you are communicating this expectation.

Speak with confidence when you address the class.

The First Days Are Critical

On the first days of school, be calm, firm, and proactive. Learn to begin many of your sentences with "You will . . ." or with "The class procedure is . . . ." The first few days are critical. This cannot be stressed enough.

Your mission is to establish student habits or routines, called procedures in this book. **Students will develop their own habits or routines in classes where teachers do not teach procedures and communicate expectations.** These patterns of behavior can spread, and soon the entire class develops its own agenda, its own curriculum, and its own set of procedures. Perhaps it's only the third day of school, and you have already lost control of your class.

The effective teacher has a classroom management plan from the very beginning to prevent the classroom from becoming a breeding ground for confusion and discontent.

Last but Not Least: Listen

It is most important to communicate your expectations and put your classroom management plan into effect during the first days of school. It is also extremely important to listen to your students. This is their classroom, their workplace, their home away from home, and it is essential that you pay attention to their needs and wants.

Dale Fillmore of Pennsylvania welcomes students and let's them know the expectations for the classroom on the first day of school.

Sharing

Learn how to get to know your students and how to let them get to know you in the **Go**ing **Be**yond folder for Chapter 12 or scan the QR Code.

Welcome them. Create a warm, caring atmosphere of trust and support. How you welcome them into the classroom will give them a very good indication of whether or not they can rely on your support. Every student expects to share their needs and wants, their dreams and ambitions, with their teacher—a kind, competent, and effective teacher who they trust knows how to ensure their success.

☆ THE EFFECTIVE TEACHER

☑ Communicates with parents, guardians, and students before school starts.

☑ Greets students warmly as they enter the classroom.

☑ Addresses the seven things every student worries about on the first day of school.

☑ Organizes the classroom so students know they can be heard and supported.

...IMPLEMENTS!

Seating Assignments or Arrangements?

One of the first questions that probably comes to mind when you are thinking about organizing your classroom is whether you should assign seats or allow students to sit wherever they choose.

How you and your students communicate will determine the success of what you want to accomplish in the classroom.

THE KEY IDEA

The main objective of classroom seating arrangements is communication.

That is not the first question that you should consider, however. You should first decide what kinds of activities your students will be doing and how you want them to be doing those activities. Then ask yourself, How do I arrange seats and desks in my classroom so different types of activities are accomplished efficiently and effectively? How do I foster and facilitate communication?

*What are they doing?
How will I set up to accomplish this?*

Seating arrangements may not be the most exciting topic, but the placement of chairs can profoundly affect the outcome of a lesson. The wrong seating arrangement can mean the difference between a controlled, constructive environment or a chaotic, unconstructive one. The right seating arrangement facilitates communication, concentration, and cooperation.

The purpose of seating arrangements is to accomplish classroom tasks efficiently and effectively.

Teachers must be clear about what they want to achieve and what students are to accomplish before arranging the seating. Each kind of activity or task has a seating arrangement that is more appropriate than others. Desks and chairs should be arranged to maximize engagement and communication and to minimize behavior problems. Consider the situation in your classroom and the options that are available to you.

Performing arts

Discussion or demonstration

Circle time

Carpet time

It is only after seats are arranged that the question of seat assignments should be considered. **Seating arrangements take priority.**

> **Classroom seating arrangements affect communication, concentration, and cooperation.**

Seating Arrangements

To determine seating arrangements for your classroom, you need to ask yourself the following four questions, in this order:

1. **What will students be doing?**
   Is it the first week of school when you will be teaching classroom procedures, rules, and routines? Are students listening to a lecture or story? Is it a class discussion, a small group activity, or individual deskwork? Are students taking a test?

2. **Who is communicating with whom?**
   Are you communicating with the students?
   Are the students communicating with each other?
   Are the students communicating with an audience?
   Are the students communicating on electronic media?
   Are the students communicating with a distance-learning teacher?

3. **What kinds of seating arrangements are possible?**
   You may be limited by the size or shape of the classroom or what desks, tables, and chairs are available. You may also have to consider other teachers or other classes that are held in the room.

4. **Which seating arrangement will I use?**
   There is no one form of seating that should be used permanently the entire school year.

At the beginning of the year, however, the only way for students to learn how your classroom is organized and structured is to have the seats arranged so that every pair of eyes is focused on you. Procedures, routines, and rules are best taught with the chairs facing you, not with the room

Can I do this?

arranged in a series of centers or circles in which half the students have their backs to you. (Procedures, rules, and routines are explained in chapters 15, 16, and 17.)

During the school year, the different activities your students engage in will require a variety of seating arrangements. Students must be in the seating arrangement that helps facilitate the task you want them to accomplish. Change the seating in your room as frequently as you deem necessary for your purposes.

- The effective teacher uses a variety of activities to engage students during the course of the school year.

- Different types of activities mean that a variety of seating arrangements will be used.

- The best seating arrangements are conducive to communication, concentration, and cooperation.

Some Different Seating Arrangements

Diana Greenhouse sets up a double circle of chairs for her "Inner-Outer Discussion." The inner circle of chairs faces in, and the outer circle of chairs faces out. The chairs are back to back, making an inner and an outer circle of seats. (See page 255.)

Lecture, test, or video

Group work

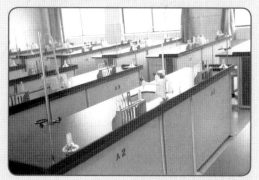

Science lab

Students sit in a circle with their backs to each other.

Chris Bennett teaches theater arts. His class is held in the auditorium and the seats are bolted to the floor. He communicates with students, and they communicate with each other from the stage, or to the stage, seated in rows

Seating Arrangements

Arrange seats, if possible, to coincide with the specific task or activity you have designed.

Examples

- First-day registration and procedures
- Cooperative learning
- Listening to a lecture
- Sitting to hear a story
- Class discussion and interaction
- Small-group activity
- Taking a test
- Individual research or deskwork

Seating Assignments

Assign seats to maximize learning and classroom management, and to minimize behavioral problems.

Examples

- By height or age
- In alphabetical order
- For peer-group tutoring
- For paired problem solving
- Placing lower-performing and more challenging students at the front of the room

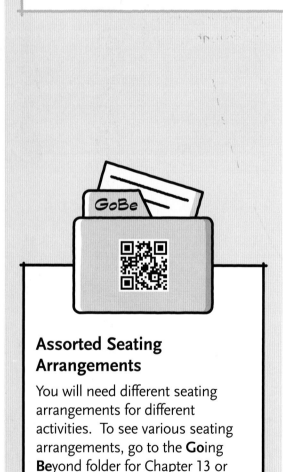

Assorted Seating Arrangements

You will need different seating arrangements for different activities. To see various seating arrangements, go to the **Go**ing **Be**yond folder for Chapter 13 or scan the QR Code.

facing the stage. What better way to have a sense of being in the audience, or to learn how to face and address an audience, than to have those students who are not on stage sitting as people do in a theater.

LaMoine Motz is a high school science teacher. His classrooms feature inquiry-based science activities. The students are in "lab groups," meaning they are in small groups engaged in activities. This same arrangement is used whenever small groups are engaged in work, regardless of grade level or subject.

Patricia Candies starts each day with students sitting for "circle time."

Tony Tringale teaches fifth grade. During social studies, he finds that a horseshoe-shape arrangement is best because of his lecture-discussion style. He talks, and he leads lots of discussions. In this seating arrangement, the students see him and they see each other.

Angelica Garcia teaches performing arts. During choir, her younger students sit on the floor facing her. An "x" on the floor indicates where they are to sit. Her older students stand in rows of risers facing her.

Robin Barlak teaches preschool special education. Her students, several of whom are severely disabled, sit in a half circle on the rug, in the same place each day, facing her during large-group time.

Steve Geiman teaches physical education. There are no seats, unless you consider the bleacher seats in fixed rows. Sometimes the students stand in columns and rows, sometimes huddled around the coach, and sometimes in lines facing different directions for drills.

All Arranged and Ready to Assign

When the school year begins, you should be ready. Before you stand at the classroom door and greet your students, have these items prepared:

- A classroom management plan (page 12)
- A classroom seating arrangement (page 121)
- Procedures to organize the classroom for student work (page 125)
- A method to assign students to seats (page 125)

> **How students respond to your first set of instructions will be determined by how prepared and organized you are when they enter the classroom.**

As students cross the threshold into the classroom, your very first instructions to them will most likely be to tell each one of them where to sit. How they respond to these directions will be an indication of how students will react to your directions for the remainder of the year.

There are two possible scenarios.

1. If you are prepared and have positive expectations for the year ahead, students will sense that you have done everything possible to ensure their success in the classroom. They will trust your decisions. They will follow your orders promptly and courteously.

2. If you have not adequately prepared and feel negatively about starting the school year, students will sense that you are not in control. They will mistrust your decisions. They will be reluctant and recalcitrant no matter what you say.

What If the Chairs Cannot Be Moved?

You may be in a room where the chairs are bolted in place. Or you may be sharing a room that is used primarily for a different grade level or subject. Or you may be sharing a room that is the primary room of another teacher.

If you are restricted to a seating arrangement that can't be changed, simply adapt activities, adjust classroom instructions, and modify your teaching techniques. You have no doubt been in many situations where circumstances and budgets dictated the terms. For your own wellbeing and that of your students, learn to be flexible and adaptable when different circumstances present themselves.

Accept that all things are not the way you want them, and that some things can't be changed. Don't become obsessed or defeated by these things.

Learn to nourish your heart, mind, and body. Continuously strive to improve the quality of your life.

At the start of the school year, desks do not have to be in traditional rows, but all chairs should face forward so that all eyes are focused on the teacher.

Seating Assignments

The effective teacher assigns students to their seats on the first day of school. Don't make finding one's seat a frustrating treasure hunt or an anxious exercise trying to be next to or away from certain classmates. The task should be over in a matter of seconds. It is not a topic for class discussion. You are the teacher, the conductor and facilitator, who is very much in charge.

It is no different when you host a dinner party, board an airplane, go to a restaurant, or attend the theater. It is more efficient and effective for people to have assigned seats. It eliminates confusion and disagreements.

Deal with changes in seating assignments in the same expedient way whenever it is appropriate to rearrange the furniture, equipment, or seating. For group work, for example, you should assign students to their groups and then direct the groups to their workstations or seating assignments. Seating assignments are not permanent. For the first few days of school, use small sticky notes with students' names on them. This will allow you to easily move a student.

You will have a much more effective class, most of the time, if you assign students to their seats. Seating assignments sometimes need to be made for social and behavioral reasons. When you do not want certain students to sit together, separate them. Before going to an assembly, say, "Please wait for me to place you before you take your seat."

Finally, seating assignments will help expedite roll taking, which should be done without interrupting students during the opening assignment.

Love this!

"Good morning. Here's your seating assignment."

Reasons for a Seating Chart

1. **Facilitates roll taking**
2. **Aids with name memorization**
3. **Separates potential problem students**

Help Students Find Their Assigned Seats

Step 1. Have place cards with names on the desks.

Step 2. Have names written on a seating chart or a PowerPoint slide to project at the front of the classroom.

Step 3. Greet students at the door, acknowledging each one. Invite them into the classroom with a warm verbal welcome such as "Hello! Come on in!" or "Glad to see you!"

Step 4. As you greet students, give them an index card with a letter and a number written on it, such as B5, A8, C3. Tell them to find their seats based on the projected seating chart. (Do not use this method if you think it will be too difficult for your students to figure out two coordinates. You want them in their seats when the bell rings, not running around confused.)

Step 5. Inform students that their first assignment is ready. Tell them they will find it at their seat, posted on a flip chart, or written on the board and that they should start to work on it immediately. The first assignment should be short, interesting, and easy to complete. It should lead to success for all students. It may simply be an information form that will not be scored.

The most important thing is to impress your students with your efficiency and competence as a classroom manager and teacher. What you do on the first day may well determine how much respect and success you will have for the rest of the school year.

It should be apparent for all to see that student success and implementing the instructional program effectively are your primary concerns.

Help students know where they belong in the classroom.

How to do this with K?

Succeeding in Your First Moments

The Effective Teacher

- Is present in the room or at the door when students arrive
- Checks each registration at the classroom door
- Assigns seating to everyone upon entering the room
- Has an opening assignment ready for students

How you behave and what you do the instant a student enters the school, the gymnasium, the office, or the classroom communicates immediately whether you can be trusted and if the student is welcome there.

People make people feel welcome. Textbooks, whiteboards, technology, worksheets, and programs do not welcome students to school. When the effective teacher is standing expectantly at the door, greets everyone with a smile, and extends a hand to shake, students receive a positive message that makes them feel secure and comfortable.

Then, upon entering the classroom, students should find themselves in a pleasant environment. The teacher's name, the room number, the period, and the class name are posted on the whiteboard. Directions for seating (whether assigned or open) are reiterated. Information about the first opening assignment, which is on the desks or posted for all to see, is clearly stated and tells students to get to work even before the bell rings.

The message an effective teacher conveys is that the classroom is a safe, positive, work-oriented environment where every second will be devoted to learning and success.

When students feel welcomed and included, they are much more likely to accede to your directions and requests.

Your First Moments Will Be Effective . . .

- If you welcome each student into the classroom
- If you check registration cards as they enter the classroom
- If you tell students your name, room number, period or grade level, and the class
- If you explain what kind of seating arrangements students will find in the classroom (open or assigned)
- If you have prepared an assignment so students can begin work immediately

A genuine welcome says, "I am glad you are here."

Failing in Your First Moments

The Ineffective Teacher

- Is nowhere in sight when students arrive

- Arrives looking disorganized and in an unpleasant mood

- Reshuffles the whole class after everyone has found a seat

- Grumbles about all the administrative details that must be done before class can begin

Imagine students walking into the classroom with no teacher in sight. Some students find a chair; others wander around. But they all ask, "Who's the teacher? Is this the right room? Is this history?" And they all respond, "I don't know."

The bell rings and suddenly a person who must be the teacher appears in the classroom, a misplaced creature who seems to have no idea why they are there and what they are supposed to be doing. It's your run-of-the-mill ineffective teacher. These teachers can always be found in the faculty lounge, gulping coffee, griping and complaining about the same old things year after year.

Students immediately register the unpleasant expression and attitude that dares anyone to breathe out of unison. Ineffective teachers see no need to introduce themselves or even identify the class or period.

The roll begins. "When I call your name, come up here! Bring your registration card for me to sign," they say, barking orders.

When seemingly everyone has been registered, the ineffective teacher finally looks up and asks, "Has everyone been called?" One hand goes up. Discovering that the student is in the wrong classroom, the teacher sends him or her out. The student leaves as all eyes stare and send two silent messages: "Dummy. How can you be so stupid as to be in the wrong room?" and "Aren't you lucky

not having to put up with this horrible, ineffective teacher for the rest of the year!"

That student was needlessly humiliated because the teacher was not prepared and acted in a non-invitational manner. And the students' first impression of this disorganized, unwelcoming, and unhelpful person who is their teacher will be reflected in their work and attitude for the rest of the year.

Your First Moments Will Be Ineffective . . .

- If you are not in the classroom to welcome students

- If you do not check registration cards before students enter the room

- If you do not tell students your name, the room number, the period or grade level, and the class

- If you reshuffle the class after everyone has taken a seat

- If you grumble about the administrative work you have to do

- If you have provided no assignment and students have nothing to do while you register the class

- If you appear disorganized and unprepared for another school year.

☆ THE EFFECTIVE TEACHER

☑ Considers what seating arrangements are effective for different kinds of activities.

☑ Creates seating arrangements that facilitate communication.

☑ Assigns seating on the first day of school.

☑ Has all seats facing the teacher on the crucial first day of school.

...IMPLEMENTS!

Ready to Show Up and Work

Societies around the world run by the clock. Any employee at any workplace knows the time when they must be at their desk or workstation ready to commence working, not chatting with fellow workers or getting another cup of coffee.

> Your very first priority when class starts is to get students to work.

Airplanes, movies, and meetings are scheduled for a certain time. Television programs and sporting events start on time. Stores open at a scheduled time. Students who have part-time jobs know they must get to work punctually to start their work shift.

It is no different in a classroom. Effective teachers start class on time. They greet students at the door with a smile and say, "Here's your assignment." Or they say, "Look at the agenda. Your first work assignment is posted there."

Each day of the school year and at the beginning of every class, your first priority is to start students working immediately. It is not to take roll. This is no different in the private sector. Employees do not stand around waiting for directions or asking questions like, "What do you want me to do?" They are expected to know what to do and to begin working at the appointed hour.

Watch the pregame practice before a sporting event. The players all know what to do; the coach isn't telling them what to do. Watch musicians before a performance. They know how to warm up and tune their instruments or voices; the conductor isn't telling them how. A carpenter has tools ready; a surgeon has instruments ready; a chef is ready for the first order.

Watch students in an effective classroom. They start each day or class with a structured routine that sets the tone for the day and prepares them for the scheduled activities. The teacher doesn't have to tell them what to do.

THE KEY IDEA

Prepare an agenda and an opening assignment for students each and every day.

Be Prepared and Show Up

Daniel Furman, the director of education policy for the Fund for Colorado's Future, reports that employers complained that high school graduates "would not come into an interview dressed appropriately. They would not come prepared to talk about the job they were interviewing for.

"If they were lucky enough to land a job," he says, "they didn't realize they had to show up to work on time Monday through Friday."[1]

---

[1] Lynn Olson, "What Does 'Ready' Mean?" *Education Week* (June 7, 2007).

One Month of Instruction Lost

Shirley Hord, of the Southwest Educational Development Laboratory, discovered that three to seventeen minutes are wasted at the beginning of each class period each school year. That is, from the time the first student enters the classroom until instruction actually begins, wasted time can range from 9 percent to 32 percent of total class time.

Assuming ten minutes are wasted per class period, that translates into one hour for a six-period school day. Multiplying that by a 180-day school year equals 180 hours lost during a school year. **This equates to one month's worth of opportunities to learn lost each year!**

Policymakers talk about extending the school year. There is no need to extend the school year. There is only the need to make the most of the instructional time that already exists.

Effective teachers know instructional time is their most precious resource. They make every minute meaningful.

Starting on time yields these results:

- It maximizes instructional time.
- It establishes a learning environment immediately.
- It reduces tardy and referral rates.

The Agenda

Preparation is critical. Organizers of meetings prepare agendas so that when the meeting begins, everyone uses their time effectively. **The most effective way to get students straight to work is to prepare and post a daily agenda.** An agenda provides a framework or plan for the day or class period. It defines what class activities students will be doing and when. It brings structure and prevents them from asking the perennial question, "What are we doing today?" The purpose of the agenda is to get students on task the moment they enter the classroom. It allows them to take responsibility for learning. It helps students organize themselves.

Effective teachers ensure that their students sit down and get to work, right away every day.

This is no fantasy. It happens every day in thousands of classrooms and it can happen in yours. Students walk in, sit down, and get to work. No one needs to tell them to do this. Even in those countries where teachers go from class to class, students in classrooms that are effectively run are busy and they all know what to do. They take responsibility for following the schedule that has been posted.

A morning routine provides a consistent start to the day or period.

1. Say, "Good Morning"
2. Take your attendance
3. Read your morning agenda
4. Work and eat

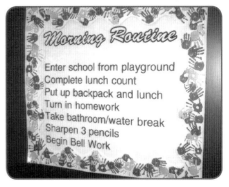

Posting the Agenda

It is ineffective to keep the agenda a mystery until it is announced, or to announce it in different ways, or to post it in different places each day. For efficiency's sake, make the format and the location of the agenda consistent. Remember, students thrive when there is consistency; students are eager to cooperate when there is consistency.

**Post the agenda
in the same consistent location every day.**

The method of posting the agenda can vary depending on your circumstances or classroom. Some teachers use a one-to-one computer format, television monitor, whiteboard, or flip chart. No matter what method is used, the important thing is that the agenda is posted every day in the same place and students know where to find it.

You can always identify classes where there is no agenda posted. In an ineffective classroom, students ask questions like this:

> "Are you going to show us a video?"
> "Are you going to read to us?"
> "Are you going to lecture to us?"
> "Are you going to let us have a study period?"

Or worse yet:

> "Are we going to do anything today?"
> "Are we going to do anything important today?"
> "Did I miss anything important while I was absent?"

In classes where students ask questions like these, they have not been given the opportunity to take responsibility for their work.

Teachers may have an idea of what is going to happen in the classroom, but if they don't communicate their plan or objectives, they are acting ineffectively. They will have difficulty creating a cooperative, successful classroom atmosphere. They leave students with no choice but to be passive and frustrated bystanders, waiting for the teacher to provide direction, entertainment, and work.

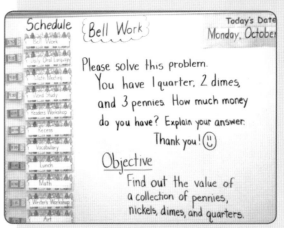

This is an elementary classroom agenda used by Stacey Allred in Muncie, Indiana.

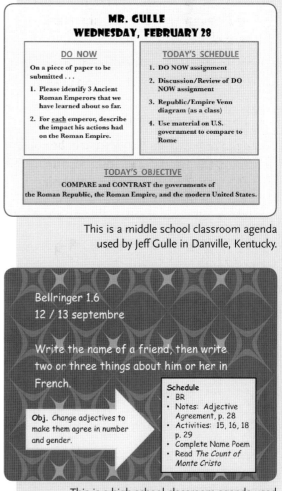

This is a middle school classroom agenda used by Jeff Gulle in Danville, Kentucky.

This is a high school classroom agenda used by Bethany Fryer in Jackson, Mississippi.

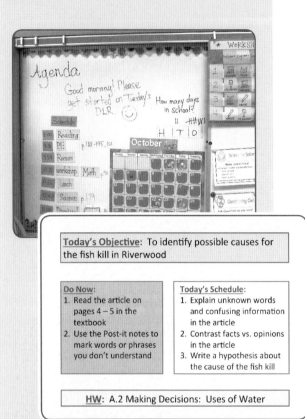

Today's Objective: To identify possible causes for the fish kill in Riverwood

Do Now:	Today's Schedule:
1. Read the article on pages 4 – 5 in the textbook	1. Explain unknown words and confusing information in the article
2. Use the Post-it notes to mark words or phrases you don't understand	2. Contrast facts vs. opinions in the article
	3. Write a hypothesis about the cause of the fish kill

HW: A.2 Making Decisions: Uses of Water

Post an agenda to motivate students to work and learn.

Assignments should be posted daily, always in the same place.

The First Assignment Every Day

Students are accustomed to the word "assignment." They know that this is something they are to DO. Tell students that their first assignment every day is to look at the agenda.

An agenda consists of three basic parts—the **Schedule**, an **Opening Assignment**, and the **Objectives** for the day or class. More parts can be added, such as homework, but the three basic parts are the essential ones and should be clearly stated.

? Objectives w/ Kinders ?

The Three Parts of an Agenda

1. **Schedule: What will occur**
2. **Opening Assignment: What to do immediately**
3. **Objectives: What will be learned**

The Opening Assignment

Once students have looked at the day's agenda, they know what they have to do. They are ready to tackle the opening assignment. **If there is one thing that ensures an effectively run classroom, it is an opening assignment.** It makes no difference what you call it. It goes by many names:

- Bellwork
- Do Now
- Bell Ringer
- Welcome Work ✽
- DOL (Daily Oral Language)
- Warm Ups
- Kick Starter ✽
- Get Going Activity
- Morning Math
- Quick Think
- Fuel for Thought
- Sizzler

One of the more commonly used terms is "bellwork." Bellwork is simply the work students do the instant they enter the classroom. It has nothing to do with the bell; the bell does not begin class. Nor does the teacher begin the class. **The bellwork assignment begins class.**

When teachers institute this simple, straightforward technique in their classroom, it provides a significant "Aha!" moment. Each school day or class begins efficiently and constructively.

Students are more productive throughout the day if they have an assignment to work on as soon as they step into the classroom. It sets the tone for the day—students are there to work and learn.

Essential Requirements for the Opening Assignment

Common sense and research on effective classrooms concludes that you should do this:

- **Post the assignment before students enter the room**
- **Post the assignment in the same location every day**

Even if it is the same assignment every day, post it. Once they know the assignment is in the same place every day, there is no need to waste class time with students asking, "What is the assignment?" or "What am I supposed to do?"

Keep bellwork simple. A bellwork assignment is short, typically five to ten minutes long, and manageable for students to work on independently while the teacher completes the attendance and other duties at the beginning of class.

Bellwork assignments are not graded. Do not begin class by pressuring students with a good or bad grade. A bellwork assignment is a procedure and a procedure is not a rule. Thus, it has no consequences or punishments. (See Chapter 15 for more on this concept.)

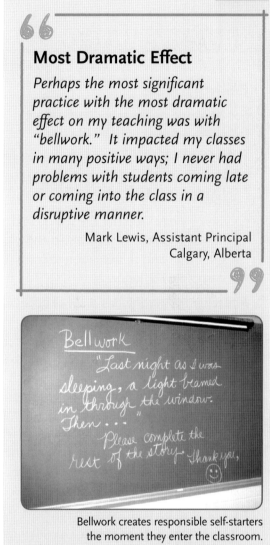

Bellwork creates responsible self-starters the moment they enter the classroom.

The P.E. teachers of Wilson Memorial High School, Virginia share their opening assignment.

Bellwork Ideas

For bellwork, one teacher wrote the following on the board as the day's opening assignment:

> Wendy she said me and josh was lying but he wasn't
>
> Task: Please reorder the words in a logical manner. Then correct the grammar and punctuation to form a complete sentence.

A teacher in Arizona has a set of bellwork assignments prepared for the entire school year. These are printed copies, one for each day, and are stored in a binder on the cart under the document camera. Each night before she leaves, she places the next day's assignment beneath the document camera ready for the next morning. She also has a student trained to turn on the document camera if she is late coming into the classroom.

As you develop your own set of assignments, keep them so you will have them ready for the following year. The best bellwork assignments are those related to that day's work, with a transition or a motivation for what is to follow. A common bellwork in elementary schools, especially K–4, is silent reading until the lesson begins.

Make bellwork a productive time for your students. If you squander this prime time with non-productive tasks such as taking roll or shuffling paper, you will jeopardize the success of the entire class period.

The most common and best use of the bellwork assignment is for it to provide a review of curriculum material, an extension of a previous lesson, or a transition to the lesson of the day. (More on bellwork can be found in **THE Classroom Management Book**.)

Posting the Opening Assignment

Opening assignments can be posted as a PowerPoint slide, on the whiteboard, a bulletin board, a document camera, a flip chart, or they can be distributed as students enter the classroom. If you are a floating, migrant, or resource teacher who has to move from room to room, have the assignment on a flip chart or your laptop ready to display the moment you enter the classroom.

In classes such as physical education and K–1, where the assignment is the same each day, it does not have to be posted. The procedure is rehearsed and repeated daily so that when students come to class, they know just what to do. The assignment becomes a routine part of their class time.

Effective Schools Have School-Wide Procedures

Wanda Bradford is a former principal in Bakersfield, California. She showed her staff various sections from the video series, **The Effective Teacher**. She did not mandate anything; rather, her teachers decided to start each day

Wanda Bradford

with a bellwork assignment. This then became a consistent and effective school-wide procedure.

She said, "We started each day with a structured opening. Each teacher had a daily opening and the students started the day on task." She described the success of her school in a poem.

14

Each day begins with learning
when students come to class.
And without a lot of chatting,
they start the day on task.

With assignments clearly posted
students need not be told,
to quiet down and get to work
while the teacher takes the roll.

If daily routines are followed
less wasted time is spent.
Classes will run smoothly
with great class management.

Research has been proven
achievement gains will rise,
when effective teachers start the day
with time that's maximized.

The goal of her poem is student achievement; teachers achieved this by using procedures that become routines to manage their classrooms.

Think about your own school. Imagine . . .

- The students walk into a class, sit down, and immediately get to work. No one tells them what to do; they know where to find the opening assignment.
- They go to their next class, sit down, and get to work.
- And on to the next class.
- The next class.
- And the next.

And this becomes the prevailing culture of the school. The next year the students go from third to fourth grade, sixth to seventh grade, and eleventh to twelfth grade, and this is the prevailing culture in the school district.

Just Think . . .

- **How much easier life would be if the teachers supported each other with routines that were consistent from classroom to classroom.**

- **What the achievement of these students would be if this was the prevailing culture of the school.**

Daily Geography Bellwork

Debra Lindsay of Alabama teaches fifth-grade science and social studies. She uses a bellwork activity called "Daily Geography Practice." It is consistent, so students do not have to ask questions. They know what to do every day.

She obtains maps from the Internet and gives students a map of the week and two questions to answer daily. The students have been rehearsed and know that the procedure is to answer in complete sentences and to use correct grammar.

Debra says that by the end of the year, not only do students have excellent map skills, they also are writing great sentences in her subject areas on daily work and tests.

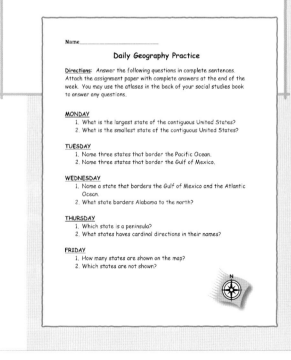

Name_____

Daily Geography Practice

Directions: Answer the following questions in complete sentences. Attach the assignment paper with complete answers at the end of the week. You may use the atlases in the back of your social studies book to answer any questions.

MONDAY
1. What is the largest state of the contiguous United States?
2. What is the smallest state of the contiguous United States?

TUESDAY
1. Name three states that border the Pacific Ocean.
2. Name three states that border the Gulf of Mexico.

WEDNESDAY
1. Name a state that borders the Gulf of Mexico and the Atlantic Ocean.
2. What state borders Alabama to the north?

THURSDAY
1. Which state is a peninsula?
2. What states have cardinal directions in their names?

FRIDAY
1. How many states are shown on the map?
2. Which states are not shown?

The Workers Start the Day

In a fifth-grade class and a high school business education class, it is not the teacher that starts the class. The students start the class. To see how this is done, go to the **Go**ing **Be**yond folder for Chapter 14 or scan the QR Code.

- How effective the schools would be if this were the prevailing culture of the entire district.

To accomplish all of this, no money need be spent. No faddish programs are installed at great expense. Nothing is controversial and the concept works regardless of what grade is taught, what subject is taught, and what educational philosophy the district espouses.

When the school staff works together as a team, it creates a sense of purpose and consistency that makes life easier for everyone. Most importantly, student achievement is increased because there is more time for instruction and learning.

☆ THE EFFECTIVE TEACHER

☑ Has the agenda and opening assignment posted daily.

☑ Posts the daily agenda and opening assignment in a consistent location.

☑ Establishes procedures and routines that maximize instructional time.

☑ Is a leader in promoting school-wide procedures.

...IMPLEMENTS!

Procedures Are Part of Life

Procedures are important in society. They help people function in an acceptable and organized manner. Procedures are evident all around us.

> The major challenge in the classroom is not enforcing discipline. It is establishing procedures that eliminate the need for discipline.

☆ THE KEY IDEA

An effective classroom is based on the teacher's ability to establish procedures.

People are taught the procedures that govern their families and culture from the day they are born. Then, to function successfully at school and in society, they must observe and learn the procedures that govern different communities. The best guideline is the old saying, "When in Rome, do as the Romans do."

Airport security. When catching a plane, you go through a series of procedures. You stand in the correct line, show your identification, put the required items on the conveyor belt, walk through the scanning machine, and collect your items. You do these things efficiently to keep the line moving.

Elevators. When entering an elevator, you step aside to allow people to exit first. In the elevator, you step back to make room when people enter. If your floor is the next stop, you step out, allow new people to enter, and then re-enter.

Wedding. At the conclusion of a wedding ceremony, the bride, groom, and wedding party leave, followed by parents and relatives in the first row, followed by guests from the front of the seating area to the back.

Manners. Manners are procedures. "Thank You, Please, Excuse Me" are reassuring words that help make interactions positive. At a dinner table, it is considered selfish and uncouth to serve oneself before the hostess or host says, "You first, please." When we say someone has bad manners, it is because that person doesn't know or doesn't care about local customs or procedures.

Unit C Recap

Chapter 10: Classroom Management – You know the four characteristics of a well-managed classroom.

Chapter 11: Plan – You have a classroom management plan.

Chapter 12: Greeting – You stand at the door and greet your students.

Chapter 13: Seating – You give assigned seating to your students.

Chapter 14: Work – You have an agenda and bellwork posted for students to be on-task when they enter the classroom.

It is up to you as the teacher to establish what procedures you want in place in your classroom. **This is why Chapter 15 and Chapter 16 are the two most important chapters in this book.** The guidance they provide will help you be an effective teacher who creates a well-managed learning environment where students thrive.

The Three C's

The classrooms of effective teachers exemplify The Three C's—**Coherency, Continuity, and Consistency.**

Coherency results when procedures are in place so that everything works together in a logical and orderly way.

Continuity results when procedures are in place to help things proceed and advance in a logical and orderly way.

Consistency results when procedures are in place to create a stable, predictable environment where learning takes place in a logical and orderly way.

Jacob Kounin did the seminal work on classroom management in the 1970s.[1] He found that a well-managed classroom has "momentum." It is essential to establish the conditions that generate momentum. The principles of coherency, continuity, and consistency ensure that your classes run smoothly and that your students are steadily moving forward.

What Is Classroom Management?

Classroom management consists of the procedures that a teacher establishes to create and maintain an optimum teaching and learning environment. The purpose of classroom management is to organize the classroom so students know what to do to succeed and are given the means to take responsibility for their own learning.

Teachers who are effective classroom managers have these characteristics:

- They have planned procedures for classroom organization.
- They have instructional procedures to maximize student engagement.
- They systematically teach and reinforce these procedures.

---

[1] Jacob S. Kounin, *Discipline and Group Management in Classrooms* (Huntington, NY: R. E. Krieger, 1977, c1970).

It is not what teachers do to stop misbehavior that characterizes effective group management, but how they <u>prevent</u> problems in the first place. Effective teachers take a systematic approach at the beginning of the school year to implement procedures that manage the classroom for the entire year.

Student success or achievement at the end of the school year is directly related to the degree to which the teacher establishes classroom procedures the very first week of the school year.

Example of a Procedure

There is a procedure for opening a lock on a locker. It's usually two turns to the right, one turn to the left, and a final turn to the right.

There is no penalty if the procedure is not followed. The lock just does not open. Likewise, there is no external reward if the procedure is followed. The reward is the lock simply opens. To do anything in life successfully, you simply follow the procedures.

Lack of Procedures

A vast majority of behavior problems in the classroom are caused by the lack of procedures. There are three main reasons why students do not have or do not follow procedures:

1. The teacher has not planned or thought out what happens in the classroom.

2. The teacher has not implemented procedures to manage the classroom.

3. The teacher has not taught students how to follow procedures.

Students cannot follow procedures that do not exist. The teacher is responsible for planning and implementing procedures that manage the classroom and ensure effective teaching and learning.

Too many teachers don't teach effectively because they don't manage. They "cover" or "do" activities. Then, when things go wrong, they discipline, pressing students into coercion and compliance.

No learning takes place when you discipline. Learning takes place when a student is at work. Discipline only stops misbehavior temporarily until it disrupts learning again.

Difference Between Rules and Procedures

Classroom management plans should not be equated with discipline plans. **Discipline is based on rules. Classroom management is based on procedures.** There is a major difference between rules and procedures.

> **Rules:** Rules are regulations that dictate conduct or action. They are created by and governed by an authority. There are consequences if a rule is broken, and rewards are given to those who act according to the rules. (Rules are explained on page 201.)

> **Procedures:** Procedures are a sequence of steps that are followed to perform a task correctly. Procedures are used to accomplish something. Procedures teach responsibility. There are no consequences if a procedure is not followed correctly. It is simply repeated until the task is completed and the desired outcome is achieved.

Please DO NOT call a procedure a rule. A procedure is not a rule. It should never be used as a threat or an order. Procedures lay the groundwork for student learning. **A procedure is simply a method or process for getting things done in the classroom.**

RULES dictate how students **BEHAVE**.
PROCEDURES determine how things **ARE DONE**.

RULES HAVE penalties and rewards.
PROCEDURES HAVE NO penalties or rewards.

> **Effective teachers teach students
> how to follow procedures responsibly.
> Ineffective teachers use controlling tactics
> to coerce students into compliance.**

Chelonnda Seroyer

I Knew That They Would Do That

I was absent one day and called the school to tell my substitute something. No one answered so I began to panic! I called the teacher next door and asked her if my substitute was there. She told me that she had seen the substitute earlier, but had no idea why the substitute was not answering the phone.

When I returned to school the next day, the teacher met me in the hallway and said, "Remember when I told you that the substitute was in your room? Well, I was wrong. She thought that it was your planning period, so she was not in the classroom."

Before I could say anything she said, "But your kids were great! They had taken the attendance, posted it outside of your door, read the lesson plan that you left for the sub, and were working quietly when the substitute arrived!"

I was so proud of my students. They followed our daily procedures and continued to move right along!

After she told me that, the administrator came around the corner and said, "Mrs. Seroyer, I need to speak with you!" I thought that I was going to be in trouble because he found out that my students were in the classroom alone.

As he was talking, I was thinking, "Oh my goodness, I'm going to lose my job!" But finally he said, "Congratulations! When the sub arrived, your students had posted the attendance and were working so quietly that no one knew that they were alone!"

With a smirky smile of relief, I said, "I KNOW. We have PROCEDURES in place! I KNEW that they would do that!"

Chelonnda Seroyer
Atlanta, Georgia

Terri L. Schultz

Could I Have the Plans Back?

Due to illness, I called for a sub. When my students came in for homeroom, I wasn't there; nor was a sub. The students took roll, filled out the Scantron attendance, listened to the announcements, recited the pledge, and dismissed on the bell.

My first-period class came in next and the sub still hadn't arrived. The students took out their daily work and began working. When most had finished, one student went to the front, used the key and led the class through the answers. He then looked at the board for the schedule and had everyone take out their grammar homework. He used that key and went over the homework with them.

Now, it is about twenty minutes into the period and they still didn't have a teacher. The self-appointed leader wrote out a pass for another student and sent him to the office to check on the teacher situation.

When the office was notified, there was concern and distress. What had been going on for the last twenty minutes? The principal went back to the room with the student.

When I returned the next day, the principal told me that when he entered the room the students were seated and working on the current grammar lesson with the student leader working it on the overhead.

The principal asked the student for the sub plans and moved to leave the room.

The student leader then asked the principal, "Could I have the plans back? I haven't finished teaching yet."

Procedures and organization have empowered me and my students. I don't have problems with discipline and I look forward to coming to work and spending time learning with "my kids" since I've been using procedures.

Terri L. Schultz
Liberty Township, Ohio

Students who follow procedures are actively engaged and take responsibility for their own learning. They know what to do to succeed.

A rule is a DARE to be broken.
A procedure is not.

A procedure is something to DO.
It is a step forward.

Students Who Work, Learn

Students readily accept the idea of having uniform classroom procedures because they simplify the task of succeeding in school.** Procedures create coherency, continuity, and consistency. They are the foundation for momentum in the classroom. They allow a wide variety of activities to take place during the school day, often simultaneously, with minimal confusion and wasted time. If there are no procedures, much time is wasted organizing and explaining each activity, even recurring activities. The lack of procedures also leads to students acquiring undesirable work habits and behaviors that are subsequently hard to correct.

Effective teachers know that the more time students spend on task, called academic learning time, the more they learn. Learning occurs when students are actively engaged and in control of their own learning.

Effective and Ineffective Classrooms: A Comparison

The Effective Classroom

Students follow established procedures and they understand how the class functions.

Students are actively and responsibly involved in meaningful work.

The teacher, having established classroom procedures, is moving around the room, helping, correcting, answering, assessing, encouraging, smiling, and caring.

The Ineffective Classroom

Students don't take responsibility for learning and procedures have not been taught.

Students are restless or apathetic in their seats doing busywork or nothing.

The teacher must continuously attempt to control the class and appears to be the only person working.

Why Procedures Are Important

Procedures establish the foundation for an effective classroom. They are necessary a for safe, calm, and productive environment for several reasons.

- Classroom procedures define the expectations you have of your students. Procedures enable them to participate successfully in classroom activities, to learn, and to function effectively in the school environment.

- Classroom procedures make it possible for various activities to take place efficiently during the school day, often several at the same time, with a minimum of wasted time and confusion.

- Classroom procedures increase on-task time and greatly reduce classroom disruptions. Procedures allow students to take responsibility for learning.

- Classroom procedures inform students how the classroom is organized, thus reducing discipline problems.

What Do I Do Next?
- Work on homework.
- Read your classroom book.
- Organize your folder.
- Study your multiplication facts.
- Make a word find puzzle.
- Make a computer card for a friend or family member.
- Write your spelling words 3 times.
- Create a picture for the Art Wall.
- Suggest a project to Ms. Tom.

Students are less likely to experience frustration, trying to figure out what they are supposed to do and how to do things correctly, if classroom procedures are clearly stated and understood.

PROCEDURE
What the teacher wants done

ROUTINES
Procedures students learn to do automatically

Students Want Procedures and Routines

Students want to know from the very beginning what they are expected to DO in a classroom work environment. They want instruction and guidance on all the how-to's—how to head a paper, how to ask for help, how to sharpen a pencil, how to get to work, how and when to use the computer, and so on.

Procedures teach students what they are to do and how. Procedures evolve into routines and routines create stability and security. Students cannot get down to the serious business of learning unless they feel secure in the classroom and certain of what is expected of them.

No Need for Discipline

I tell my new teachers that I am a lousy disciplinarian, but a good classroom manager.

If they will follow my advice—and I have a procedure for everything that they do—they should not need to discipline a student.

Judy Blassengame Davis
Hampton City Schools, Virginia

**My daughter hated school until this year.
She loves school now.**

**Why?
Because of the way her teacher
has organized the class.**

A parent

Effective teachers have procedures for taking attendance, exchanging papers, registering students on the first day, taking turns speaking, and moving from task to task. They determine what they want done, and they devise a procedure or a set of procedures that clearly state how they want it done. Without procedures, time that should be spent on learning will be wasted getting routine tasks done.

A routine is what students do automatically, without prompting or supervision. A well-managed classroom is the responsibility of the teacher and the result of the teacher's ability to implement procedures so that they become efficient routines.

For Their Benefit

Tell your students that classroom procedures are for their benefit. Following procedures will help them do their work with less confusion and thus help them succeed. Procedures allow the class to operate smoothly and efficiently. They create an environment where it is a pleasure to teach and learn.

Classroom procedures tell your students these things:

- How to enter the classroom
- What to do when they enter the classroom
- What to do if they are tardy
- Where to find the assignment
- What to do when you want their attention
- How a paper is to be done
- Where you want the paper placed
- What to do when they finish work early
- What to do if they want to sharpen a pencil
- How to use electronic media in the classroom
- Where to find assignments if they have been absent
- What to do when they have a question
- What to do when they need to go to the restroom
- What to do if they have a personal emergency
- What to do upon dismissal of class
- What to do when they hear an emergency alert signal

They Quietly Walked in and Began the Bellwork

Oretha Ferguson is one of the co-authors of **THE Classroom Management Book**.

On the first day of school, I stood at my classroom door to welcome my students. I observed as they quietly walked in the room, sat down, and began the bellwork. I also observed the students in another classroom in total chaos as the teacher tried to quiet them to begin class.

I thought, "What a waste of time."

The teacher from the other classroom one day commented that my students were "always so good!" I said, "It's not the students; it's the procedures that have been proven to work. Procedures help me manage my class, so that I can be an effective teacher."

Oretha Ferguson
High school teacher
Fort Smith, Arkansas

On the first day of school, and on other days when a new student enters the classroom, Oretha has a trifold that thoroughly outlines the coherent and consistent organization of her classroom.

She lists the basic classroom procedures in the trifold:

- Starting class
- Ending class
- Completing daily work
- Turning in papers
- Taking a test
- Making up work
- Sharpening pencils
- Throwing away trash
- Using computers
- Signaling for attention
- Getting into groups
- Getting teacher help

Her preparation before the first day of school allows her to be effective the moment students enter the classroom.

In the first few days of school,
teach only the procedures necessary at that time.

Teach other procedures
at the appropriate time when the need arises.

Reasons for Procedures

Procedure for the Start of the Period or Day. When the students enter the classroom, do they know what to do, where to sit, and what materials to have ready? Or do they roam around, wasting time, and waiting for the teacher to tell them what to do? (See page 131.)

Procedure for Quieting a Class. Do your students respond immediately when you want to quiet the classroom and you need their attention? Or do they ignore you so you become tense, yell, and flick the lights—all to no avail? If you do eventually succeed in calming things down, does it take a long time for your students to respond and focus on what you want to communicate? (See page 155.)

Procedure for Students Seeking Help. When students want your help, do they raise their hands, wagging them and calling your name to attract attention, interrupting class work and distracting everyone with muttered complaints because you do not respond instantly? (See page 157.)

Procedure for the Movement of Students and Papers. Do your students take forever to pass their papers in

GoBe

Procedures at Home

Lena Nuccio was having problems with her two kids leaving clothes all over the floor. Read how she solved this problem in the **Go**ing **Be**yond folder for Chapter 15 or scan the QR Code.

Classroom Procedures That Become Routines

- Start of the period or day
- Quieting a class
- Students seeking help
- Movement of students and papers
- Dismissal at the end of period or day

and even longer to change from group to group or task to task? And when they do turn in their papers, do they throw them in a pile on your desk or punch each other in the back as the papers are passed forward? (See page 176.)

Procedure for Dismissal at the End of the Period or Day. When the dismissal bell rings, are your students already standing at the door waiting to leave, or do they just get up and leave, even if you are in the middle of a sentence? You can always tell who is running the class—the students or the teacher—by how the students behave at the end of the period or day. (See page 153.)

The Three Steps to Teaching Classroom Procedures

Most behavior problems in the classroom are caused by the teacher's inability to teach students how to follow ← *it me!* procedures. Telling is not teaching. Students must be physically engaged in the process if you want them to learn. Procedures must be taught, rehearsed, and reinforced.

> **The Three Steps to Teaching Procedures**
>
> 1. **Teach.** State, explain, model, and demonstrate the procedure.
>
> 2. **Rehearse.** Students practice the procedure under your supervision.
>
> 3. **Reinforce.** Reteach, rehearse, and affirm the procedure until it becomes a routine.

Step 1. Teach Classroom Procedures Clearly

Effective teachers spend a good deal of time during the first weeks of school introducing, teaching, modeling, and rehearsing procedures. Do not expect students to learn all procedures in one day, especially at the elementary school level. Procedures must be taught, modeled, practiced, monitored, and retaught.

Difficulties with Procedures

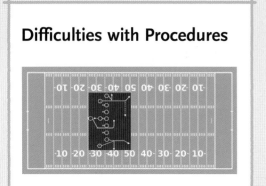

The reason many teachers cannot effectively establish procedures in the classroom is because they just tell students what to do.

If students do not do a procedure properly, you must do what all successful coaches do, what all successful music teachers do, and what all successful second-grade teachers do. Their students practice the plays, practice their instruments, and spell the words over and over again **until the procedures become routines**.

A procedure is not a rule. There are NO consequences if it is not done.

It must simply be rehearsed again and again until it is done correctly.

It is essential that you have the procedures for each opening-of-school activity ready on the first day of school. Explain, and then post or distribute, each procedure to students early in the school year or at the time when the procedure is needed in the classroom. Elementary school teachers should explain the procedures verbally and post pictures that are representative of them. Revise and hone these procedures year after year until they become models of efficiency.

Remember that the effective teacher has a script ready for the first day of school. (See page 15.)

Step 2. Rehearse Classroom Procedures Until They Become Routines

> **All procedures must be rehearsed!**

Effective teachers have students experience each procedure by doing it. Ineffective teachers only tell students what to do; they don't have their students act out what should be done. That is why many teachers fail when they want students to follow procedures.

Coaches are masters of the rehearsal technique. Observe a good music, drama, athletic, or foreign-language coach. They tell and show a technique, show videos of the technique, then have their students or athletes do it repeatedly while they watch. Some people call this method "guided practice." The more musicians, athletes, and students practice, the better and more skilled they become. The discipline of practice enables them to achieve their potential.

Rehearse

- **Have students practice the procedure, step-by-step, under your supervision. After each step, make sure students have performed it correctly.**

- **Have students repeat the procedure until it becomes a routine. Students should be able to perform the procedure automatically without teacher supervision.**

Step 3. Reinforce and Affirm Correct Classroom Procedures

Again, watch a coach. Good coaches are the best teachers. As they guide a team, class, or student through practice, corrections are made instantly. The coach tells, shows, demonstrates, cajoles, and even loudly calls out commands until the task is done correctly.

But good coaches don't stop there. They affirm and reinforce the correct technique by having the student do the acquired technique over and over again, each time exhorting the student to do it better, accompanied with words of confirmation, hugs, pats, and smiles.

Encourage a student who follows a procedure by specifically affirming the action or deed. Be SPECIFIC when telling a student what he or she did well. Say, "Marvin, I see you know where to put your backpack when you come to class," rather than "Good job, Marvin."

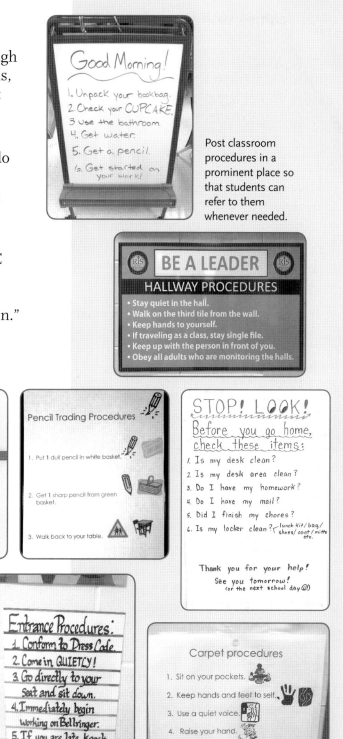

Post classroom procedures in a prominent place so that students can refer to them whenever needed.

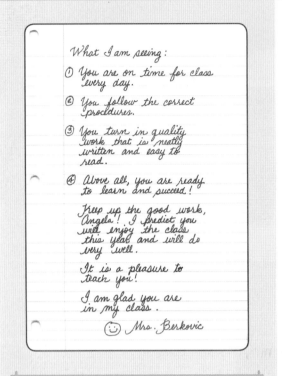

What I am seeing:

① You are on time for class every day.

② You follow the correct procedures.

③ You turn in quality work that is neatly written and easy to read.

④ Above all, you are ready to learn and succeed!

Keep up the good work, Angela! I predict you will enjoy the class this year and will do very well.

It is a pleasure to teach you!

I am glad you are in my class.

☺ Mrs. Berkovic

Praise and Polish

Praise to reinforce the deed
and polish the work.

An example of affirmation and reinforcement is shown in a note Shoshana Berkovic, a high school science teacher in New York City, used for one of her students.

Notice how she affirmed specifically what the student did with numbered items 1, 2, and 3 and encouraged her to continue her good work with the closing paragraphs.

It's worth noting that the student was a borderline student the first two weeks of school and began to flourish after this note was presented.

"Thank you class for hanging up your book bags when you entered the classroom. Please continue to do it just like that every day. Thank you."

Affirm the Deed

Avoid giving generalized compliments that carry no specific personal meaning, such as "Nice work," "Great kid," or "Good job." When students hear vague praises like these, they often have no idea what the teacher is referring to. Pep talks, too, are invigorating, but hollow. They tend to be meaningless because students are unsure to whom the message is directed.

There is a much more effective way to praise. **Affirm the deed.** When you affirm the deed, the student knows exactly what he or she did that was worthy of praise.

"Angela, you spelled all the words correctly. I know you can do it again." End with a smile, make eye contact with the student, and wait for confirmation. When you receive the student's confirmation, say, "Thank you!" and pat the student on the back, give a fist bump, or give her a high-five.

Let students know how much you appreciate the deed they have done. "Thank you for walking behind each other and for not disturbing the other classrooms."

Congratulate them for following procedures. "Class, my compliments for passing the papers across the rows using the proper procedure."

Specific Praise

General praise is nice, but it is not tangible or meaningful. For instance, "Justin, you are a bright young man" doesn't inform the student what they should do or how they should behave.

Praise what the student did, rather than the student, and then encourage him to do it again. This technique is called Specific Praise or "praise the deed, encourage the student."

"Thank you for reprogramming the software, Justin. Look at how fast the screen changes now. Pat yourself on the back. Congratulate yourself. Do it again the next time we need some reprogramming done."

If you have been specific about what the student did, he is more likely to do it again because he knows exactly what to do next time. The student thinks, "You were paying attention to me. You noticed me! And you personally thanked me for doing something. What I do matters to you." When you praise a specific accomplishment, you encourage the continuation of appropriate procedural practice.

Here are some other examples.

> "Thank you, class. That was the correct procedure when you see my hand or hear a bell. Please do the same thing each time you see my hand or hear a bell."

> "Heidi, thank you for the excellent report at the faculty meeting. The next time I need assistance, I would truly appreciate your help again."

> "Julio, thanks for helping with the dishes tonight. Mom had a meeting to go to, and you helped out. The next time Mom needs assistance, I would be glad to have you help out again."

When you praise the deed and encourage the student, you help the student do two things:

1. Accept responsibility for having done the task.
2. Develop a sense of accomplishment.

The key words are **responsibility** and **accomplishment**, two things that all people must develop to be happy and successful in life.

> With gratitude to Barbara Colorosa, author of *Kids Are Worth It*, for suggesting this technique.

Group Praise

"You are working very well as a group. You share the tasks and everyone contributes. Please continue to work like this the next time we are in groups. Thank you."

Individual Praise

"Taye, you played the piece correctly. Please continue to practice so you can play it correctly the next time you come for class. Thank you."

Using the Three Steps

The following are examples of teaching procedures using the three steps. You may not need or want these particular procedures, but note how each one is taught. Then substitute your own procedure, using the **teach, rehearse, reinforce technique** just described.

- How to dismiss a class (page 153)
- How to quiet a class and gain students' attention (page 155)
- How to have a class working when the bell rings (page 133)
- How students are to ask you for help (page 157)
- How students are to pass in papers (page 176)
- How to transition to another activity (page 178)
- How to take lecture notes (page 190)
- How to complete a rubric (page 245)

Procedure for Dismissal at the End of the Period or Day

Teach

On the first day of school, teach students how the period or day will end.

"Students, there is a procedure at the end of the period. You are to remain in your seat (or at your desks with the chairs pushed in) until I dismiss the class. The bell does not dismiss the class. You do not dismiss the class. The teacher dismisses the class. Thank you."

Explain the criteria for dismissal, such as how clean you want the desk or work area, and where and how you want the chairs and equipment to be positioned. Show and demonstrate this procedure. Have several students (never one, because it creates a show-off situation) demonstrate the procedure. Affirm the deed so students know that you are validating the correct procedure.

Rehearse

Have students practice the dismissal procedure on the first day and every day until it becomes a routine. By the end of the third or fourth day, the procedure will have become automatic.

I Missed the First Day of School

You've been hired and school has already started. Or you just want to wipe the slate clean and start all over again. Help for starting your first day, after the real first day has already come and gone, can be found in the **Go**ing **Be**yond folder for Chapter 15 or scan the QR Code.

Thereafter, all you need to do a few seconds after the bell rings is smile and say, "It's been nice seeing all of you. See you tomorrow. Have a nice day." Saying words like these is much better than, for example, "You're dismissed." Let students know you enjoyed your time with them.

Reinforce

Be alert a few seconds before the bell rings on the first day of school. Anticipate that you will need to make an immediate correction if the dismissal procedure is not followed. If the class starts to file out, it is too late to correct the procedure. Failure to correct a procedure will only escalate the problem. Students will decide to dismiss themselves, and they will be the ones in control of the class.

Just before the bell rings, remind the class of the dismissal procedure. This will reduce the need to correct the class. However, if any students begin to leave at the bell, do not scold, yell, or demean. And do not use meaningless phrases or questions like, "Listen to me!" or "What did I say about the dismissal procedure?" You do not want a discussion, an argument, or a response. You want all students at their desks. Calmly, in a confident and certain tone of voice, tell the students who began to leave to return to their desks. "Tom, Joel, Anne, please return to your desks. That's not the procedure."

At the appropriate time

- **REMIND the class of the procedure.**
- **AFFIRM that the procedure has been done correctly.**

Remind: "Class, I would like to remind you of the procedure at the end of the period. You are to remain standing at your desks with your chairs pushed in until I dismiss the class."

Affirm: "Look around the room. You are all at your desks and your chairs are pushed in. This is the correct procedure, and I thank you for doing it correctly. Well done. Please do it again tomorrow. Have a nice day!"

For Whom Does the Bell Toll?

The school's bell, buzzer, or chime at the end of the period or day is a signal for teachers, notifying them that their instructional time has come to an end.

The bell is not directed at students. The bell does not dismiss the class. The teacher dismisses the class with a consistent signal and a pleasant expression of farewell.

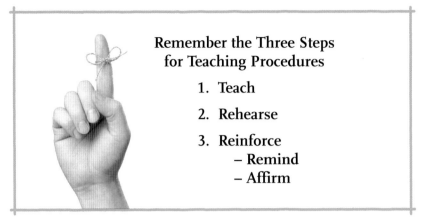

**Remember the Three Steps
for Teaching Procedures**

1. **Teach**

2. **Rehearse**

3. **Reinforce**
   – **Remind**
   – **Affirm**

Procedure for Quieting a Class

Teach

"Students, I have a procedure when I want your undivided attention. You will see me stand with my hand up. Or I may tap a bell because some of you will not be able to see my hand while you are working in a group. When you see my raised hand or hear a bell, the procedure is as follows:

> First, freeze.
>
> Second, turn and face me, pay attention, and keep your eyes on me.
>
> Third, be ready for instruction. I will have something to say. Let me repeat and demonstrate what I just said."

Repeat and call on students to verify understanding. "Geno, please tell me the procedure when you see my hand or hear a bell."

Geno does so. "Yes, yes, yes. Thank you, Geno." Repeat this with several more students.

Ask: "Is there anyone who does not understand or know what to do if you see my hand or hear a bell?"

Rehearse

When everyone agrees that they understand the procedure, say, "Good, let's rehearse the procedure. We will be working together this year, so let's get to know one another. Please look at the person to the right of you. You will have two minutes to introduce yourselves and get acquainted."

Modeling Manners

If the teacher says, "Have a nice day" every day to farewell the class when students are being dismissed, then the teacher is modeling respect and manners. Students are getting a lesson in appropriate behavior—that well-mannered people acknowledge others when they leave a place.

It is the same when teachers greet students at the classroom door. Well-mannered people greet each other before they begin to work or socialize.

Manners are procedures. Teachers should repeatedly model appropriate behavior so that students learn and experience what they need to do and how they should act to succeed in school and society.

Calmly and without saying anything, raise your hand when you want students' attention and silence in the classroom.

> No matter what grade level
> or subject you teach,
> all procedures need to be rehearsed.

After two minutes, hold up your hand or ring the bell, perhaps doing both this first time. Do not say a word when you raise your hand. Do the demonstration exactly as you will be doing it for the rest of the year. Be patient and wait until the class does the three steps and pays attention.

Do not give up as you wait for the students to give you their undivided attention. Affirm their actions when you have their attention. "Thank you. You practiced the procedure correctly. Now please look at the person to the left of you. You may have two minutes to introduce yourself and get acquainted."

After two minutes, hold up your hand or ring the bell. Compliment and affirm that they have done the procedure correctly. "Thank you. You followed the procedure correctly."

Reinforce

Say, "We are not finished learning this procedure. You will often find yourself out of your seat—working in groups or alone somewhere in the room away from your seat. So let's try a different scenario. I would like two of you to stand by

The Greatest Gift

One of the greatest gifts a caring teacher can contribute to students is to help them learn

- to sit when they feel like running,
- to raise their hand when they feel like talking,
- to be polite to their neighbor,
- to stand in line without pushing, and
- to do their homework when they feel like playing.

By establishing procedures in the classroom, you are also preparing students for a disciplined, fulfilling, happy, and successful life.

How to Teach a New Student Procedures

You have spent a few weeks practicing and rehearsing classroom procedures. Your class is now a smooth-running, well-oiled learning environment.

Suddenly, a new student joins the class. What do you do? First, be confident that your existing students are well versed in classroom procedures. If they aren't sure what to do, it will be difficult to orient and teach a new student.

But if you have a class in which students have learned the procedures to the point that they have become automatic routines, you have developed a classroom culture. Students perform in a manner appropriate in your classroom community.

- When a new student joins the class, give the student a copy of the classroom procedures.

- Explain what procedures are and why you have them.

- Tell the student that you will help with the procedures, but that the student will probably be able to learn them by observing how the rest of the class functions.

For example, the bell rings at the end of the period and the new student stands up. Then, he or she notices that all other students still remain in their seats. The student says mentally, "Oh, I'd better stay seated, too, like the rest of the class." The student has just learned the dismissal procedure.

the pencil sharpener, two of you at the sink, two of you at the bookcase, and one of you at the computer."

Hold up your hand and wait for the seven students to pay attention and follow the procedure.

Say, "Thank you. That was the correct procedure when you see my hand or hear a bell. Please do the same thing each time you see my hand or hear a bell."

Use the same language each time to reinforce the procedure until it becomes a routine.

Hand signals are not the only way to quiet a class or group. Create your own technique or steal from what other teachers do.

- A principal holds up an orange card at an assembly and can quiet an entire student body in seconds.
- Many teachers simply say, "May I have your attention, please?"
- A Texas teacher says, "S-A-L-A-M-E," which stands for **S**top **a**nd **L**ook **at ME**.
- A football coach says, "Gentlemen, please."
- A teacher in Arizona plays a tabletop chime.
- A pre-K teacher sings a song.

Procedures for Students Seeking Help

Raising a hand is not an effective procedure for students to use when they want your attention. There are more effective procedures to use.

The class is at work and you are walking around the room helping. You see a hand up and say, "Layne." The whole class stops to look at you and Layne. Layne says, "May I sharpen my pencil?"—a reasonable request. You say, "Yes," or "No," and the class goes back to work.

A few seconds later, you see another hand up. You say, "Carlos," and the whole class stops to look at you and Carlos. Carlos says, "I need your help"—an appropriate request. You say, "Wait a minute," and the class goes back to work.

Every time you speak, you interrupt the class. These interruptions can occur frequently, often two or three times a minute. You would be distracted if the principal

She Quieted One Hundred People in Five Seconds

We were invited to our daughter-in-law's class to attend the annual International Day celebration. Students from three sixth-grade classes were gathered in a large room for the culmination of their study of the country of their ancestry or choice. The students were dressed in native attire and had information and food samples typical of their selected countries.

The three classes and an assortment of guests— parents, teachers, administrators, school board members, and friends—numbered about one hundred people. As we were walking from display to display, talking with the students and tasting food, we suddenly heard the students call out, ". . . 3, 4, 5."

Then there was silence in the room, including those of us who had no idea what was going on. Everyone faced the teacher, Cindy Wong, and she spoke. Then everyone went back to what they were doing.

Later we asked Cindy what she did to quiet the room so quickly. She said, "Dad, it's a variation on your three-step technique. I have a five-step procedure called 'Give Me Five' because I teach younger students than you do, so I wanted to be more specific as to what I wanted. These are my five steps:

1. Eyes on speaker
2. Quiet
3. Be still
4. Hands free (put things down)
5. Listen

"The way it works is, I say, 'Give me five.' They go through each of the five steps in their mind.

"We have rehearsed this procedure, so when I say, 'Give me five,' it takes them no more than five seconds before I have their attention.

"In addition, all three sixth-grade teachers have the same procedure. So, when another teacher, an aide, a substitute teacher, an administrator, or another student says, 'Give me five,' they have the students' attention. It's the consistent culture for all the sixth graders."

Cindy Wong and the Give Me Five procedure posted in her classroom.

beamed announcements two or three times a day, no less two or three times a minute. Before you complain that the principal creates too many interruptions during the day, consider how many times a day you might allow some students to interrupt fellow classmates when they are trying to concentrate on their work.

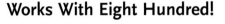

Works With Eight Hundred!

Susan Galindo from San Antonio, Texas, shared her Give Me Five story with us. She was at a Fiesta Event for the River City Christian School. There were over six hundred mentally and physically challenged public school children (from ten different school districts across south Texas) attending and it was time for lunch under the big tent.

During lunch there was an awards presentation for several community members. Susan kept trying to focus the attention of the very loud and boisterous gathering.

After several unsuccessful attempts, she yelled out to the nearly two hundred teachers who were also attending, "How do I get these kids' attention?"

A unanimous reply from the teachers was, "Say, give me five!" So she calmly said, "Give me five," and held up her hand. The whole group of eight hundred became quiet IMMEDIATELY.

The honored community members were quite impressed.

Methods for Getting the Teacher's Attention Without Interrupting the Class

Help sign:	The student places a "Help" sign on the desk.
Hand signal:	The student signals with different numbers of fingers.
Cardboard tube:	The student signals with a colored tube.
Styrofoam cup:	The student signals with the position of a cup.
Index card:	The student signals with a message on an index card.
Colored cups:	The student signals with a different colored cup.
Textbook:	The student signals with an upright textbook.

There are many other methods for students to use to get your attention.

Help Sign

Alicia Blankenship of Texas tapes a sign with six pertinent procedures on each desk so the students see them every day, along with a list of commonly misspelled words, as she is an ESOL teacher. There is also an envelope with a card that says, "HELP." When the student needs help, the procedure is to take the card out and place it on top of the envelope and **continue to work**. When the teacher comes to help, the card is then returned to the envelope.

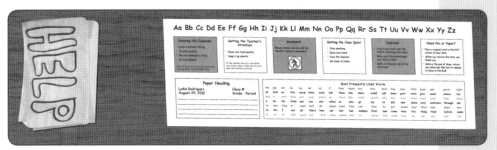

A HELP card is on every desk in Alicia Blankenship's classroom.

Hand Signal

With this technique, students signal the teacher with a predetermined number of fingers. The number of fingers raised corresponds to a request established by the teacher.

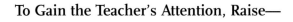

To Gain the Teacher's Attention, Raise—

One Finger: "I wish to speak."
Two Fingers: "I wish to leave my seat."
Three Fingers: "I need your help."

Pencil in the air.
I have to sharpen my pencil.

I have to use the bathroom.

Be quiet. Silent signal.

I need water. I'm thirsty.

A sign posted in the halls of Locke School in New York City.

Post a sign on the wall with your hand signal chart. Then teach your students to use the system.

- If they wish to sharpen a pencil, they hold it up.

- If they have to use the bathroom, they raise one finger.

- If they see two fingers (from anyone in the classroom), they become quiet.

- If they need a drink, they raise three fingers.

When you see a signal, silently respond to it with a nod or shake of the head or a hand gesture. **The important thing is that the class is not disturbed.**

These are hand signals used in Ayesa Contreras' classroom in Cozumel, Mexico. *Participar*: I know the answer and wish to participate; *Agua*: May I have a drink of water?; *Baño*: May I use the restroom?; *Termine*: I'm done with my work; and *Ayuda*: I need help, please.

Cardboard Tube

Take an empty cardboard tube, a toilet tissue tube works well, and wrap one end with red construction paper and the other end with green construction paper. The tube is placed with the green end up on the student's desk. When the student wants the teacher's attention, the procedure is to turn the tube so the red end is up and **continue to work**. When the teacher comes to help, the green end is turned back up.

Styrofoam Cup

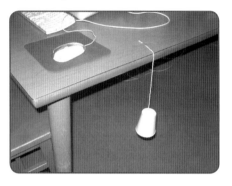

Tape a short length of string to the bottom of a Styrofoam cup. (Styrofoam cups are noiseless.) Tape the other end of the string near the edge of the desktop, and leave the cup dangling off the top. When the student wants the teacher's attention, the procedure is to place the cup on the desk and **continue to work**.

Index Card

Fold and tape an index card into a three-sided pyramid. On one side write, "Please help me." On another side write, "Please keep working." Leave the third side blank. Place the card on the table so the blank side is facing the student. When the student wants the teacher's attention, the procedure is to turn the card so that "Please help me" is facing forward. The student sees "Please keep working" and is reminded to **continue to work**.

HELP ME
PLEASE

PLEASE
KEEP WORKING

Faces teacher   Faces student

Colored Cups

This is a good device to use when groups work together and need to signal the teacher for help. Give each group two plastic cups, one green, and one red, one inside the other. All cups should show green, except when red is used to signal for help. Tell students that they are to signal for help only when they have thoroughly discussed their work, have exhausted all resources, and finally need the teacher. This technique is good because it makes students reach out to each other, collaborate, and decide on a whole-group question.

Textbook

High school teachers may appreciate this simple system. When a student wants the teacher's attention, the procedure is to take a textbook, place it in an upright position and **continue to work**.

Instructional Procedures for Student Learning

Just as there are procedures for Classroom Management, there are Instructional Procedures that govern the academic work of the students. Some basic instructional procedures include the following:

- How to work in groups (page 183)
- How to take lecture notes (page 190)
- How to do the assignment (page 239)
- How to read the textbook (page 190)
- How to summarize each day's learning (page 189)
- How to do the homework (page 192)
- How to study for a test (page 239)

These procedures apply to any subject or content area. Classroom management procedures lay the foundation for structuring the classroom; instructional procedures lay the foundation for acquiring information and learning. See Chapter 16 for a discussion of specific instructional procedures.

Structure for the At-Risk Student

Students who are at-risk need structure. At-risk has nothing to do with the student's intelligence, gender, skin color, national origin, or socioeconomic background. At-risk means the student is in danger—at-risk—of failing or dropping out of school.

Students who are labeled at-risk are really **"at-promise,"** a much more positive expectation of what you want the outcome to be. The reason students fail is typically because they have not done the work, and failure to do the work results in failing grades in the classroom. Most at-promise students are failing because they have not been taught many of the instructional procedures discussed in Chapter 16.

> **The number one solution for at-promise students: STRUCTURE!**

In a well-managed classroom, students are taught HOW to do things and WHAT they need to do to succeed. They are taught procedures and given structure. If at-risk students are placed in a classroom that lacks structure (translation: a classroom that is disorganized and chaotic), their disadvantage is compounded. Many students come from dysfunctional (unstructured) homes. They want and crave structure. An at-promise student said:

> "I want to do what is right,
> but no one ever taught me how to do things.
> Do you understand me?"

The effective teacher provides procedures and structure to give students the confidence and knowledge to be actively engaged and in control of their own learning.

- The effective classroom has STRUCTURE.
- Procedures and routines create STRUCTURE.
- Effective teachers manage and instruct with PROCEDURES and ROUTINES.

Procedures don't have to be elaborate. They just need to be coherent, continuous, and consistent. They can be as

It's a Happy Place

Principal Edward Aguiles says, "I can only tell you that teachers and students love to come to this school." Read how he did it in the **Go**ing **Be**yond folder for the Chapter 15 or scan the QR Code.

simple as knowing where to line up for an elementary student and knowing what to do in an emergency for a secondary student.

As stated before, procedures simplify the task of succeeding in school. They give students the opportunity to participate successfully in classroom activities, to learn, and to function effectively in the school environment. They make it possible for students to be responsible for their own learning.

At-risk students become at-promise students when they can be responsible for their own learning by following the classroom and instructional procedures the teacher has established.

> *You seemingly waste a little time at the beginning to gain time at the end.*
>
> Lim Chye Tin
> Esteemed educator
> Singapore

Procedures to Rehearse With Students

Imagine the consistency that would be established in every school, if students walked into every classroom knowing the teacher was going to teach these procedures. This listing is just a start for creating a coherent and continuous learning environment for student and teacher success.

Entering the classroom
Getting to work immediately
Listening to and responding to questions
Participating in class discussions
Keeping a desk orderly
Checking out classroom materials
Indicating understanding
Coming to attention
Working cooperatively
Changing groups
Keeping a notebook
Going to the office
Knowing the schedule for the day or class
Keeping a progress report
Finding directions for each assignment
Passing in papers
Exchanging papers

Returning student work
Getting materials without disturbing others
Handing out playground materials
Moving about the room
Going to the library or tech center
Structuring headings on papers
Returning to a task after an interruption
Asking a question
Walking in the hall during class time
Responding to a fire drill
Responding to an earthquake
Responding to a severe weather alert
Saying "thank you"
Knowing what to do when tardy
Dismissing at the end-of-period or class
Needing a pencil or paper
Knowing what to do when absent
Asking for help or conferencing
Finishing work early
Listening to schoolwide announcements
Responding to visitors in the classroom
Proceeding when the teacher is out
Taking action when suddenly ill

The Benefit of Procedures

Procedures and routines established early in the school year free up the rest of the year to be devoted to teaching and learning. They ensure coherency, continuity, and consistency. They are the foundation for momentum in the classroom. They create a classroom culture and community where everyone is an active participant, and it is a pleasure to teach and learn.

☆ THE EFFECTIVE TEACHER

☑ Has planned and structured procedures for every activity.

☑ Teaches the procedures for each activity early in the year.

☑ Rehearses the class so that procedures become class routines.

☑ Reinforces procedures when appropriate and reteaches procedures when necessary.

...IMPLEMENTS!

Classroom and Instructional Procedures

As discussed in Chapter 15, classroom management procedures lay the foundation for structuring the classroom. They create coherency, continuity, and consistency.

> When students are taught procedures, they are taught responsibility for their learning. They are given the techniques they need for all future endeavors.

Procedures minimize confusion, disruptions, and wasted time. They create a cooperative classroom culture where everyone understands exactly what they need to do and how they should behave. Procedures ensure that the classroom is the optimum environment for teaching and learning

Instructional procedures lay the foundation for acquiring information and learning. They teach students how to learn. They give students the means to control and take responsibility for their own learning. Instructional procedures will not only help them succeed in the classroom, they will help them succeed in life. They are techniques and methods that will be used in all professions. In today's world, things change rapidly and everyone has to be flexible and adaptable. Procedures help students to learn how to learn—confidently and effortlessly.

An effective teacher has a management plan that consists of classroom and instructional procedures.

> **Procedures do not control students.**
> **Procedures allow students to have ownership and be in control of their own lives.**

Reactive Teachers

In classrooms where there are no plans or procedures you will find a **REACTIVE** teacher, one who reacts to every misbehavior incident in the classroom. This teacher teaches and then stops instruction to react to misbehavior while the rest of the class sits, watches, and waits. Instruction

Ahhh!

THE KEY IDEA

Classroom and instructional procedures improve teaching and learning.

> *Good fortune is what happens when opportunity meets with planning.*
>
> Thomas Alva Edison
>
> *If you don't have a plan for yourself, you'll be part of someone else's.*
>
> American proverb
>
> *Plans are nothing; planning is everything.*
>
> Dwight D. Eisenhower
>
> *If you don't have a plan for managing your classroom, then you are planning to fail.*
>
> Harry and Rosemary Wong

Behavior Management

Managing the behavior so
the student will act in a proper, civil,
and responsible manner.

Classroom Management

Organizing the classroom so
that student learning and
achievement can be accomplished.

resumes, only to stop again. This repeats itself all day long—teach-react; teach-react; teach-react.

Soon, the reaction becomes scolding, yelling, threats, punishments, and coercion to whip students into compliance. The reactive teacher goes home angry, tired, and stressed out. To solve the problem, the teacher looks for an intervention program, some fast-acting potion that will get students to comply. Unfortunately, such interventions are usually "too little, too late," as we say.

As discussed in Chapter 15, discipline is behavior management; it is not classroom management. Because classroom management is so grossly misunderstood, teachers spend more time disciplining students rather than managing the classroom for learning. (See Chapter 17 for behavior management.)

Proactive Teachers

Effective teachers have a discipline plan and a classroom management plan. **They are PROACTIVE.** They know that 80 percent of classroom problems are caused by not having plans in place that prevent problems from occurring. They know that the number one problem in the classroom is not discipline; it is the lack of procedures and routines—the lack of a plan that organizes a classroom for academic success.

All good schools have a vision for creating student success. When effective classroom and instructional procedures are planned and established, there is increased time for teaching and learning. The result is improved student achievement. Proactive teachers go home at the end of the day happy and satisfied with the knowledge that their students have learned.

The INEFFECTIVE TEACHER begins the first day of school attempting to teach a subject and spends the rest of the year being reactive, trying to control students.

The EFFECTIVE TEACHER is proactive and establishes classroom and instructional procedures so that students can take responsibility for their learning.

A Plan in Place

Sarah Jondahl

Sarah Jondahl, a teacher in California and one of the co-authors of *THE Classroom Management Book*, was ready the first day of her teaching career with a binder that contained a specific, consistent classroom management action plan. Although it took months of work to compile the binder, it ensured her success from the very first minute of her teaching career. Her classroom was organized before students walked through the door.

Two major problems in a classroom are movement and noise. Sarah had these solved on her first day of school. She planned exactly how her students were to enter the classroom in the morning, come in from recess, line up to leave the classroom, get ready for lunch, walk in the halls, and get ready for dismissal. She then taught, rehearsed, and reinforced the procedures until they became routines.

Today, Sarah is an experienced teacher and she says, "My classroom management plan is based on establishing procedures I learned from *THE First Days of School*. Having procedures in place from day one and teaching my students about these procedures made the educational experience in my classroom extremely effective."

Teachers like Sarah Jondahl will succeed in any kind of school. It truly makes no difference what grade level or subject you teach, whether you teach in a public, private, or charter school, whether your school is traditional or year-round, or whether your students are urban or rural.

> **All effective teachers have procedures to assist in managing a classroom and maximizing learning time.**

Sarah Jondahl is an example of a successful and highly effective teacher. Steal from her list of procedures, routines, and ideas as you plan for your classroom.

Create a Classroom Management Plan

Sarah's classroom management action plan is the heart of our eLearning course. Find it at www.EffectiveTeaching.com.

The outcome of the course is the creation of a Classroom Management Plan binder filled with procedures to help you be effective the moment you enter the classroom.

Proactive and Preventive Procedures

I present my classroom procedures as a PowerPoint presentation. Then I cut and laminate each one and paste them on black construction paper. They are posted on an easel up on the bookshelf near the hooks where backpacks hang. I put them there because the students see them each morning when they arrive after they shake my hand and are reminded.

At the beginning of the year we spend time going over and practicing each procedure one slide at a time. I don't want to boast, but I have no discipline problems as seen on my "How am I doing?" chart.

Mary Braunstein
New York, New York

Red, yellow, and green disks are posted in Mary Braunstein's classroom. Students strive to keep their name pinned to the green disk.

Before the First Day

Sarah's plan includes a letter she sends to her students before the first day of school. It tells a little about her background and establishes expectations for lots of work and learning. It also contains the class's first homework assignment.

The First Day of School

Greet Each Student at the Door

- Direct them toward their assigned seats (alphabetical)
- Tell students to read and follow the instructions written on the board (the bellwork)

Introduce Self

Teach Classroom Procedures

- Teach classroom procedures
- Communicate the expectations of the classroom and rewards

Teach Classroom Rules

- Tell students the rules and the consequences if they are not followed

Entering the Classroom

Students enter the classroom quietly and calmly, put their belongings away quickly according to the morning routine, and do the bellwork.

Bellwork

Each morning there is a bellwork assignment on the board. Students enter the classroom and get started on the assignment.

Quieting the Class

Teach that when the teacher raises a hand, it is a signal for quiet.

Taking Attendance

A student is taught the procedure of how to be the "Attendance Keeper." If students are absent, the Attendance Keeper places "Absent" folders with yellow stickers on their desks so the teacher can glance around the room to know who is absent.

When a Student Is Absent

When students are absent, copies of all papers passed out during class or any notes that need to go home are placed inside the "Absent" folder for students to complete when they return. The folders are placed on a shelf in the front office for pick up after 3:00 P.M.

Class Motto

At the start of the day, everyone in class stands together and says the classroom motto, which is posted on the wall in the front of the room.

Turning in Work

There are two baskets placed in the front of the room, one labeled "Class Work" and the other "Homework." Students place their work in the appropriate basket.

Collecting Seatwork (More on page 176)

Work is collected according to the configuration of the desks. If desks are arranged in rows, students collect their seatwork by passing papers across their rows. Students seated at tables place finished papers in the middle of the table. A student picks up each table's stack of papers, and puts them in the basket.

Notes from Home

Students place any notes from home in a basket labeled "Notes from Home."

Restroom Breaks

Individual students are allowed to go to the bathroom four times a month without having a tally pulled. They use their daily agendas as their pass that the teacher signs and dates when they are going. Only one student may use the restroom at a time. Students are excused as a class to go to the restroom during lunch and recess.

Going to Lunch

Students form a "Home Lunches" line and a "School Lunches" line by the outside door. Those buying their lunches line up in alphabetical order. After lunch, students wait to be picked up in their classroom area. (Numbers are painted on the blacktop.)

Entering the Classroom

Your students can enter the classroom properly. Learn how to do this at the **Go**ing **Be**yond folder for Chapter 16 or scan the QR Code.

Hallway Procedure

With a schoolwide procedure in place, this school makes the movement of students in its hallways very efficient. Read how it's done in the **Go**ing **Be**yond folder for Chapter 16 or scan the QR Code.

Cafeteria

Students follow cafeteria procedures. They clean up their sitting areas when done. They are expected be courteous, saying, "Please" and "Thank You."

Working in Learning Groups (More on page 183)

Students are placed in teacher-chosen groups called "support groups." They are reminded of the procedures.

- You are responsible for your own work.
- You are to ask a "support buddy" for help if you have a question.
- You must offer help if you are asked for help.
- You may ask the teacher for help after the entire group agrees on a question.

Selecting Monitors

Each student's name is written at the end of a Popsicle stick, and the sticks are placed in a "Pick a Stick" can. The teacher draws a stick to randomly select students.

Pinning Up Class Work

When an activity requiring glue or paint is completed, students pin their work on a rope at the front of the classroom to dry. At the end of the day, students remove their papers and place them in the "Class Work" basket.

Keeping the Noise Level Down

A cardboard stoplight is used to control classroom noise levels. It has three black circles with a hook on each and is placed at the front of the room. A red circle is hung to indicate "Silent Time," a yellow circle for "Whisper Time," and a green circle for "Talk Freely Time."

Classical music is played during class time. Students keep their noise levels lower than the sound of the music.

Sending Notes Home

Notes to parents at the end of the day are placed in cubbies by the "Cubby Keeper." Students are responsible for sharing notes with parents each evening.

Transitions (More on page 178)

The teacher gives a verbal announcement of "five minutes left" before changing lessons, activities, or centers, etc. When it is time to change, a variety of methods are used such as playing music; a snap/clap rhythm pattern led by teacher; ringing a bell. Students know what these different signals mean and make the change quickly and quietly.

If the Teacher Is Out of the Classroom

Students remain on task while the teacher is out of the room. Classroom procedures and rules are followed as they continue their work. The classroom aide or a teacher next door is available for help if needed.

Daily Closing Message

At the end of the day, one student is chosen to read the daily closing message to the class. The message is prepared by the teacher during the day and printed for each student to share at home that evening, an effective way to communicate upcoming events, important information, and what happened during the day.

Common Courtesy

Students are reminded to say "Thank You" and "Please" to one another.

End-of-Class Dismissal

The bell does not dismiss the class; the teacher dismisses the class. Students are dismissed when called upon, either individually or by groups.

Transportation

Students follow rules and procedures on school outings. When walking to or from the school bus or car, hall procedures are followed. Students stay seated while on the bus or in the car and respect the property. Seat belts are worn at all times. Low voices are always used in the vehicle. There is no eating in the car or bus unless the driver agrees.

Teacher success can be traced to the ability of the teacher to manage the classroom.

I'm Managing My Attitude, Too

I had a disastrous first year as a teacher. I could not control my students and, as a result, I was asked to not return to teach.

*Well, I got another job the second year in an alternative high school. That summer I got a copy of **THE First Days of School** and I began to map out a plan. On the first day of school I started to work that plan.*

Now, it felt really weird because it just didn't match my personality. However, the students seemed to be responsive and so I kept on the plan. What happened is that the very positive student response drove me to work the plan even harder. Soon I had the lowest referral rate in the school.

Now, these were students who had to leave their regular home school and come to my alternative classroom. In fact, one of them is now in prison. But they enjoyed my class.

They made astonishing progress and they liked my class. Several of them even went back to their home school and became star performers.

What happened is that gradually I realized that not only was I managing my classroom, I was also managing my teaching and managing my attitude.

Margery T.

A Teacher of Teachers

Karen Whitney

Classroom management plans are not just for individual classrooms. They can be applied schoolwide so there is consistency, coherency, and continuity from classroom to classroom. This doesn't happen by chance—an effective leader who has a plan makes it happen.

The most effective administrators are instructional leaders; they know how to instruct their teachers in effective practices. Such an instructional leader is Karen Whitney, who took on the challenge of being a principal at Sisseton Middle School, a school on a Native American reservation in South Dakota. During her first year, she spent 95 percent of her time handling discipline issues. A year later, she had it down to 5 percent. How did she do this?

She knew the school had to develop a culture of consistency—predictability, reliability, and stability—for students. The most logical way to start was with procedures, and she used *THE First Days of School* as her guide. Rather than just telling teachers what to do, Karen became a "teacher of teachers" as she modeled techniques and expectations. She allocated the time needed for her teachers to understand how to transform their classrooms into cooperative, well-managed learning environments.

To help teachers implement procedures, **Karen created a Classroom Management Plan template the teachers could use for self-assessment, and that she could use for formative assessment when she observed each teacher.** The procedures were implemented schoolwide. New teachers received personalized instruction from Karen to get them up to speed and veteran teachers found that procedures allowed them to be even more effective in the classroom. One Sisseton teacher said, "I was at a conference the other week, and my sub left this note for me, 'All in all a great day! I expected middle school to be more stressful!!' What wonderful words to read as I came back to my classroom—all because of consistency!"

Using a template such as this one will help you organize each day in your classroom to create consistency.

Classroom Management Plan Template

Teacher	Date	Class

EXPECTATION	SCORE	COMMENTS
Teacher is at the door greeting students as they enter the classroom.		
Bellwork is posted.		
Students enter the classroom and immediately begin working.		
Agenda for the day is posted.		
A beginning of class or morning routine is in place.		
Objective(s) for the day are posted.		
Transitions are smooth with minimal loss of teaching/learning time.		
Teacher can quiet the room quickly.		
Individual classroom procedures are evident.		
Students know how to correctly set up an assignment.		
Students know how to ask for help.		
Teacher dismisses the class.		
Teacher is at the door as students exit the classroom.		

1	Exceeds minimum expectations	3	Does not meet minimum expectations
2	Meets minimum expectations	N/A	Not observed

school (skül), A place for teaching and learning: place where children are taught, nurtured, enlightened and loved. *n*.

A Place of Acceptance

School is a sanctuary for many
  students.
They do not come to school to be
  disciplined and controlled.
They come to school to belong.
They want to be accepted, they
  want to learn, and they want to
  be given the opportunity to do
  their best.

Procedures Produce Results

The Sisseton Middle School students also readily accepted and appreciated the school's new organization and the resulting culture of consistency. Students thrive when they know what they have to do and how they have to do it to learn and succeed.

In a school with a culture of consistency, students know what to do, when to do it, and how to do it.

With consistency, a teacher has taught responsibility, and when students become responsible learners, they have been given the greatest opportunity to succeed.

Procedures produce permanent change. Students who follow procedures take pride in being actively engaged participants who work together to create a consistent classroom culture that gives them the opportunity to succeed. There are fewer behavioral problems and increased academic learning time. **Procedures produce results.**

The Power of Predictability

When you walk into a room, you do not pay attention to the floor. But if it were missing you would. It's the same with classroom management. Teachers who have a well-managed classroom have well-established, invisible procedures. The class just flows along smoothly and students are learning. There are no surprises; the teacher and students know how the class is structured and run. The students know what to do.

Remember, there are specific steps for teaching a procedure —**Teach, Rehearse, and Reinforce.** If you need to review this technique, please see Chapter 15.

More Classroom Procedures

Classrooms in each country, each city, and each school will require a different set of procedures. Procedures are infinitely adaptable and flexible. Create and adjust procedures to best serve your particular set of circumstances.

Here are some more classroom procedures to teach, rehearse, and reinforce in your classroom:

- Emergencies
- Moving Papers
- Transitions
- Pencils
- Groups

It is essential to be prepared. Emergencies come without warning. The better you and the students are prepared with a well-rehearsed procedure, the greater the chances are of coming through it unharmed.

Procedure for Moving Papers

If your students are sitting in columns and rows, it is more effective to have them pass their papers across the rows to the side of the room rather than up the columns to the front of the room. Why?

- You cannot see what is happening behind each student's back as you stand at the front of the room waiting for the papers. Some students tap, poke, shove, and hit the back of the student in front to announce that the papers are coming up the column.

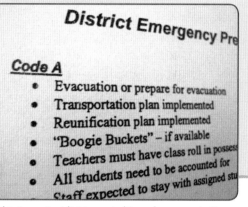

This important list is posted in a classroom in Texas.

Procedure for Emergencies

The most important procedure is for an emergency drill. This may be for an impending weather problem such as a tornado, hurricane, or severe thunderstorm, or for an earthquake. It may be for a possible lockdown, a hostile intruder on campus, or for campus violence.

You may have been in a store and heard a message like "Code 99 in Women's Shoes" over the sound system, an in-house code used to call someone for assistance or to alert employees of an emergency. In some schools, "Code Red" comes through the speakers to tell teachers to put a procedure into place pending further information.

To guard against upsetting students and parents, letters explaining the drill should be sent home before the students are rehearsed in the procedure. Tell students, "We don't expect anything terrible to happen to you. This is just to keep you safe."

"Drop and cover" is a signal to get out of harm's way and protect oneself. Some law enforcement people recommend this if anyone is near gunfire. In California, where an earthquake can strike instantly, the students have two seconds to duck under a desk when the teacher shouts, "Duck and cover!"

In Saskatchewan, Canada, teacher Laurie Jay has the class roster Velcroed next to the door. She is ready to grab it when the class leaves for a fire drill or if they have to evacuate quickly.

Passing papers across the row gets the task done.

Distributing and Collecting Materials

Students are more engaged and thus learn more if hands-on activities are provided. Learn how to do this in less than a minute. Go to the **Go**ing **Be**yond folder for Chapter 16 or scan the QR Code.

Others wave the papers in the face of the student in front. No matter what is done, students become irritated, words are spoken, and the class is disturbed.

■ There are frequently more students in a given column than across rows. As papers are passed, some may fall to the floor, so it follows that the more students handle papers, the more likely it is that papers will fall. This detracts from learning time. The task takes longer to do and is often accompanied by student agitation.

> **Students should pass their papers across the rows, not up the columns.**

This is the procedure for passing papers across rows:

Step 1. Have students place papers on the desk next to theirs, starting with the student at one end of the row. Students can see the papers coming across.

Step 2. The next student adds his or her paper on top of the stack and places them on the next desk.

Step 3. As students pass papers from desk to desk, walk to the side of the room and look across the rows to monitor the procedure. Make corrections when necessary and praise when appropriate.

Step 4. Pick up the papers, or ask a student to pick up all the papers.

If students are sitting at tables instead of rows of desks:

■ Have students place their papers at the head of the table (point to the designated spot).

■ Have a student or an aide pick up the papers, or do so yourself.

It is not a good procedure to have students place their papers in a basket on the teacher's desk. This procedure involves too much movement and often results in a mess.

> **Whatever procedure you choose, rehearse it until it becomes routine.**

The C-P-R Procedure for Transitions

Transitions happen all day long. Times and schedules are mandated. Students go from one activity to another, from one class to another, from one teacher to another. There's recess, break time, lunch time, library time, assembly time, club time, and a host of other things happening at school. Transitions also include moving from reading books to completing worksheets; from watching a video to participating in a discussion; from writing to recitations; from clean up to preparations for dismissal.

You want transitions in your classroom. Nothing would be so boring as to sit in one chair for seven hours doing one task day after day. No matter what the transition is, a procedure will help it happen smoothly, without turmoil or commotion. **Effective teachers have procedures that facilitate transition time.**

> **The key to a good transition is clarity and simplicity of instruction. Keep it short, simple, and easy to do.**

Students do not react well when given an abrupt order to do something else. To help students ease into a transition, you must prepare them for it. It's best to say, "In two minutes, I will want you to . . ." Autistic students, especially, need a two-minute warning.

Transitions can be difficult because they require students to do three things at once:

1. **C**lose one task.
2. **P**repare for another task.
3. **R**efocus on a new task.

Step 1: **Close.** Announce that is time to perform C-P-R. Students complete and stop the activity they are working on and put away all materials related to it.

Step 2: **Prepare.** Students gather the materials needed for the next activity.

Transition Tunes

Robin Barlak teaches preschool Special Education in Ohio. The students in her class sing their transition procedures. They have a good morning song, a snack song, a clean-up song, and a good-bye song. Her students eagerly anticipate each sing along time and happily perform moving from one activity to the next.

The most important procedure for you to follow during transition time is keeping your lips zipped.

Step 3:   Refocus. Make the new activity clear to students verbally or by posting it prior to announcing transition time. Students cannot listen to directions while performing Steps 1 and 2. If verbal instructions are given, write them on the board so students can refer to them. If a student is having difficulty, give a firm smile and a hand signal, or point to the directions on the board.

Most failed transitions are the result of interruptions: the teacher announces another bit of information; a student asks what needs to be done because the directions were not clear. Talking distracts students and impairs their ability to switch properly, particularly those students who are autistic or ADHD. If constant directions need to be given, then your procedure for transitions is not short, simple, and easy to do.

The Procedure for Pencils

Don't get annoyed. Don't listen to students whine, "I forgot my pencil. I can't do my work today." Don't spend time muttering about the lack of responsibility these days. Don't waste another precious moment of learning time in the classroom.

Don't fight it. Just give them a pencil.

Can the problem! Have pencils readily available for those who need them.

Notice the two cans pictured. One is labeled, "New Pencils" and has sharpened pencils in it. The other is labeled, "Used Pencils" and indicates the pencils need to be sharpened.

Put the cans at the classroom entrance. As students enter, they can select a sharpened pencil to use during the class period or school day. At the end of the class or day, students return their pencils to the "Used Pencils" can as they exit the room. Appoint a "Pencil Keeper" to sharpen the pencils for use the next day or period.

The same procedure applies to pencil points that break during class time. Students put the pencil with the broken point in "Used Pencils" and take one from "New Pencils." Simple—the class need not be interrupted.

This is just one way to handle the pencil problem. As part of an end-of-day procedure, some elementary teachers have students put a sharpened pencil in their mail cubby that they retrieve the next morning. With their pencils sharpened the day before, students are ready to write as soon as they enter the classroom.

The concept is simple—have sharpened pencils available in the classroom. Design a procedure that works for you and your students.

Procedure for Groups

Benefits of Working in Groups

Developmental psychologist Jean Piaget is credited with saying that students learn best by doing and then thinking about what they've done. **Hands-on, minds-open learning in structured groups is one of the best methods to engage students in their own learning.**

Analyzing data from A Policy Information Center Report on 14,000 eighth grade math and science tests, Educational Testing Service found this to be true:

Students whose teacher conducted hands-on learning activities outperformed their peers by about 70 percent of a grade level in math and 40 percent in science.[1]

> **Students who know how to work together achieve more.**

Compete Only Against Yourself

The message to your students is this:

- There is only one person in the world you need to compete against, and that is yourself.

- Strive each day to be the best person possible.

- Your mission in life is not to get ahead of other people; your mission is to improve yourself.

- While you are improving yourself, you are expected to work with everyone else in this classroom cooperatively and respectfully.

- You are responsible not only for your own learning, but for the learning of your classmates as well.

[1] Harold Wenglinsky, *How Teaching Matters: Bringing the Classroom Back Into Discussions of Teacher Quality* (Princeton, NJ: Educational Testing Service, 2000).

Before the Lesson Begins

*From the moment my students enter the classroom, they know **what** we will be doing and **how** we will be doing it. The Agenda with the Content Standard, bellwork, and the day's objective are posted every day in the front of the room. They know what I expect of them **before** I begin teaching the lesson. My instructional strategies, guided and independent practice, and daily assessment are all executed in the same way, every day.*

Deb Thompson
Sisseton Middle School math teacher
Sisseton, South Dakota

Group learning is a structured situation. Procedures have to be in place so that students clarify opinions, compare impressions, and share solutions. A group of people who are committed to achieving a goal will do so more efficiently together than if each were to attempt the task alone. Students involved in group activities are being trained in leadership, group decision-making, teamwork, and conflict management—essential skills for success in life.

Dividing Into Groups

The question is not how to divide the class, but rather how quickly and smoothly the class will divide itself when students are asked to do so.

Some teachers have no problems dividing their students into groups. When told to do so, students do it rapidly and with ease. Other teachers have problems getting their students to divide into groups. When told to do so, the students whine, complain, and even refuse to work with other people. Why? There are two reasons.

> **Effective grouping is dependent on two major factors:**
> 1. The class culture
> 2. The explanation

1. The Class Culture

Quite simply, if students dislike the class or the teacher, or do not feel they are learning and achieving, grouping will be difficult. **It is important that all the determinants of successful student cooperation be in place before the class is divided into groups.**

There are many factors that affect student cooperation. When students do not cooperate, the ineffective teacher wonders helplessly, "What am I supposed to do?" and looks for a quick fix or disciplinary measure to resolve the crisis. There are no quick fixes in education. Implicit in the "Factors of Success" list (page 195) is the fact that **it is the teacher who is responsible for creating an effective classroom culture from the beginning.** Doing so requires planning, effort, and determination. Once done, the rewards are immeasurable.

2. The Explanation

How quickly students move into groups depends on how explicitly the teacher explains why groups will be formed and how.

"OK, divide into groups of four" is not how groups should be set up. Vague, purposeless directions like this are sure to provoke comments and complaints like these:

> *Can I work with Andrew?*
> *Do I have to work with Charlotte?*
> *How long do I have to stay in this group?*

The best approach is to include students in the rationale behind group formations. There is no need to solicit class input on grouping, but it is necessary for students to understand the purpose of the groups being formed. They should also be reassured that groups are not permanent. They are formed to accomplish particular tasks and will change for different tasks and activities.

Simply discuss these issues with students.

- **Number of People in a Group:** The class will be divided into groups many times. Each time there is a need for a group, the size of the group and the people in the group will depend on the nature of the activity. Some activities may need two people; others may need four, eight, or whatever. In fact, whatever number is needed, that will be the number of people in the group.

- **Length of Time in a Group:** Each time the class is divided into groups, the length of the group activity will depend on the nature of the activity. Some activities may take two minutes; others may take two days or two weeks. When the activity is finished, the group will be disbanded.

Corporations spend hundreds of millions of dollars to find and train people to work together. Likewise, the effective teacher invests time in teaching and training students to work together.

Teaching young people to work well in groups does not happen overnight. Teaching the procedures for group work occurs incrementally and requires time, patience, and constant reinforcement. Society has changed from teaching

How to Motivate Your Students

Lack of structure often interferes with the learning process. Ways you can motivate your students to learn are in the **Go**ing **Be**yond folder for Chapter 16 or scan the QR Code.

They Knew the Names of Only Six Students

This is part of a letter we received after presenting a workshop to a group of student teachers at a local university.

One of the student teachers tried something in her class to test out one of your ideas. She handed out a blank seating chart to her ninth-grade class and asked all the students to fill in the seating chart, giving first and last names. Only about 80 percent of the kids seemed to have more than two-thirds of the names correct. Many of them knew only first names, and there were even a few students who could name only six or eight students sitting right around them out of a class of thirty-five.

The letter was dated May 20, so these students were in a classroom that had been together for nine months. In addition, there were two teachers in the room: a cooperating teacher and a student teacher. Yet at the end of the year, few of the students really knew one another.

When you have a situation like this, students will misbehave. They will refuse to work together, be reluctant to participate in group activities, and have a negative attitude generally.

When confronted by such difficulties, the teacher needs to reflect on the problem and establish procedures to correct the situation. The teacher has to find effective ways to change the classroom culture.

students to "think for themselves" to "thinking collaboratively" in an ecologically sustainable culture.

Students inherently like to work—and play—together. So the problem is not student participation or interaction. It is the failure to have a set of procedures for group work.

When the directions, whether verbal or written, do not state what is to be done, how it is done, and what is to be accomplished, students will create their own version.

The teacher must structure and write the activity for maximum understanding.

How to Structure Group Activities

How smoothly students move into groups depends on how clearly the teacher explains the procedures and responsibilities of the group assignment.

Group Structure

- Specify the group NAME.
- Specify the group SIZE.
- State the PURPOSE, MATERIALS, and STEPS of the activity.
- Teach the PROCEDURES.
- Insist on INDIVIDUAL ACCOUNTABILITY for the work of the group.
- Teach EVALUATION METHODS students can use to determine how successfully they have worked together.

Specify the Group Name. Learning together is epitomized by the concept of a support group. There are support groups for people trying to lose weight, stop addictions, overcome fears, and learn parenting skills. Support groups exist for single parents, senior citizens, abused children, battered wives, and military veterans. Networking groups, start-up groups, even CEO groups support each other in expanding their businesses.

> Consider calling groups **SUPPORT GROUPS** and each member of the group a **SUPPORT BUDDY.**

People in support groups have similar needs and goals. They join together to help each other solve problems and achieve success. Support groups in the classroom are formed for the same reasons.

Specify the Group Size. The size of the group is determined by how many jobs need to be accomplished to complete the activity. This is an example of how responsibilities can be allocated in a group of four students.

- Student 1 is responsible for getting the materials and returning them to the appropriate place when the day or period is over.

- Student 2 is responsible for seeing that the steps of the activity are followed.

- Student 3 is responsible for making observations, recording data, and taking minutes while the activity progresses.

- Student 4 is responsible for overseeing the writing of the group report.

State the Purpose, Materials, and Steps of the Activity. The activity assigned must be structured enough so students will know what is to be done and how to do it successfully. See the activity on page 187 for an example of how to do this.

Teach the Procedures. Here are four procedures to establish with students for group work.

- **You are responsible for your own job and the results of the group.** (In the working world, you are responsible for your own job and the results of the people you work with.)

- **If you have a question, ask your support buddies.** Do not ask your teacher. (In the working world, you do not raise your hand for help. You seek, ask, research, and Google it because you are expected to act on your own initiative.)

How to Raise Test Scores

If you want to raise test scores, you have to have time to teach. The only way I know of to do this is to have procedures for everything.

It is amazing how much time one has to teach then!

Kathryn Roe
William Penn University
Oskaloosa, Iowa

*I teach troubled kids and
procedures work.
They have made all the difference
in my first two years of teaching.*

Dick Doucett
Quebec, Canada

- **You must be willing to help if a support buddy asks you for help.** (In the working world, you are expected to apply teamwork skills.)

- **If no one can answer a question, then agree on a consensus question and appoint one person to raise a hand for help from the teacher.** (In the working world, negotiating and reaching agreements are the keys to success.)

Post procedures so students know how to successfully work in groups. One person speaking to the teacher asking for help is one of the hallmarks of effective group interactions.

Hold Individuals Accountable for the Work of the Team. The teacher acts as consultant to the group after setting the objectives, assignments, and procedures. Problems are turned back to the group for resolution.

The support groups write reports cooperatively and give team presentations. The students are accountable for the quality of their group work and the results of their work. The support group will get a group grade, and that grade will be each individual's grade, so it is important that each member of the group supports the efforts of other members and contributes equally to the group's success.

Teach Evaluation Methods Students Can Use to Determine How Successfully They Have Worked Together. Tell your students to write down the group procedures. (See the activity on page 188 for a list of the procedures.) Beside each procedure, students should evaluate whether their support group followed the procedure most of the time, sometimes, or not at all.

Then, for each procedure, have the support groups discuss how they can improve their team skills. The procedures they should pay particular attention to are those that received a rating of "most of the time." By reviewing them, and being aware of why they followed certain procedures *most of the time*, students can apply their successful ways of working together toward improving those procedures that were rated lower.

The more time students work together and the more students take responsibility for their work, the greater the learning that takes place.

Working together equals greater learning.

We, NOT Me

Learning is
an individual activity
but NOT
a solitary one.

It is most effective
when it takes place within
a supportive community
of fellow learners.

Sample Activity

In this activity, you will be working in **support groups** of four. Your teacher will choose the members of the **support group**. The reason you work in support groups is because when you discuss new ideas with your classmates, you understand the ideas better.

Sometimes you will work with your friends, and sometimes not. No matter who your support buddies are, your responsibility is to help one another understand and complete the activity. This is why you are called **support buddies**.

Your teacher will explain what jobs need to be done. Either the teacher will choose or you will be asked to choose who does which job.

You need to work together and talk about your assignment so that each member of the support group understands what your group has done and why. When it is time for your support group to report to the class, your teacher will call on only one member of your group. That member will explain the support group's results, so make sure that you all know what is happening before you get called on. When your support group looks good, you look good!

How Do Propellers Work?

Background

Some airplanes and helicopters fly because of propellers. As the shape and pitch (angle) of the blade change, different results are obtained.

Problem

How many different ways can you design a propeller blade?
How does each design perform?
What is your evaluation of each design?

Support Group Jobs

Equipment Manager: Your job is to obtain the materials needed for the activity and to make sure that they are returned to the appropriate place at the end of the designated time.

Facilitator: Your job is to make sure that the group is following each step of the activity carefully and correctly.

Recorder: Your job is to observe, take minutes, and record data. You need to see that the support group has the proper forms to record the results of the activity as they occur.

Reporter: Your job is to coordinate the writing of the group report.

Materials

Binder paper, scissors, and a paper clip

Activity Steps

1. Cut a piece of binder paper across its width into 2-inch strips.
2. Cut and fold the paper as shown in Fig. 1.
3. Hold and release the paper as shown in Fig. 2.
4. Try different versions of the helicopter.
5. Observe and record each result.

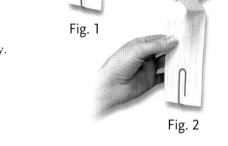

Fig. 1

Fig. 2

Support Group Procedures

Move into your groups quickly and quietly.
Stay with your group in your area.
Do your job.
Help each other.
Follow the Activity Steps listed above.

Support Group Responsibilities

1. The **facilitator** needs to make sure that everyone has read and discussed the activity before beginning to work. Do not start until everyone knows the purpose of the activity, what needs to be done (Activity Steps), and what everyone needs to do (Support Group Procedures and Responsibilities).

2. The **equipment manager** needs to see that the materials are collected.

3. The **recorder** needs to see that a record page is set up on which to record what is to be observed. This can be a form for taking minutes, a table for recording numbers, or a chart for writing observations. Do not start until the record page has been set up.

4. The **facilitator** takes the group through the activity steps, as a moderator would take a meeting through its agenda.

5. At all times, the members of the **support group** must cooperatively and respectfully help each other by following the Activity Steps and the Support Group Procedures.

6. The **support group** must help the recorder record the results of the activity.

7. The **reporter** coordinates the writing of the group report. Make sure that everyone in the support group can explain the activity:
   its purpose,
   steps, and
   results.

When everyone can explain the purpose and results of the activity, all the members of the group should sign their names to the group report.

Thank you!

Instructional Procedures to Enhance Student Learning

Procedures are not just used to manage the classroom. Instructional procedures are techniques used to enhance learning in the classroom. They may seem like common sense, but the adage, "The problem with common sense is it's not so common," certainly applies.

Here are some instructional procedures to teach, rehearse, and reinforce in your classroom:

- Taking Notes
- Reading a Textbook
- Homework Assignments

Procedure for Taking Notes

> **Note taking is the embodiment of one of life's greatest skills: LISTENING.**

Effective people have learned the skill of taking notes. That is why they are effective. People take notes watching television, during a telephone call, listening to a conference speaker, synthesizing something that is being read, and during an endless array of situations where they want to recall information and refer to it later.

Notes are particular to each person. They are what someone wants or needs for personal edification. Teach a note-taking procedure and you teach a student something useful for life, a technique for collecting information and ideas for any number of purposes.

Walter Pauk invented the most commonly used note-taking technique while he was at Cornell University: the Cornell Note-Taking Method. In its simplest form, it is a piece of paper divided into three sections: Record, Reduce, and Review. There is an Internet site where you can draw your own Cornell page, download it, and duplicate it for your students.

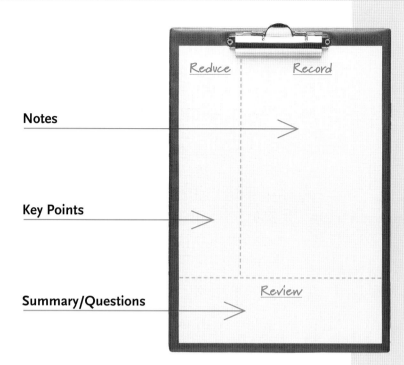

Notes

Key Points

Summary/Questions

The Cornell Note-Taking Method

1. **Record.** Record notes in this space. Teach students to use abbreviations and to write in phrases. Leave spaces between thoughts. Neatness is not important; organization is important.

2. **Reduce.** In the left column, write simple phrases, cue words, and key points based on the notes taken. Encourage brevity and simplicity.

3. **Review.** At the bottom, write one sentence or phrase that summarizes the notes on the page. Add any questions that remain, or write ideas for further research.

The benefit of the Cornell Note-Taking method is that notes do not have to be rewritten. They can be reviewed instantly. They are reminders of the details of the lesson and are used for review and study prior to tests or class discussions.

Procedure for Reading a Textbook

Effective readers do not necessarily start at the beginning of a book, magazine, or newspaper. Newspaper and magazine publishers know this, which is why some content is put on the cover to grab your attention.

They know that effective readers skim, scan, and skirt from one page to another. This method for reading a textbook is called SQ4R, which stands for **S**urvey, **Q**uestion, **R**ead, **R**ecite, **R**eview, and **R**eflect.

Here's an easy way to understand this technique. Have you ever been in line at a buffet restaurant with no clue as to what is being served? Wouldn't you like to know so you can make decisions and ration the space on your plate? Do a SQ4R of the buffet before you serve yourself.

Survey the layout of the buffet. Is there a section for hot foods? Is there a carver slicing meats? Where is the dessert table?

Question what is under the lids of the chafing dishes. Look at the sauces. Are there any low-sodium, heart-healthy foods available?

Read the labels on all the food items.

Recite all the choices you made as a result of examining the spread.

Review what you have just surveyed and plan how you will proceed through the line to take what you have selected.

Reflect on the promises you made to yourself about not overeating. Then, get in line, ready to dine responsibly at the all-you-can-eat buffet.

Teach students the SQ4R technique for reading a textbook.

SQ4R

■ **Survey**
  – Read the summary of the chapter first.
  – Look for any indication of a key idea or concept.
  – Read all bold-print sentences, and all highlighted text in caps, italics, or in boxes.
  – Look at the pictures and read the captions.
  – Read the section headings to understand the organization of the material.

These initial steps provide an overview of the information to be learned.

- **Question**
  - Ask what this chapter is about.
  - Ask what the subsections are about.

The better the student has a sense of what questions to ask, the better the student will understand the primary message the chapter or subsection conveys.

- **Read**
  - Read each section with the questions in mind.

- **Recite**
  - Answer the questions being asked verbally.

- **Review**
  - Review the questions or key ideas to check for understanding.

- **Reflect**
  - Reflect to reorganize any new ideas and compare them to each other.

Procedure for Homework Assignments

Any homework given must be part of the lesson objective and it must help when learning is assessed. Otherwise, it's just busy work and has no value as homework. Understanding this concept, Elmo Sanchez in Miami calls homework "home learning." He assigns only what reviews and cements concepts the students have learned in class.

Homework must fit the lesson objective and the assessment.

Just as effective teachers use guided practice followed by independent practice, homework or home learning should be additional practice to reinforce what was learned in the classroom. If a student takes skating or music lessons, the teacher sends the student home to practice the lesson, not to create something new. **Homework is not for new learning.** If it is it will only frustrate students and many parents who will be called upon to teach what has not been taught in the classroom.

The key word is "practice." Ask these questions:

- What have students learned in class?
- What can students do to practice this new knowledge?

This becomes the homework for the day. In many primary classes, students get a "take-home" folder with all their work for home learning.

Practice doing homework in the classroom. Spend time during the first two weeks in class teaching students how to do the homework before sending them home with assignments. A variation is to have students start the homework in class and then finish it at home.

Students become responsible learners when procedures are in place that give them the opportunity to be responsible.

What If Procedures Do Not Work?

There is no doubt that procedures are extremely effective management and learning techniques. There is also no doubt that establishing them in your classroom requires thorough planning, patience, and persistence. Here are four of the most frequently asked questions about procedures:

1. **What if they do not do the procedure?**
   My fear
   "I tell them, I remind them over and over again and they just will not do it" is the anguished statement made most often. Students won't stop talking; someone always blurts out; the transition dissolves into chaos. If you just tell students what the procedure is, there is no guarantee they will do it. A procedure must be rehearsed and rehearsed, and then reinforced and reinforced. It has to be so well known that it becomes a routine. (Review pages 148–151.)

2. **What if they forget the procedure?**
   Students forget. We all forget. A student knows and has practiced the procedure, but just forgets to do it. There is no need to rehearse it again as there is a much better, quicker, and saner way. Just ask, **"And what's the procedure, please?"**

   Stand in front of a mirror and calmly repeat this question over and over again a thousand times until it becomes automatic. "And what's the procedure, please?"

"And what's the procedure, please?" Repeat it a thousand times. Say it patiently, with a firm, kind smile.

The next time you see a student do something that should not be done, the next time a student blurts out, simply go over to the student and with no anger or stress, and with that firm, kind smile, ask, "And what's the procedure, please?" The question and body language are not confrontational. It's just a simple question.

After the student makes the correction, acknowledge the response with a smile and go on with teaching.

3. **What if a new student comes into the classroom?**
(Review page 157.)
When a new student joins the class, give the student a copy of the classroom procedures. Explain what procedures are and why you have them. Tell the student that you will help with the procedures, but that he or she will probably be able to learn them by observing how the rest of the class functions.

Enlist the aid of the other students, and guide and correct as necessary.

4. **What do I do if all else fails?**
Assuming you have mastered the skill of how to teach procedures (page 148) and there is a student who will just not cooperate or participate, you have the alternative of turning the procedure into a rule. First, ensure you know the difference between a procedure and a rule (page 141).

Procedures that have become routines are the hallmark of an effective classroom.

If you choose to convert the procedure into a rule, inform the student there will be consequences if the rule is not followed. Then you must ensure that there are consequences the next time the new rule is not followed. With consequences comes enforcement and compliance, maybe even coercion.

Think twice about converting a procedure into a rule, because it may still be easier to try and teach the responsibility of doing a procedure. The decision is yours to make.

Planning for Success

When teachers ask us, "How do I get students to stop doing . . . ?" our reply is "We can help you, but we need to see the context of what is happening in your classroom. Please send us your Classroom Management Plan with the procedures that spell out what it is you want your students to DO." (In over thirty years of asking, not a single classroom management plan has ever been sent in response to this request.)

In other words, teachers are asking the wrong question. The question should be, "How do I get students to DO . . . ?" That's when it is possible for them to address issues constructively and make a comprehensive plan that establishes procedures to prevent or minimize problems. That's when a teacher decides to be proactive rather than reactive.

Factors of Success

- **Enhancing positive expectations** (Chapter 6)
- **Using first-day-of-school activities** (Chapter 7)
- **Using invitational learning** (Chapter 7)
- **Dressing for success** (Chapter 8)
- **Using the five appropriate words** (Chapter 9)
- **Implementing effective classroom management strategies** (Chapter 10)
- **Having the classroom ready with a positive atmosphere** (Chapter 11)
- **Introducing yourself properly** (Chapter 12)
- **Involving the home** (Chapter 12)
- **Arranging and assigning seating** (Chapter 13)
- **Posting and starting assignments immediately** (Chapter 14)
- **Teaching and rehearsing procedures and routines** (Chapter 15)
- **Creating a consistent environment** (Chapter 16)
- **Investing time on teaching the discipline plan** (Chapter 17)
- **Sharing the purpose of the lesson** (Chapter 18)
- **Giving tests that have purpose** (Chapter 19)
- **Explaining that students can govern the grade they earn** (Chapter 20)

The Last Days of School

I am beginning my third year as principal at a year-round middle school. After I heard you speak, I had an epiphany of how to create an effective school with effective teachers.

Even though the school year was coming to an end, I did not think waiting to next year would be a wise decision. Timing was important and just as important was involving the faculty and staff in this process.

*Before the students returned for the fourth nine weeks, we had a teacher workday. I showed DVD 3: "Discipline and Procedures" from **The Effective Teacher** and used that as a springboard for discussion on schoolwide procedures that needed to be established. My approach was simple: **We must create procedures and establish routines as we move into the "Last Days of School."***

Next, I had teachers get into groups to list the top six procedures that we needed to address. Finally, each group presented their list and teachers were given three sticky dots to vote for what they believed were the top four procedures:

1. *Walk quickly on the right side of the hall with whisper voices and hands to self.*
2. *Enter each class quietly, sit quickly, and put book bag under your desk.*
3. *Teachers are the first into the hall after each bell.*
4. *Hand raised in the air is the quiet signal.*

Parents were informed and procedure posters of our new schoolwide procedures were displayed around the building and in every class. Teachers spent several days having the students practice the procedures. The students realized the importance of the procedures and liked the structure. Teachers felt less stressed and were able to focus on teaching and learning.

The story does not end here. In July of this school year, when teachers returned for their workdays, we viewed DVD 4: "Procedures and Routines." Once again teachers revisited our procedures and decided to keep the four school procedures and add three additional ones:

5. *All students will sit in their assigned seats.*
6. *Students will write the lesson objective and homework assignment in their planner.*
7. *Every class will start with a bellwork activity.*

We have just finished our last nine weeks. Many teachers have commented on how well behaved the students are this year compared to prior years. One teacher even stated that this was the best nine weeks of teaching she has ever had. The number of student disciplinary incidents is lower compared to previous years. Teacher morale in general is higher.

You are right! The secret is CONSISTENCY with schoolwide procedures to create an effective school with effective teachers.

Thomas Hatch, Principal
Anne Chesnutt Middle School
Fayetteville, North Carolina

☆ THE EFFECTIVE TEACHER

☑ Is proactive, rather than reactive.

☑ Has a management plan with comprehensive classroom and instructional procedures.

☑ Creates a classroom culture that is consistent, coherent, and continuous.

☑ Gives students every opportunity to take responsibility for their own learning.

...IMPLEMENTS!

Discipline

Discipline is a good word. Successful individuals are disciplined people. The self-discipline of athletes, performers, and leaders guides their success. Discipline can be taught and learned.

> Discipline is behavior management, not classroom management.

The most compelling reason for establishing and practicing procedures in your classroom is that they allow students to take responsibility for their own learning. Students who act responsibly learn self-discipline. They know what they have to do to succeed and they do it.

Everyone agrees that there must be good behavior in the classroom. Learning happens in an orderly environment where students follow classroom and instructional procedures to accomplish tasks, such as participating in class discussions and working in groups. They are being taught respect as well as responsibility. Schools are effective when they give students structure, focus, guidance, and direction in the form of classroom management plans that include discipline plans.

Discipline is learned in an organized classroom.

Prevention, Not Intervention

Little or no learning takes place when a teacher has to take time away from teaching to enforce rules. Behavior or discipline problems will occur in the classroom—they are inevitable. But disciplining students and managing the classroom are not the same. Discipline is behavior management, not classroom management.

Classroom Management: Organizing the classroom so that student learning and achievement can be accomplished.

Behavior Management: Managing behavior so students will act in a proper, civil, and responsible manner.

THE KEY IDEA

The ultimate aim of any discipline plan is to teach students self-discipline.

> 66
>
> ### I Did Not Even Have a System
>
> *I was going insane and then I realized that I did not have a fair system or even any system . . . .*
>
> *My students, after we had the plan in effect, commented on how quiet the room was and how easily they could do their work. The principal commented about the plan and said how pleased he was to see quiet, working, well-behaved students!*
>
> *As for me, I was thinking of quitting teaching because I was so uptight—until you shared a plan with me.*
>
> Sheila
> Lethbridge, Alberta, Canada
>
> 99

Behavior is caused.
Discipline is learned.

Misbehavior can be caused by what happens in the classroom and by what teachers do or do not do. Medical reasons, home conditions, and social-emotional problems can affect behavior, too. It may not be the student's fault, or in his or her control, that a behavior issue has arisen. It is important to consider what may have provoked the behavior and to give time to some calm analysis and discussion. Then it may be possible to work together to find a solution to the problem.

Classroom management should not be confused with behavior management, but the two are linked simply because a well-managed classroom will minimize discipline problems. When procedures are used to manage a classroom, students know what to do. If students know what to do, they will not do what they are not supposed to do. Effective teachers implement a classroom management plan that includes a discipline plan to prevent problems from occurring in the first place. In other words, effective teachers are proactive rather than being reactive when problems occur.

Prevention is much more effective than intervention.

It comes down to a choice between these two scenarios of Three C's:

- Managing a classroom with Three C's: Coherency, Continuity, and Consistency

- Disciplining a classroom with Three C's: Compliance, Control, and Coercion

Classrooms with well-established procedures operate with coherency, continuity, and consistency. Misbehavior is minimized. Classrooms that develop an abundance of misbehavior problems typically operate with compliance, control, and coercion. If a student does not <u>comply</u>, office intervention or in-class scolding is used to <u>control</u> the student. <u>Coercion</u> is used to <u>control</u> the class—whatever it takes for the teacher to survive and restore some sort of order.

In an ineffectively run classroom, energy is used to stop misbehavior.

In an effectively run classroom, energy is used to enhance learning.

According to a report from the Alliance for Excellent Education, "Middle and high school students subjected to harsh school discipline policies and practices, such as suspensions and expulsions, are more likely to disengage from the classroom and course work, and increase their chances of dropping out . . . . The report recommends implementing measures that address discipline in fair and equitable ways so that schools and districts can improve school climate and ensure that all students graduate from high school ready for college and a career."[1]

[1] Jessica Cardichon and Martens Roc, *Climate Change: Implementing School Discipline Practices That Create a Positive School Climate* (Washington DC: Alliance for Excellent Education, September 2013).

No Foolproof Discipline Plan

To repeat: behavior or discipline problems will occur even in the most well-managed classroom—they are inevitable. So every classroom management plan has to include a discipline plan.

If you have a behavior or discipline problem, manage the problem, not the classroom.

Discipline plans are like diet plans. There are dozens of them, yet most do not work because people are looking for quick-fix solutions that don't involve changing their lifestyle, eating, and exercise patterns. So if you read this chapter looking for a quick fix, you will be disappointed. You will never find a foolproof discipline system that is guaranteed to effortlessly solve all the potential behavior problems in your classroom.

There are many different kinds of discipline plans. They all have their good and bad points. Today, we are encountering a student population with diverse skills, languages, and needs, so it is obvious that one plan will not work in all situations. In fact, effective teachers may use two different discipline plans for two different kinds of classes.

Love this!

Motivation to Respect Her

Lois Austin teaches in Rochester, New York, and uses a "Respect Me" procedure to easily quiet the class.

With student Amy Amaya demonstrating, Lois explains that the class is to come to attention and be quiet when they see the teacher or a student raise a right hand high in the air. With the hand in the air, the person states clearly in a gentle but firm tone, "Respect me."

After stating, "Respect me," the person lowers the raised hand and places it over the heart.

By the end of two weeks, when a hand touches a heart in Lois's classroom, the class is silent.

The class now reminds their classmates of the procedure. When someone is engaged and doesn't notice the procedure, rest assured there will be a student who chimes in, "Respect her!"

Lois said that she was recently in a grocery store and ran into a student she had last year. A tear ran down her face as she saw him put his hand high in the air and lower it over his heart.

What a gesture of respect!

What Can I Do?

It is ineffective to ask, "What do I do with this student?" You cannot really DO something to someone to modify their behavior any more than they can DO something to change you. You can only communicate expectations and delegate responsibilities. Have a classroom management plan to proactively prevent problems and a discipline plan to take care of problems should they arise.

Have a plan and work the plan.

In this chapter, you will find two distinct approaches to behavior management:

1. The teacher monitors the classroom and enforces rules with consequences and rewards.

2. The teacher and students work out a cooperative discipline plan to solve problems together.

You will need to decide what approach will work best with your students and circumstances. Let's now transition from a discussion about classroom management to one about behavior management; from procedures to rules.

Behavior Management with Rules and Consequences

A discipline plan based on rules has three parts—Rules, Negative Consequences, and Positive Consequences.

1. **Rules:** What students are expected to follow.

2. **Negative Consequences:** What happens to students if rules are broken.

3. **Positive Consequences:** What students receive for appropriate behavior.

All rules should be discussed so students know that they are not orders or punishments. Explain that the purpose of rules is to set limits or boundaries, just as there are rules in games to maintain order and achieve a certain outcome.

Rules are used to define what is acceptable and what is not. Students expect teachers and school administrators to set boundaries. They need to feel confident that someone is in control and responsible for their safety and that of their environment—someone who not only sets limits but maintains them.

It is also important to state the rules in your classroom very clearly because different kinds of behavior are expected or tolerated by different teachers. For example, some teachers permit wandering around the room, but not others.

School must be a safe, protected, and controlled environment where students come to learn and interact with each other without fear.

The Two Kinds of Rules

The function of a rule is to prevent or encourage behavior by clearly stating the expectations you have of students. There are two kinds of rules: general and specific.

General rules encompass a wide range of behaviors.

- Respect others.
- Be polite and helpful.
- Keep the room clean.

Advantage: General rules address numerous behavior concepts and expectations in broad terms.

Disadvantage: General rules must be explained. For instance, students must be told that respecting others includes no hitting, no stealing, no tattling, no name-calling, and so on.

General rules are more successful when used by effective veteran teachers who have learned how to encourage good classroom behavior over the years. These teachers know how to calmly give the student a signal, a wave of the hand, or a stare, and the student behaves.

Specific rules focus on particular behaviors.

- Be in class when the bell rings.
- Keep hands, feet, and objects to yourself.
- Do not use offensive language.

Advantage: Specific rules clearly state expectations of student behavior without ambiguity.

Disadvantage: Specific rules need to be limited to no more than five, as explained in How Many Rules?

Specific rules are generally better for the newer teacher or the experienced teacher who is looking for a better discipline system. You can always move from specific rules to general rules during the school year as students learn more about your expectations for their behavior.

HARRY WONG PUBLICATIONS
943 N SHORELINE BLVD
MOUNTAIN VIEW CA 94043-1932

call us toll free:
1-800-248-2804

How Many Rules?

Have you ever noticed that your phone number, credit card, social security number, vehicle license number, and ZIP code are written in groups of five numbers or less? That's because people find it easier to remember numbers in groups of three to five.

- Limit your rules to a number that you and the students can readily remember—never more than five.

- If you need more than five rules, do not post more than five at any one time.

- The rules need not cover all aspects of behavior in the classroom.

- It is the teacher's prerogative to replace one rule with another at any time.

- As a new rule becomes necessary, replace an older one with it. The rule you replace can be retained as an "unwritten rule," which the students have learned. The students are still responsible for the one you have replaced.

Not Good Rules

Academic behavior should not appear on your list of rules. Such things as doing homework, writing in ink or typing, and turning in assignments fall into the realm of procedures (chapters 15 and 16) and academic performance (Unit D). Your discipline plan should be concerned with behavior, not academic work.

If possible, state rules positively. But recognize that sometimes a negative rule can be more direct, understandable, and incontestable:

- No cursing or swearing.
- No smoking.
- No fighting on the playground.

For rules to be effective, they must have consequences.

Rules Have Consequences

Rules must have consequences. Some students think they can break certain rules because the aftermath is consistent and predictable: nothing will happen to the violator. The responsible adult may find this hard to accept, but many people—children and adults—believe they have done nothing wrong until they are caught.

There have to be consequences, both positive and negative, for rules to be effective. Rules and their consequences require consistency and constant vigilance.

The Two Kinds of Consequences

- **POSITIVE** consequences or **REWARDS** result when people abide by the rules.

- **NEGATIVE** consequences or **PENALTIES** result when people break the rules.

Understanding Choice and Consequences

It's a fact of life. **Every action results in a consequence.** Consequences are not punishments. They are simply what happens when a person does something. For instance, if you overeat, smoke cigarettes, or park in a no-parking zone, there is a consequence for each action. Study hard, save money, or show kindness, and there is a consequence for each action as well.

Help students understand that if they break a rule, they are not being punished. Rather, they have consciously made a choice to accept the negative consequence of their action.

A consequence is the result of a person's chosen action.

The key to understanding consequences is **CHOICE.** People who cannot accept choice as part of responsible living cast themselves as victims.

Victims blame others for their actions or circumstances. Discuss this openly with students so that they clearly understand that they are responsible for their actions and the choices they make and that those actions or choices result in consequences.

It is far more helpful to spend time examining choice and consequences than it is to emphasize rules. Successful people accept that one's life is formed by choices and consequences, and consequences can be positive or negative.

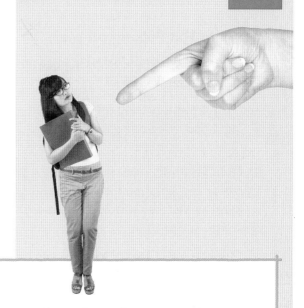

Punishment Doesn't Work

Armstrong Middle School (a pseudonym, but the facts are correct) was a miserable place for teaching and learning. Student misbehavior was out of control. Fights erupted. Fed-up teachers threw students out of class so often, long lines snaked outside the doors of the principal and assistant principal. The miscreants in those lines, waiting to be punished for their classroom behavior, often got into it with one another, compounding their original offense with yet another hallway fight.

Suspended students often went home, got their bikes, and came back. They would ride up and down the sidewalks outside, hollering for their friends to come to the windows to admire their freedom. It was cool to be bad, which only infuriated the teachers more.

Like many schools, Armstrong's philosophy about disciplining bad behavior relied on the assumption that adults can punish a student into compliance.

Actually, punishment does not improve behavior, because it does not cultivate cooperation or respect. Trying to rule over students by threatening them with a nasty consequence invites rebellion and resistance.

Punishment might work as a last resort. But in general, its costs outweigh the benefits.

So Armstrong was caught in a cycle of retributive discipline. Adults punished the students. Students found obnoxious ways to punish the adults. And so it went. Miserably.

I always point out the difference between having control of your classroom and trying to control students.

I also talk about the difference between structure and control. Students welcome and need structure, and teachers who provide the right structure don't have behavior problems and don't feel the need to control kids.

What you and I advocate for and teach teachers doesn't overpower students. It empowers students. Once the structure (procedures, organization, etc.) is in place, teachers can give students ownership of their learning.

David Ginsburg
Instructional coach

Why Are You Picking on Me?

What do you say to the following questions asked by students worldwide?

"Why are you picking on me? What did I do? Everyone else is doing it. Why look at me?"

Stand in front of a mirror and practice the following one hundred times until you can respond calmly and automatically every time one of these questions is asked:

"Because you CHOSE to break the rule. Because you CHOSE to break rule X."

Do not argue. Do not ask the student if he or she is questioning your authority. Do not yell, scream, or raise your voice. Just respond calmly every time:

"Because you CHOSE to break the rule."

After a few days, no one will ever ask, "Why are you picking on me?" because everyone will know exactly what you will say.

The key word in the phrase is CHOSE. Choosing means that one is responsible and accountable for one's actions. You are teaching your students responsibility and accountability. You are saying, "I, the teacher, am not picking on you. There are five rules in the classroom. The rules were discussed, agreed on, and signed. So when you CHOOSE to break one of the rules, you have chosen to accept the consequence."

After a few weeks or months, if someone should ask you, "Why are you picking on me?" all you have to do is stand and smile at the student. The entire class will respond for you,

"Because you CHOSE to break the rule!"

What About Rewards?

A reward is a positive consequence. After all, everyone likes and expects special recognition, rewards, and incentives when good work is done. Perks, incentives, honors, prizes, and awards are commonplace.

Although rewards are a fact of life, the wholesale bribery system of giving out endless supplies of stickers, candies, and other tangibles in schools today has got to come to a halt. Let's stop the "What's in it for me?" attitude prevalent in classrooms.

In addition, the Child Nutrition and WIC Reauthorization Act of 2004 makes the use of food items to reward good behavior no longer acceptable; it can actually nullify the efforts of your school and district toward compliance with the Act.

Research has shown that rewards do not necessarily increase desired behavior, and that in some situations rewards can, in fact, have negative effects. Rewards can be considered a way of controlling a student's behavior and when students quickly figure out that they are being controlled or extrinsically manipulated, it will decrease intrinsic motivation, the inner satisfaction of a job well done.

Carrots are as ineffective as sticks in helping young people to make responsible choices. They are totally ineffective in cultivating intrinsic motivation.

B. F. Skinner is famous for his work in operant conditioning—conditioning mice to press a lever in a cage in order to receive a reward. Rewards were used to reinforce behavior. You can see this in classrooms where the only reason students are motivated to come to school is to get something each day from the Treasure Box.

Neither carrots nor sticks teach students how to make responsible choices.

Marvin Marshall, an expert in promoting responsible behavior in students, shares this story about rewards.

The elementary school hired a substitute during the absence of the regular teacher.

Upon returning from lunch, a student asked if the class had earned a star to put on the bulletin board for the quiet way in which the class had returned.

The substitute didn't understand the request and asked about the procedure.

Another student explained that when students enter the classroom quietly, the teacher puts a star on the bulletin board. When a certain number of stars are reached, the class is given an afternoon without any work.

The substitute asked, "But aren't you supposed to walk quietly in the hall so that you don't disturb the other classes? Why should you earn a star for doing what is right?"

Students looked at each other, puzzled. Finally, one student explained, "We always get a reward. Why else should we do it?"

Specific Praise

To acknowledge a task done correctly, use specific praise instead of a reward. (This was introduced in Chapter 15.) **A reward results in momentary extrinsic motivation. Specific praise results in intrinsic motivation.** It helps students become aware of exactly what it is they are doing that is worthy of praise. You are praising the appropriate decisions and choices they have made.

- Praise the specific procedure, task, or action, not the student.

- Make the praise dependent on the specific learning target.

- Focus on the academic work rather than behavior. (Do you want the students to produce results or to just behave?)

Carol Dweck, professor of psychology at Stanford University, has found that educators cannot hand students confidence on a silver platter with general remarks praising their intelligence (for example, "Aaron, you are so smart").

More Help with Preventing Misbehavior

Books have been written on the subject of discipline and no definitive solution has been found. For a quick refresher course in discipline basics go to the **Go**ing **Be**yond folder for Chapter 17 or scan the QR Code.

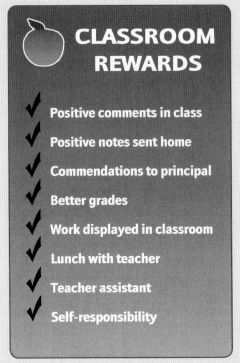

CLASSROOM REWARDS

✔ Positive comments in class

✔ Positive notes sent home

✔ Commendations to principal

✔ Better grades

✔ Work displayed in classroom

✔ Lunch with teacher

✔ Teacher assistant

✔ Self-responsibility

A set of rewards posted by a teacher.

Specific praise allows students to see what they, as individuals, are doing well, and this helps them gain the tools they need to maintain their confidence in learning by keeping them focused on the process of achievement.

> **The best reward is the satisfaction of a job well done.**

The goal of education to keep students focused on their own individual path to achievement and success.

Reward the Class

If you must use a reward, one that is popular for any grade level, give some minutes of free time on Friday as a whole class reward. Everyone has to work together cooperatively the entire week for the reward. The special minutes of free time on Fridays is effective and simple because it is not a tangible prize—and your students will never grow tired of it. Besides, the time is used, mostly, for schoolwork. There are no popcorn parties, pizza parties, or videos to plan for and clean up after—just free time to work!

66

Win-Win Procedures

You would not believe how many times I have to explain this.

1. *Management in the classroom is too often misinterpreted as controlling the herd.*

2. *Using discipline as punishment to force behavior management is a losing proposition.*

3. *Teaching procedural skills, which put students in control of their behavior and learning, is the win-win.*

Our purpose as teachers is to set our students free, with a hunger for knowledge that is never quite satisfied.

Bruce Kendall
www.teachers.net commentary

99

Schoolwide Reward System

Rather than individual class rewards, a schoolwide reward system works well for Cheyenne Traditional School in Scottsdale, Arizona.

1. Identical signs that promote positive behavior are posted in every classroom, hallway, playground, and cafeteria. The signs look the same, but the expectations for behavior are very specific to the location.

2. Adults carry tickets, and when a student is "caught being good," behaving in accordance with the signs, they are given a ticket with the location marked. These are dropped into a glass jar in the cafeteria.

3. One ticket per grade level is drawn each week and the rewards are a mix of donations from community members and intangible things like time with a requested teacher.

Behavior Management with Cooperative Discipline Plans

In the book, *Building Classroom Discipline*, C. M. Charles reports that the discipline approaches considered most effective dismiss punishment and other forceful tactics and favor approaches that are non-coercive.

The trend in education is to move from a punitive to a supportive, cooperative approach.

Each edition of his book reports on the most current trends in addressing discipline issues and he says:

"Although the Wongs' work is not a discipline plan, I want classes to run like well-oiled machines, where students are pleasantly doing what they know they are supposed to be doing.

"I wanted to include their work in my book because I use the term 'discipline' to include whatever teachers do non-coercively to encourage and help students conduct themselves civilly (meaning courteously) and responsibly (meaning doing what they know they should be doing).

"I see their work contributing powerfully to that goal, and my readers would miss ideas of great importance if I did not include the Wongs' approach in my book."

Imposing discipline is a thankless task; encouraging self-discipline is endlessly rewarding.

My Action Plan — Think Sheets

The most common form of a cooperative **discipline plan is a contract, or some type of an agreement, from the student.** My Action Plan is a simple technique that addresses specific problems and simultaneously teaches the student responsibility, problem solving, and self-discipline.

My Action Plan

1. What's the problem?
   I have too many tardies.

2. What's causing the problem? (Please list the factors.)
   I can't make it here in 7 minutes from P.E.
   It's too far away.
   I have to shower.
   I have to return the towel.
   I have to get a drink
   I have to go to the bathroom
   I have to go to my locker.
   The locker is hard to open.
   I have to return my library book.
   I have to see my girlfriend.
   I have to see the counselor.
   I have to check and see if I have made the team.

3. What plan will you use to solve the problem?
   I will shower.
   I will return the towel.
   I will see my girlfriend quickly.
   I will go to my locker.
   I will get a new lock for my locker
   I will move faster.

   Will Watson
   Student's Signature

   Thurs., October 3
   Date

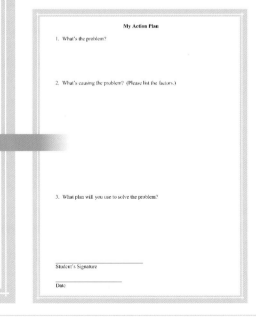

My Action Plan

1. What's the problem?

2. What's causing the problem? (Please list the factors.)

3. What plan will you use to solve the problem?

Student's Signature

Date

When a problem happens in the classroom, direct the student to a desk set aside with a pencil and a copy of My Action Plan. Follow the three steps.

Step 1. Show the student a copy of My Action Plan, and be prepared to work with him or her on answering these questions:

- What's the problem?
- What's causing the problem?
- What plan will you use to solve the problem?

What's the problem?
State the rule or rules the student has violated.

What's causing the problem?
Have the student list all the factors that are causing the problem to occur.

Work with the student in a **PROBLEM-SOLVING** mode. Tell him or her that the only way a person can solve a problem is to first isolate and identify it. You are not interested in degrading or scolding the student. You want to teach the student how to analyze and rectify a problem, a technique that the student can use throughout life.

What plan will you use to solve the problem? *Love This explanation*
Have the student write the action plan needed to solve the problem.

Guide the student to look at the factors causing the problem. Explain that the way to solve a problem is to change or eliminate the factors causing the problem. Help the student see the logic of this.

Have the student write a plan based on the causative factors listed under the second question. The student now takes **RESPONSIBILITY** for the plan. You did not tell the student what to do. The student, through problem solving, devised his or her own plan to correct the problem. You are teaching responsibility.

When students play a part in solving the problem, they have buy-in to carrying out the solution. Responsibility is chosen by the student as an outcome, rather than a stern punishment imposed by and forced on to the student the teacher.

My Action Plan Template

Download a copy of My Action Plan **Go**ing **Be**yond folder for Chapter 17 or scan the QR Code.

> **Using My Action Plan gives students
> the opportunity to learn**
>
> 1. **Problem-solving**
> 2. **Responsibility**
> 3. **Self-discipline**

Step 2. Have the student commit to responsibility by signing the action plan. This formality helps ensure that the student agrees to the plan and is committed to taking action. Make the student aware that, in the real world, signed contracts are serious and binding.

Step 3. For the student to carry through with his or her responsibility, encouragement and support are needed from home and the school so that the student achieves SELF-DISCIPLINE. Be generous with specific praise when the student is making an effort and the problem is being addressed as planned.

If at First You Don't Succeed . . .

If the problem is not being corrected, go back and work together again to modify the action plan. It is much better to put effort and energy into teaching problem-solving, responsibility, and self-discipline than to yell, criticize, and flunk. Yelling, criticizing, and flunking do not ultimately benefit, or result in positive consequences, for anyone.

Learning to be a self-disciplined and responsible person who knows how to take action to solve problems benefits all of humanity. With patience and persistence, have the student work on the action plan repeatedly until the problem is corrected.

*Energy and persistence
conquer all things.*

Benjamin Franklin

Being quick to solve a problem is not always the best solution. Dedication to the process does have its rewards.

The Self-Manager Plan

Jane Slovenske of Arizona uses a Self-Manager Plan that teaches students to be responsible for managing their own behavior. Students are presented with a Self-Manager Application—a self-evaluation form outlining responsible behavior, appropriate treatment of others, and efficient work habits. Each application is tailored to each student's abilities to bring out the best possible outcomes.

This is the process used to achieve a Self-Manager Plan.

List of Appropriate Behaviors. The class discusses a list of appropriate behaviors and standards for a Self-Manager and is then given an opportunity to revise the list. Once it is agreed upon, students complete an application evaluating themselves against the list of appropriate behaviors and take it home for review. When the adults at home are in agreement with their child's self-evaluation, it is signed and returned to school.

Teacher–Student Evaluation. The teacher must agree with the student's evaluation. If the teacher disagrees, evidence must be provided to support this. Student and teacher discuss their differences of opinion and come to an agreement. Jane says this is rarely necessary, because most students, with input from adults at home, are honest about their performance. Students rated "almost always" in each category become Self-Managers.

Each qualifying student wears a badge that says, "I'm a SELF-MANAGER." Staff and students recognize and acknowledge Self-Managers by the badges.

Student's Self-Evaluation. About once every six weeks, all students, including Self-Managers, complete a self-evaluation. It is important that Self-Managers maintain and reflect on appropriate behaviors. Remaining members of the class continue to have chances to refine their behaviors and become Self-Managers, too.

If a student loses or misplaces the badge, it can be replaced for a fee. This fee comes from their personal classroom checking accounts. Students earn "money" for their checking accounts by applying for a class job from a list of job descriptions. Only students who apply are given jobs. Checking account balances are used to pay fines for classroom infractions throughout the year.

The class determines and agrees to privileges granted to those with a Self-Manager badge. Types of privileges include walking ahead of the class to P.E., music, and art; sitting in beanbag chairs while the teacher reads aloud or during silent reading; not having to ask to use the restroom; and being first in line for dismissal.

Self-Manager Help Group. Self-Managers pair up with students who have not yet achieved Self-Manager status. Each Friday, after all students have received their weekly completion sheets, pairs of students review the list of missing assignments, work together to find them, and

Jane Slovenske's students manage their own behavior.

organize for completion. This is strictly on a voluntary basis, but all students who are not Self-Managers must request assistance from a peer who is a Self-Manager.

Students and former students take great pride in this form of recognition. Many students have older siblings who were Self-Managers. They still have their Self-Manager badges and are proud to show them to their younger brothers and sisters.

Self-Manager Application Template

Download a copy of the Self-Manager Application in the **Go**ing **Be**yond folder for Chapter 17 or scan the QR Code.

The Power Center©

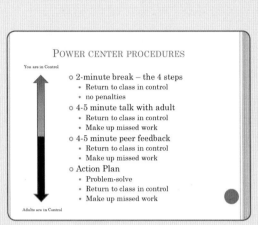

POWER CENTER PROCEDURES

You are in Control

○ 2-minute break – the 4 steps
  • Return to class in control
  • no penalties
○ 4-5 minute talk with adult
  • Return to class in control
  • Make up missed work
○ 4-5 minute peer feedback
  • Return to class in control
  • Make up missed work
○ Action Plan
  • Problem-solve
  • Return to class in control
  • Make up missed work

Adults are in Control

This slide explains to students how time is spent in the Power Center©.

GoBe

Power Center© Details

The PowerPoint presentation, the Power Center© steps, and the Action Plan for the Power Center© can be accessed in the **Go**ing **Be**yond folder for Chapter 17 or scan the QR Code.

It is common to see "Time Out Centers" in some classrooms—an area off to the side of the room where students who are causing problems are told to sit. Similar to penalty boxes in hockey, the problematic student is expected to reflect on the error of their ways and cool off. However, this is usually not enough to help most students assess and correct the actions that led to their being placed in the area. Most students need a more structured process to analyze their thoughts and decisions.

Margot Parsons, a special education teacher in the Lakeland School District, Scott Township, Pennsylvania, developed and uses a Power Center© method in her class where students are taught how to make choices. When school begins, she shows a PowerPoint presentation to her class on "The Power Center: Developing Your Power to Make the Right Choices."

She teaches them the concept that they have the power to choose. When needed, students are sent to a small area in the classroom where they take a short break and reflect on their behavior. Students are taught that this is a special space where they can consider their choices and the consequences of those choices. The objective is that they come out saying, "I have the power to discipline myself and act responsibly." If the student starts to waver, Margot asks with a smile, "Do you have the power?" She gets a smile in return.

The Power Center© process is not only for students with behavior issues. If a student feels frustrated, or the teacher notices a student's frustration, a two-minute Power Center© break may be recommended to refresh and recharge.

During the two-minute break, the student is asked to consider four steps:

1. Do a self-assessment
2. Describe the situation
3. Weigh the choices or consequences
4. Make a choice and return to class in control of yourself

If the student cannot make a choice, the next step is to request a "talk time" with a trusted adult and then get "peer feedback," as necessary. If the student is not ready to return to class after these opportunities, the student will be asked to complete an Action Plan.

The Raise Responsibility System

In the book, *Discipline Without Stress, Punishments, or Rewards: How Teachers and Caregivers Promote Responsibility & Learning*, Marvin Marshall explains a totally non-coercive, but not permissive, discipline and learning system. The core is the Raise Responsibility System that teaches students the Hierarchy of Social Development.

In this hierarchy, there are four levels: two levels of unacceptable behavior and two levels of motivation.

Hierarchy of Social Development

(D) Democracy: Student is self-disciplined, self-reliant, and takes the initiative to do the right thing because it is the right thing to do.

The motivation is *internal*.

(C) Cooperation/Conformity: Student cooperates, does what is expected and follows procedures, prompted by rewards, imposed punishments, or negative peer influence.

The motivation is *external*.

(B) Bossing/Bullying: Student bosses, bothers, or bullies others, breaks classroom standards and needs to be bossed to behave.

Unacceptable level of behavior.

(A) Anarchy: Student makes own standards and is only interested in self-gratification with no concern for consequences or impact on others.

Unacceptable level of behavior.

Once the levels are introduced, no time is spent differentiating between Level B and Level A— neither is acceptable. The goal of the system is to have students reflect on their behavior and be motivated to be at level D. For instance, if the student takes the initiative to pick up trash without being asked (internal motivation), that is Level D. If the teacher asks a student to pick up trash and the student cooperates, that is Level C (external motivation).

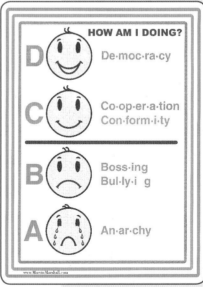

Posters are hung in the classroom so students can be reminded where they are on the Hierarchy of Social Development. Posters with smiley faces are used in primary classrooms.

The Raise Responsibility System is used to help misbehaving students self-evaluate by first asking them to reflect on their chosen level. The teacher continually focuses on the difference between the two levels of *motivation* so students naturally aim to achieve at the highest level—both in behavior and learning.

The Raise Responsibility System is implemented in three phases.

Phase 1. Teaching (Being Proactive). Before problems occur, teach and elicit examples of each of the levels from the students in different situations in and out of the classroom. After the four levels are taught, reference is made only to the letter D, C, B, or A, rather than to the vocabulary describing the level.

Jim Mann, a high school teacher, uses an alarm clock analogy to teach his students the differences between the levels of responsibility.

Level D – You set your alarm clock, wake up, and get to school on time.

Level C – You depend on your parents to wake you up to get to school on time.

Level B – You ignore your alarm clock and come to school late.

Level A – You don't even set your alarm clock because you are only interested in what you want and do not consider how your actions affect others.

Phase 2. Checking for Understanding (Asking). If a student acts on Level A or Level B (unacceptable levels of behavior), the student is prompted to reflect on the level chosen. Referring to a level, rather than to the behavior itself, the natural tendency to defend one's behavior is completely bypassed and the relationship between the teacher and student is not damaged.

Phase 3. Guided Choices (Eliciting). If a student continues to behave on Level A or B, a procedure or consequence is elicited that will help the student control future unacceptable impulses. In more severe cases, a series of self-reflecting forms are used.

66

Discipline Is a Positive Way

To many people, discipline means punishment. Rather, discipline should be a positive way of helping and guiding children to achieve self-control. Unless the teacher empowers by communicating in positive ways, offers choices to decrease coercion, and prompts reflection, the greatest discipline system will not be successful.

Use a system that teaches responsibility to help people change themselves.

Marvin Marshall

99

Schoolwide Behavior Plan

A schoolwide behavior plan is used at Paul Rowe Jr. & Sr. High School in Manning, Alberta, Canada. The plan is called SOLE (Respect for **S**elf, **O**thers, **L**earning, and **E**nvironment) and is presented as a behavior matrix for the school.

SETTING	Respect for **S**ELF	Respect for **O**THERS	Respect for **L**EARNING	Respect for **E**NVIRONMENT
ALL SETTINGS	▪ 4 Bs—no bras, bellies, butts, or backs ▪ Be respectful, friendly, and welcoming to visitors, staff, and fellow students ▪ No profanity	▪ Use manners ▪ Respect others' personal space ▪ No bullying	▪ Respect that the school is a learning environment	▪ 3 Rs—reduce, recycle, reuse ▪ Wear appropriate footwear ▪ Respect for school property ▪ Clean up after yourself and help keep the entire school clean ▪ Remove your hat

The matrix describes how students are to behave in every classroom and in specialized classrooms and areas. The staff introduces SOLE at the beginning of the year and continues to reaffirm good behavior throughout the year.

SOLE works well for the teacher, because the plan is schoolwide. It is for every class, every year, and there is no need for each teacher to develop their own discipline plan.

There are consistent expectations and students know whether the choices they make are appropriate or inappropriate.

There are no consequences. The staff continues to reaffirm good behavior.

SOLE Behavior Matrix

To see and duplicate the SOLE behavior matrix, go to the **Go**ing **Be**yond folder for Chapter 17 or scan the QR Code.

> ## There Is No Room for Ambiguity
>
> *I teach in the UK. Over the summer, I wrote a list of procedures and a classroom management plan. We've been back at school for about three weeks now. I spent a lot of time going through the procedures.*
>
> *There is no room for ambiguity. Every student knows exactly how things are done.*
>
> *I now have the most productive classes I've ever had, the calmest start to a school year I've ever had, and the most fun my students and I have ever had!*
>
> Jon Eaton
> Devon, United Kingdom

The Choice Is Yours

Now that you have read chapters 15, 16, and 17, you have been made aware of the advantages and disadvantages of different approaches to classroom and behavior management. Once again, behavior or discipline problems will occur in any classroom—they are inevitable. Your classroom management plan has to include a discipline plan. What plan you decide to use in your classroom is your choice.

Be sure to convey whatever plan you choose to use to the adults at home so they are aware of your policy. They will support you in helping their child succeed in your classroom.

However, prevention is more effective than intervention. Teach, rehearse, and reinforce procedures so students know "what to do" and "what to learn" in a calm, orderly classroom. (See Unit D for "what to learn.") Whatever system you choose to implement, the ultimate aim should not be external control and the enforcement of rules. Every effort should be made and every opportunity used to teach students about choice and consequences, and to instill responsibility and self-discipline.

So Students Can Learn

Griselda Almonte teaches high school in Paterson, New Jersey, where the school district has been under state control since 1991. Griselda's classroom is always consistent. Everyone follows the same set of procedures and knows what to do to succeed. Griselda does not lose her temper or yell. Instead, Griselda's system of classroom procedures is easy to learn and easy to follow.

Griselda allows students to select their working environment as long as they are quiet and do not disturb others. Her students were initially shocked that they were being given options and choice for their learning. The result is that students became responsible for their own learning. News soon spread at the school that "Ms. Almonte is fair."

With procedures in place, Griselda's focus is on instruction instead of discipline. Her students welcomed the change in the classroom. Instead of being reprimanded for their behavior and getting into trouble, they are now focused on learning and succeeding.

The reason for having well-managed classrooms is so students can have the opportunity to learn.

Carolyn Evertson is one of the foremost authorities on classroom management (page 97). **In her research, she shows that the purpose of classroom management is to create a "productive classroom environment so students have the opportunity to learn."**

Unit C has given you the tools to create a productive classroom environment. Giving students the opportunity to learn is the subject of Unit D.

---

[2] Carolyn M. Evertson and Carol S. Weinstein eds., *Handbook of Classroom Management: Research, Practice, and Contemporary Issues* 1st ed. (Mahwah, NJ: Lawrence Erlbaum Associates, Inc., 2006).

> ## A Productive Classroom Environment
>
> *Supporting and developing orderly and productive classroom environments is the foundation of good classroom management. Organizing the classroom takes into account the many students' characteristics and issues that will influence what students have the opportunity to learn.*[2]
>
> Carolyn Evertson
> Vanderbilt University

⭐ THE EFFECTIVE TEACHER

☑ Thinks through a discipline plan before school begins and conveys the plan to students when school begins.

☑ Discusses the plan so that students understand its logic and accept it as reasonable.

☑ Involves the home to help guarantee and enforce the plan.

☑ Uses discipline to help teach students self-discipline and responsible behavior.

...IMPLEMENTS!

Unit

Third Characteristic—Lesson Mastery

The effective teacher knows how to design lessons
to help students achieve.

Chapters

The Heart of Education

You have finished Unit C on Classroom Management. With the written plan you've created, you are ready to proceed like a coach with a game plan. This ensures that for the rest of the school year you will have a classroom that is a well-oiled learning environment where you can teach effectively and students are given every opportunity to learn.

> **Learning has nothing to do with what the TEACHER COVERS.**
> **Learning has to do with what the STUDENT ACCOMPLISHES.**

Teaching and learning are the heart of education. Unit D, the most important unit in this book, specifically addresses how to teach so that your students progress steadily toward the ultimate goal of being prepared for further education, careers, and life. **Schools exist and teachers are hired for one reason only—to help students learn and achieve.** Good, sound instruction created for student success is fifteen to twenty times more powerful than family background, income, race, gender, or other explanatory variables.[1]

Teachers must be effective instructors who know how to design lessons and create assignments that help students achieve what they should know, understand, and be able to do from day to day. Reflecting on the definition of "effective" as introduced in Chapter 1, page 3, it is "successful in producing intended results." The results that are intended are determined by education standards, curriculum, and learning objectives. **Success is achieved when teachers write lessons with crystal clear objectives and precise instructions so that students understand what the outcome or result of the lesson will be.**

It is not what students manage to discover on their own. The research is very specific about teaching and learning. **Teachers are responsible for what students learn.**

THE KEY IDEA

When lesson objectives are clear, and instruction and assessment are aligned to objectives, the greater the chances are that students will succeed.

Schools exist and teachers are hired for one reason only—to help students learn and achieve. Students come to school so that they are prepared for further education, careers, and life.

[1] Theodore Hershberg, "Value-Added Assessment and Systemic Reform: A Response to the Challenges of Human Capital Development," *Phi Delta Kappan*, vol. 87, no. 4 (December 2005): 276–283.

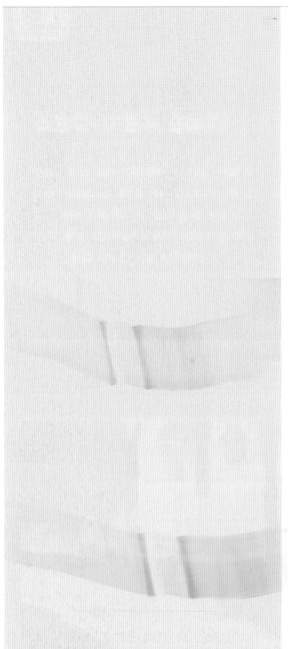

- Former superintendent Mike Schmoker says, "Lay out a sound set of standards and then actually teach these standards and there will be an immense increase in levels of achievement almost immediately."[2]

- Educational researcher Robert Marzano reported on a study of what affects student achievement and says, "It is what gets taught!"[3]

- Andrew Porter, Dean of the Graduate School of Education at the University of Pennsylvania, says, "What gets taught is the strongest possible predictor of gains in achievement."[4]

This chapter will show you how to get the intended results.

> **Student learning and achievement must be the focus of all decisions made in school.**

What Is an Education Standard?

The term "standard" has become the measuring rod of quality used in many fields. When buying a car, we look at the performance standards. We buy from companies that produce goods and services of high standards. We expect the food and drug industries to enforce the highest quality standards. We assume the buildings we work in are constructed to rigorous standards. The city checks to see that the plans meet codes or standards for the proper use of plumbing, electricity, structure, roofing, and other construction factors. If you were to buy a home, you would want to know that your home was built to code, which signifies that it meets the standards.

> **Every enterprise has standards, including education. We expect and demand high standards to protect and enhance our lives.**

In education, standards provide the foundation for teaching and learning. They indicate what each student is to learn at

[2] Mike Schmoker, "Results: The Key to Continuous School Improvement" (Alexandria, VA: Association for Supervision and Curriculum Development, 1996). (Retrieved from an email with author April 2007.)

[3] Robert Marzano, "What Works in Schools: Translating Research into Action" (Alexandria, VA: Association for Supervision and Curriculum Development, 2003).

[4] Andrew Porter, "Measuring the Content of Instruction: Uses in Research and Practice," *Educational Researcher*, vol. 31, no. 7 (October 2002): 3–14. (Updated from an email with author August 2007.)

each grade level. They set grade specific, clear, and consistent learning goals. They form the base point from which to design lessons and assignments so that learning objectives are met.

Standards state what students are to accomplish, not what to teach or how to teach it.

Although standards set recommended learning goals, following standards does not deprive you, the teacher, of creativity. Quite the contrary—standards don't regulate how things should be taught or what materials should be used.

Architects can design homes in an unlimited number of ways, provided they are in accordance with the city's standards. Poets express their thoughts and feelings in an infinite number of ways within the parameters of rhyme and rhythm patterns.

When you know the learning objectives, you are free to decide the most effective way of achieving those objectives in your classroom with your students.

These are some typical standards from state guides:

Elementary Math, Colorado
Use place value and properties of operations to perform multi-digit arithmetic.

Seventh Grade Physical Education, California
Explain the effects of nutrition and participation in physical activity on weight control, self-concept, and physical performance.

High School Language Arts Literacy, South Dakota
Determine a central idea of a text and analyze its development over the course of the text, including its relationship to supporting ideas; provide an objective summary of the text.

Standards provide the foundation for student learning.

Standards provide the foundation for teacher ingenuity.

The building industry has standards to safeguard our safety by ensuring that plans meet codes for plumbing, electricity, structure, roofing, and other construction factors.

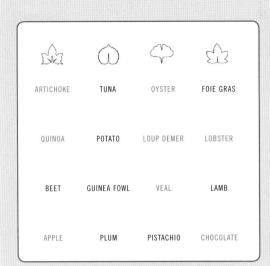

ARTICHOKE	TUNA	OYSTER	FOIE GRAS
QUINOA	POTATO	LOUP DEMER	LOBSTER
BEET	GUINEA FOWL	VEAL	LAMB
APPLE	PLUM	PISTACHIO	CHOCOLATE

A list of food items allows the chef to be creative in meeting your needs.

What Is a Curriculum?

A **curriculum is the course of study that determines what knowledge and skills students are to learn.** It is a school document that identifies the content to be taught and the suggested methods to be used. If standards provide the foundation, a curriculum provides the framework. Or, in other words, standards form the core or backbone of the curriculum. With standards in place, schools can create curriculum guides.

The purpose of curriculum guides is to tell teachers what students are to master. They recommend ways to teach the content so that students achieve high levels of proficiency in content areas. They are like menus in restaurants listing the different wholesome food items available and how they are prepared. It is then up to the chef to create the dishes each day so diners can enjoy the food.

A committee of teachers, administrators, and curriculum specialists create the school or district curriculum. They take the Common Core, state, or professional organization's standards and design curricular and instructional strategies that best convey the content to students. This work is then assembled into a curriculum guide.

Most district curriculum guides address these areas:

- Identify the content (facts, concepts, topics, themes, musical selections, skills)

- Suggest instructional methods to be used (discussion, case studies, role playing, rehearsals, real-life experiences, cooperative learning, experiments)

- Suggest assignments to teach the content or illustrate the method to be used

Get Your Curriculum Guide

I f you have not already been given the curriculum guide for your school or district, ask for it. You must have a guide as you teach, just as you must have a map as you travel. **It is not your job to develop a personal curriculum for your classroom. It is your responsibility to deliver the district curriculum.**

I was so excited as I came to the office for my first day of school. I checked in at the counter and met the school secretary (no principal) and was given my key and the schedule. When I asked for the curriculum, she said, "Oh, you'll figure it out."

Too many teachers are handed a key to the classroom and sent off to teach without adequate information about the curriculum and available resources. Too often, new teachers have little or no access to information about what exactly they are to teach their students. Often they don't even know what their students are expected to learn before going on to the next grade.

The Project on the Next Generation of Teachers, a research group at the Harvard Graduate School of Education, discovered this:

> **Few teachers began teaching with a clear, operational curriculum in hand, and even fewer received curricula that are aligned with state standards.**[5]

This is a recipe for floundering, discouragement, and failure. The problem can be alleviated for new teachers and their students if school districts have curriculum guides for each subject and grade level and then show teachers how to implement them.

The Learning Triangle

Once you have a curriculum guide in hand, you are ready to prepare lessons and assignments. Everything you need to know about ensuring your students learn, succeed, and progress can be explained and implemented with The Learning Triangle.[6]

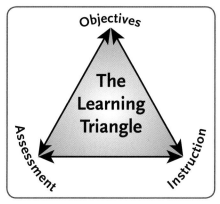

The use of The Learning Triangle in all of your lesson planning will improve the quality of your instruction.

[5] David Kauffman, Susan M. Johnson, Susan Kardos, Edward Liu, and Heather G. Peske, "Lost at Sea: New Teachers' Experiences With Curriculum and Assessment," *Teachers College Record*, vol. 104, no. 2 (March 2002): 273–300.

[6] Developed in collaboration with Sarah Powley, Tippecanoe School Corporation, Lafayette, Indiana.

Every lesson must have the three components of The Learning Triangle for optimum student learning to take place: Objectives, Instruction, and Assessment.

- **Objectives:** Every lesson must begin with objectives, the target for teaching and learning. (Chapter 18)

- **Instruction:** Every lesson must have instruction that is made up of activities directly related to the lesson objectives. (Chapter 21)

- **Assessment:** Every lesson must have a way to assess students' understanding of the lesson objectives. (Chapter 19)

That's the essence of The Learning Triangle. It shows how the beginning (objectives), middle (instruction), and end (assessment) of a lesson are all related and must all be aligned to be effective. It provides the solid structure needed to prevent a mumbo jumbo, smorgasbord of classroom activities that fill in time but are not achieving any continuous, coherent, or consistent content.

Keep a diagram of The Learning Triangle posted in your personal work area. Keep it foremost in your mind every single day—whether you are creating a lesson, a unit, a semester plan, or even an entire course. Use it to advance, step-by-step, though the curriculum.

The Learning Triangle will help you with lesson planning:

- **Articulate** the objectives at the beginning of every lesson

- **Adhere** to those objectives as you create lessons so that students focus on them as they work through activities

- **Assess** for student learning against the objectives

Lesson Objectives

You can't teach for learning if there are no stated lesson objectives to be learned, and you can't assess what students have learned if there are no stated objectives to assess against. **Objectives drive all decision points in a lesson.**

The Instructional Coach

Crafting the perfect learning triangle is the work of Sarah Powley. To see how she uses The Learning Triangle to coach teachers, go to the **Go**ing **Be**yond folder for Chapter 18 or scan the QR Code.

Objectives serve two purposes:

1. The lesson objectives tell the teacher what is to be taught.

2. The lesson objectives tell students what is to be accomplished.

Objectives are sometimes called learning targets. They tell students what they are aiming for. They tell students what they are responsible for learning. They tell students the purpose of the lesson. Objectives can also be called outcomes—they tell students what they will achieve.

> **Objectives are what a student is to learn, accomplish, and master.**

The work of John Hattie was introduced in Chapter 5. Hattie's research, published in *Visible Learning: A Synthesis of Over 800 Meta-Analyses Relating to Achievement*, has found that the foremost and most powerful method for improving student achievement is to make students aware of what they are to learn.

> **Tell students what they will be learning (objectives) before the lesson begins and student achievement can be raised as much as 27 percent.**

If you were to ask one of your students, "What are you learning?" could that student state or point to a posted or listed objective? Could they tell you what they are going to accomplish? Or are they just dutifully going through the motions without any sense of purposeful engagement?

Objectives Give Purpose

Objectives help students understand the purpose of a lesson. They help students focus on what they must do. They also help students anticipate how they will be assessed. The research of Kevin Wise and James Okey showed that "the effective classroom appears to be the one in which the students are kept aware of instructional objectives and receive feedback on their progress toward these objectives."[7]

One Out of 12

Wise and Okey wanted to know what teaching strategies were most important in helping students achieve. They looked at these twelve possible factors:

- Audiovisual
- Grading
- Inquiry/discovery
- Focusing on objectives
- Hands-on manipulation
- Modifying the textbooks and instructional materials
- Presentation mode of teacher
- Questioning strategies
- Testing
- Teacher direction
- Wait time
- Miscellaneous

Out of the twelve possible factors influencing student achievement, there was one that stood out above and beyond the rest. They found that **focusing on objectives** had the biggest influence on student achievement.

[7] Kevin Wise and James Okey, "A Meta-Analysis of the Effects of Various Science Teaching Strategies on Achievement," *Journal of Research in Science Teaching*, vol. 20, no. 5 (1983): 419–435.

The Activity Is Not an Objective

Too many teachers think that doing an activity is the learning target or objective of the lesson. Likewise, many students when asked the purpose (the lesson objective) of what they are learning will tell you, or point to, the activity they are doing. An activity is not an objective.

An activity is an instructional device used to teach an objective.

Objectives make a lesson meaningful. They include the student in the process of teaching and learning. Students are more engaged and get more done when they understand why, where, what, and how—why they are doing something, what they are doing, where they are going, and how they are going to get there.

**Students who are given objectives
at the beginning of assignments
make it their responsibility to accomplish them.**

Objectives are important for teachers too, because they specify and clarify what is to be taught. Purposeful, meaningful, and effective lessons are those that teachers create with the end results in mind.

When thinking about lesson objectives, refer to the standards in your area and your school's curriculum guide. They will identify what content is to be taught and suggest methods to be used.

When the objectives of a lesson are matched to the district and state standards, it is called alignment. What the student is to learn and how you teach it must fit together smoothly.

**When both student and teacher are moving toward
the same target or objective, learning will occur.**

When to Write Objectives

Teachers must know the objectives of the lesson before designing the instruction and creating the assessments. Students must know what they are responsible for learning before the lesson and instruction begins.

Objectives must be formulated before you create the lesson.

- When you know the objectives, you know what is to be taught.

- When you know what is to be taught, you can decide how it will be taught and what instruction you will use.

- When you know what instruction you will use, you will know what type of assessment is appropriate to see if the students have learned what has been taught.

Instruction

Your students should become accustomed to hearing the terms learning objective, lesson objective, lesson outcome, or learning target. In order to explain how they are to achieve lesson objectives, you might want to use a simple archery metaphor.

Tell them that if you were to give them a bow and arrow, you would, of course, also give them a target. Without a target, there is nothing for them to aim for when shooting the arrow.

- The bull's-eye is the lesson objective or learning target.

- The arrow is the instruction and assessment used to reach the bull's-eye.

Objectives tell students what they are to learn. Instruction and assessments show students how they will achieve the learning. When students are made aware of WHAT they are to learn and HOW they are to learn it, you increase the chances that they WILL learn.

Remember, Hattie found that when you tell students the lesson objectives, you increase student achievement by 27 percent. He also found that if you provide students with specific feedback about their progress, achievement can be raised by as much as 37 percent. (Chapter 19)

The Three Major Aspects When Writing an Objective

1. **Structure: Use a consistent format.**
2. **Precision: Use succinct, clear sentences.**
3. **Accomplishment: Tell what is to be achieved.**

> *To begin with the end in mind means to start with a clear understanding of your destination.*
>
> Stephen Covey

Lesson Objectives Begin with Verbs

Verbs are action or thinking words that do two things:

1. **They tell the student what is to be accomplished.**

2. **They tell the teacher what to assess to determine whether the student has accomplished what the teacher specified.**

How to Write Objectives

As previously stated, **determine** and **articulate** the objectives before you create a lesson and **adhere** to those objectives as you formulate the instruction so that students focus on them as they work through the lesson activities.

There are two steps when writing objectives:

Step 1: Pick a verb.
Step 2: Complete the sentence.

Step 1: Pick a verb. Refer to the list on page 231, and select a verb to use as the first word in a sentence. Only you know which verb to pick because you know what you want or need to teach. Only you know the level of competence and readiness of your students. Only you know what level of thinking they are able to achieve. Only you know how to challenge your students so that they keep progressing.

Refrain from choosing verbs from one category only, because this would limit your students to only one level of thinking.

Step 2: Complete the sentence. The verb you choose tells the student what action is to be taken. The rest of the sentence tells the student what is to be accomplished or mastered.

Ensure that the sentence is simple and direct enough to be easily understood by you, the students, and their parents and guardians.

> To teach for learning, use thinking or action words that state HOW the student is to demonstrate that learning has taken place.

Bloom's Taxonomy

In 1956, Dr. Benjamin Bloom and collaborators from the University of Chicago devised a framework for categorizing educational goals into six main categories. This method of classification is known as Bloom's Taxonomy.[8] In 2000, Lorin Anderson and David Krathwohl revised Bloom's Taxonomy and organized instructional verbs into levels of knowledge like floors in a building from the most basic to the most sophisticated.[9] The verbs—"action words" and "thinking words"—are categorized into six related groups, ranging from the lowest thinking skill, Remembering, to the highest thinking skill, Creating.

These categories are a useful guide as you plan lessons that are direct, achievable, and challenging.

6 – Creating
5 – Evaluating
4 – Analyzing
3 – Applying
2 – Understanding
1 – Remembering

Commentary on Bloom's Taxonomy

For a comparison and commentary of the original and revised Bloom's Taxonomy, go to the **Go**ing **Be**yond folder for Chapter 18 or scan the QR Code.

Recap and Remember
Creating Objectives
Step 1: Pick a verb.

Step 2: Complete the sentence.

Examples:

List four collective nouns.

Create a logo for a new health food company.

Posting Objectives

Post lesson objectives for students to see or give students a copy of the objectives. Do this before instruction begins.

[8] Benjamin S. Bloom and David R. Krathwohl, eds., *Taxonomy of Educational Objectives Handbook 1: Cognitive Domain* (New York: Longmans, Green 1956).

[9] Lorin W. Anderson and David R. Krathwohl, eds., *A Taxonomy for Learning, Teaching, and Assessing: A Revision of Bloom's Taxonomy of Educational Objectives* (Boston, MA: Allyn & Bacon, Pearson Education Group, 2000).

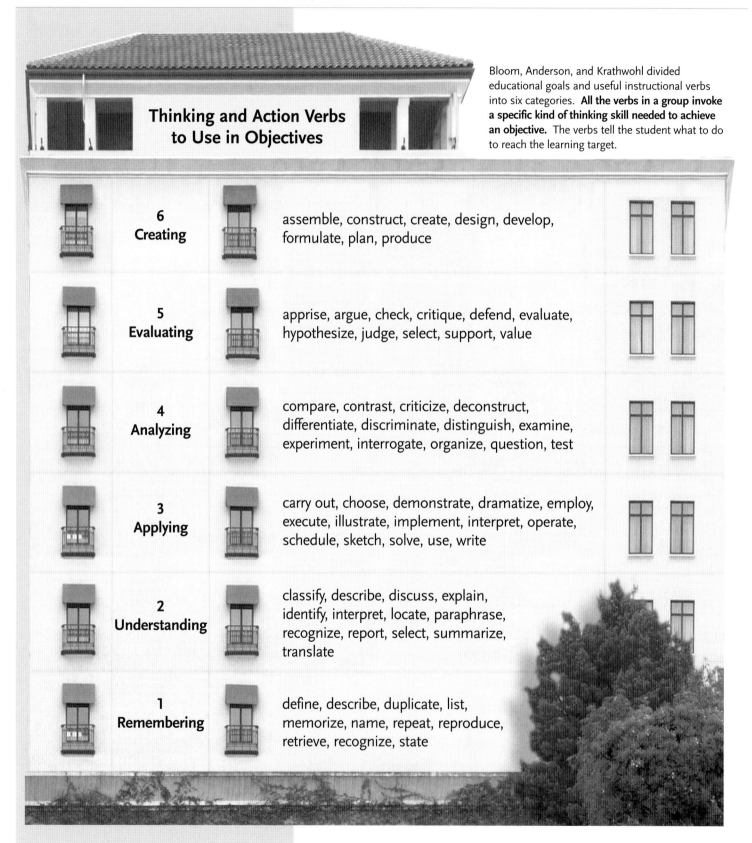

Thinking and Action Verbs to Use in Objectives

Bloom, Anderson, and Krathwohl divided educational goals and useful instructional verbs into six categories. **All the verbs in a group invoke a specific kind of thinking skill needed to achieve an objective.** The verbs tell the student what to do to reach the learning target.

6 Creating
assemble, construct, create, design, develop, formulate, plan, produce

5 Evaluating
apprise, argue, check, critique, defend, evaluate, hypothesize, judge, select, support, value

4 Analyzing
compare, contrast, criticize, deconstruct, differentiate, discriminate, distinguish, examine, experiment, interrogate, organize, question, test

3 Applying
carry out, choose, demonstrate, dramatize, employ, execute, illustrate, implement, interpret, operate, schedule, sketch, solve, use, write

2 Understanding
classify, describe, discuss, explain, identify, interpret, locate, paraphrase, recognize, report, select, summarize, translate

1 Remembering
define, describe, duplicate, list, memorize, name, repeat, reproduce, retrieve, recognize, state

Levels of Student Thinking Desired in a Lesson

The level of thinking you want to elicit from a student during a lesson is based on the level from which you select the verb. The type of thinking required at each level becomes more complex as you go from Remembering to Creating.

6 Creating

To take parts of information and produce an original whole

Accomplishment: The student can create a new product or point of view.

5 Evaluating

To make a judgment based on criteria

Accomplishment: The student can justify a stand or decision.

4 Analyzing

To show understanding of parts and relationships

Accomplishment: The student can distinguish among the different parts.

3 Applying

To use learning in a new situation

Accomplishment: The student can use the information in a new way.

2 Understanding

To show knowledge or comprehension

Accomplishment: The student can explain ideas or concepts.

1 Remembering

To recall information

Accomplishment: The student can recollect or remember the information.

Applying Bloom's Taxonomy to the Study of Antarctica

1. **Remembering:** Name the first person to reach the South Pole.

2. **Understanding:** Describe the difference between the Arctic and Antarctic regions.

3. **Applying:** Choose an example of modern technology that, had it been available to the explorers, would have made a difference in their trip.

4. **Analyzing:** Compare the weather at the South Pole on December 1 and June 1 in any given year.

5. **Evaluating:** Defend your position: Should Antarctica remain a continent free of development and left with its natural habitat?

6. **Creating:** Imagine that you made the journey. Write a diary entry describing your emotions on the day you reached the South Pole.

There are some verbs—for example: appreciate, enjoy, like, understand—that are not on Bloom's list and should not be used when writing objectives because it is difficult, if not impossible, to determine from them what students are to do, nor is it possible to assess whether they have achieved the intended result. Here are some examples of ineffective objectives:

- The students will appreciate the poetry of e. e. cummings.
- The students will enjoy reading about the creation of the World Wide Web.
- The students will like the music of Mozart.
- The students will understand the difference between Celsius and Fahrenheit.

Learning Targets

The second way to write an objective is to start the sentence with the words "I can." Objectives written in an "I can" form are usually called learning targets or lesson outcomes.

There are two steps when writing learning targets.

1. Start with the stem, "I can . . . "

2. Add what the students will be able to *do* at the end of the instruction.

 - I can label the cell bodies in a diagram correctly without using a word bank.
 - I can create a still life drawing of a three-dimensional object.
 - I can defend my choice of nutritional drinks.
 - I can summarize the main idea of the article.
 - I can solve a two-digit division problem.
 - I can label the New England states on a blank map of the United States.
 - I can explain the water cycle by drawing a picture and labeling the stages.
 - I can plan a snack of less than 200 calories.

Learning targets are ideal for younger, more challenged, and ESL students. This is because a learning target is designed to capture a daily goal—just a bite-sized piece of learning.

The "I" in "I can" is critical. When a student reads a statement that begins with "I can," the learning target is personal. The goal is about what *the student* will be able to do at the end of the instruction. The "I" creates ownership. It creates responsibility. "I" speaks directly to the student and the student must respond with "I can" or even "I cannot." Either way, the teacher is there to help the student make progress.

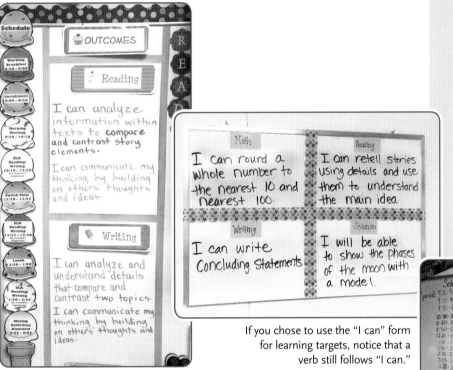

If you chose to use the "I can" form for learning targets, notice that a verb still follows "I can."

Creating an Effective Assignment

Lessons are what teachers create to accomplish an intended result. Lessons consist of assignments that students are to do to achieve the lesson objectives. Look at the word "assignment." It means that someone will be given a task and, at the end of the task, a result or product will be evident. You say to an assistant, "Please type this letter and then give it back so I can sign it." The assistant has been given a clear assignment and the expectation is a completed and correct letter. Or, you go to the bakery to select a cake for a wedding. You say, "On Saturday, July 18, I want that cake delivered to the reception hall at 3 P.M."

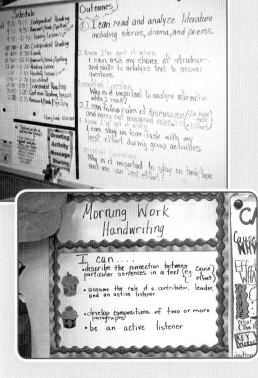

The Objective Is the Object of the Lesson

- Post the objectives for everyone to see. Write objectives on the board or make them part of the daily agenda. Students are more likely to engage with lessons and participate in activities if they understand why they're doing them.

- Begin a lesson by pointing to the objectives so that everyone knows where they are going.

- Refer to the objectives during a lesson to allow students to check for their own understanding. This helps them recognize when they are having trouble with the lesson.

- Bring closure to a lesson by reviewing the objectives and reinforcing what students have learned.

The baker has been given a clear assignment—a specific product is to be delivered at a specified time and place.

Effective assignments clearly specify what students are to do or learn and what the teacher wants produced as evidence of having completed the assignment.

Assignments are always created to produce an intended end result. And the end result always relates to accomplishing the objective of the lesson. As research has clearly shown, students accomplish more and achieve more when they are given objectives. They have been given the opportunity to see what has been planned for their learning. They are on a path to success through clearly signposted "mastery learning," rather than being bogged down in a fog of "mystery learning."

Mastery learning is when students do knowing why and how.
Mystery learning is when students do without knowing why or how.

Effective teachers ask this when creating assignments:

- What do I want students to learn (the lesson objective)?

- What do I want students to accomplish (the lesson product)?

The Four Steps to Creating an Effective Assignment

Creating an Effective Assignment in Four Steps

Step 1: Determine what you want students to accomplish.

Step 2: Write the objectives of the lesson as single sentences.

Step 3: Ensure students know the objectives.

Step 4: Post or send objectives and instructions home with students.

Step 1: Do NOT ask, "What am I going to cover in class?" or "What activity will I have students do?" Determine what you want students to accomplish. The question that must be foremost in your mind is, "What do I want my students to learn?"

What you want your students to learn will be predetermined by the school or district curriculum guide, which, in turn, was probably written by a district committee of teachers based on designated standards.

**Standards identify
what is essential for students to master.**

Every state and most districts have curriculum standards. In Texas, they are called Texas Essential Knowledge and Skills (TEKS). In Arizona, the standards are called the Arizona College and Career Ready Standards. Check with your administrator for the standards that correlate to what you are assigned to teach.

Step 2: Write each objective as a single sentence. The sentences must clearly and precisely state what is to be accomplished. The most important word in a lesson objective is the verb. Verbs help clarify and identify whether or not the intended result has been accomplished.

Objectives should be in student-friendly language. They should be clear, concise, explicit, and aligned to assessments and tests. Do not write complex objectives like the following, taken from a published elementary science program:

> Given two different molds growing on the same plate, the student will describe the inhibiting reaction at the interface of the molds.

The same objective could have been written in a straightforward and simpler way:

> Describe what happens when two molds grow together.

**Write precise objectives that explicitly state
what you want the student to accomplish.**

These are examples of typical objectives or learning targets:

- Name, in order, the parts of the digestive system.
- Summarize the class discussion on photosynthesis.

What Objectives Accomplish

Objectives or learning targets must be written to accomplish three things: Assign, Assess, and Evaluate.

1. **Assign.** Objectives give direction or tell a student what is to be comprehended or mastered in an assignment. (Chapter 18)

2. **Assess.** A rubric is written to correlate to the objectives. (Chapter 19)

3. **Evaluate.** A test is written to correlate to the objectives. (Chapter 20)

Students will be much more likely to succeed in class if they know what **Procedures** (do) and **Objectives** (learn) they are responsible for.

- Critique the use of drones that fly over foreign countries.
- I can categorize the contents of the box.
- I can create a new ending for the story.
- I can judge the effects of global warming.

Step 3: Objectives do not have to be written; they can be stated verbally. This is a useful approach in the primary grades and certain special education situations. You need not present all the objectives at one time, either. For elementary students, it may be more appropriate to state the objectives one or two at a time.

**Ensure students know the objectives
to guide them through the assignment.**

Most importantly, you must continually look at the objectives to make sure the class is on course.

Just as you would with a map, a blueprint, or a conference program, refer frequently to the objectives.

Step 4: Enlist the home to help students learn.

Post or send objectives home with students.

> **Students can be in control
> when they know
> what objectives they are responsible for learning.**

Communicating with Parents and Guardians

It is important that any person—teacher, student, parent, or guardian—be able to easily read and understand lesson objectives. The more understandable they are, the greater the chance that the student will accomplish what is intended.

Schools typically have an open house soon after school begins. When parents or guardians ask you, "How do I know what my child's assignment is?" explain how you create lessons and assignments.

You Teach the Students, Not the Textbook

Teaching is not covering the textbook. Neither is the textbook the curriculum. For more on this concept, go to the **Go**ing **Be**yond folder for Chapter 18 or scan the QR Code.

Explain that lesson objectives are like the final destination of a journey. They are what the student is to learn, accomplish, and master. Explain that your instruction and assessments will guide students so that they are able to achieve objectives. This will help parents and guardians understand the teaching, learning, and assessment process. It will enable them to help their children accomplish what's required of them so they can progress and succeed.

Students Who Need Additional Directions

Lesson objectives generally work well with most students. When they understand the objectives, they assume responsibility and take pride in accomplishing the goal of the lesson. They are able to translate the lesson or assignment into concrete results. They are eager to solve problems and achieve on their own.

What about those students who need additional assistance and guidance in understanding objectives and following instructions? These students are not necessarily below-average students. They, too, are probably eager to learn and achieve on their own. But they may have no background in your subject, or they may face linguistic or cultural barriers.

For these students, you will need to elaborate on the lesson objectives. You will need to break them down into accessible assignments with multiple, specific goals for each objective.

Here is an example of how to elaborate on a lesson objective.

Objective: Give examples of the different types of nutrients.

Further elaboration:

1. Name the different kinds of nutrients.
2. Define and give examples of proteins.
3. Define and give examples of carbohydrates.
4. Define and give examples of fats.
5. Explain why proteins are important for your body.
6. Explain why carbohydrates are important for your body.
7. Explain why fats are important for your body.

For students who may need even more support, give the page number or location where the answer may be found next to each question.

The Optimum Length of a Lesson

The shorter the lesson, the MORE likely the student will complete it. The longer the lesson, the LESS likely the student will complete it. There are optimum lengths for assignments:

- No high school lesson should exceed five days.

- No junior or middle school lesson should exceed four days.

- No intermediate school lesson should exceed three days.

- No primary school lesson should exceed a day, or occasionally, two.

- No special education lesson should exceed fifteen minutes.

How Study Guidelines Help Students Achieve

Study guidelines assist students, parents, and guardians in clearly defining the expectations for success in, and mastery of, the concepts presented in a lesson.

Here is how study guidelines should be introduced and incorporated into your lesson plans.

- The first time you give students the assignment, explain to them why they are called study *guidelines*. They are guides that you have prepared to help them complete the assignment.

- Use the analogy of a map to explain the use of study guidelines. Explain that just as a traveler would use a map or GPS as a guide to a destination, each sentence serves as a map to guide them in their study. The study guidelines are to be presented as "user-friendly," not intimidating.

  - Tell students that the best way to use study guidelines is to place them next to whatever source they are studying, such as their textbooks, worksheets, or notes. Tell them to use the guidelines just as they might use a road map or a recipe while cooking.

  - Tell students that the content standard for the lesson is at the top of the page. They are to focus on this to accomplish the objective, learning target, or outcome of the assignment. It will be specific and achievable as opposed to vague assignments like "Chapter 24," "decimals," "clouds," or "China."

- Point out the numbered sentences. These are the lesson objectives, learning targets, or outcomes. Explain that these sentences tell students exactly what they are responsible for, and that they must master these specifics if they are to understand the content standard.

- Tell students that each objective, learning target, or outcome will be the subject of questions when they are evaluated on the lesson. They will be tested for their comprehension and mastery of each objective. (See Chapter 20.)

Study guidelines help students by telling them directly what they need to know to achieve learning objectives, targets, or outcomes.

The examples of study guidelines shown here have been used for years with great success. They are presented as examples only. Ignore the subjects and focus on how the objectives for the assignment are written. Then apply the examples to your own subject matter.

How to Maximize Student Achievement and Your Effectiveness

- Write assignments based on lesson objectives, not coverage of content.

- Write the objectives so succinctly and clearly that even outsiders, such as parents and guardians, can understand the assignment.

- Give students the objectives in advance so they know what they are responsible for accomplishing.

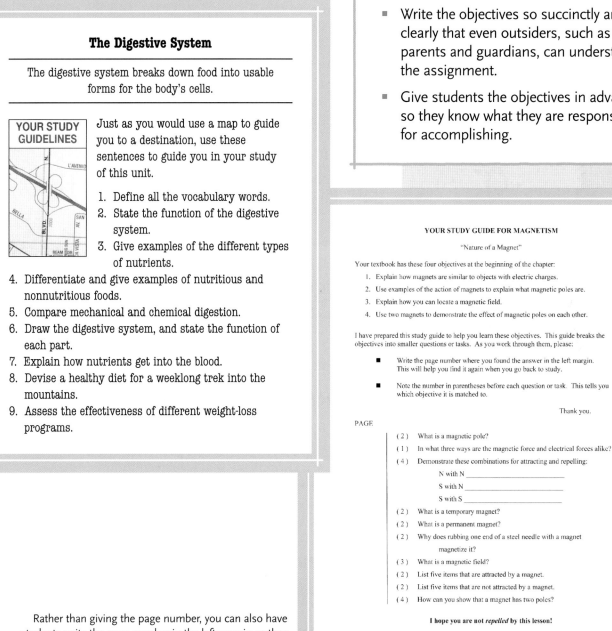

The Digestive System

The digestive system breaks down food into usable forms for the body's cells.

YOUR STUDY GUIDELINES

Just as you would use a map to guide you to a destination, use these sentences to guide you in your study of this unit.

1. Define all the vocabulary words.
2. State the function of the digestive system.
3. Give examples of the different types of nutrients.
4. Differentiate and give examples of nutritious and nonnutritious foods.
5. Compare mechanical and chemical digestion.
6. Draw the digestive system, and state the function of each part.
7. Explain how nutrients get into the blood.
8. Devise a healthy diet for a weeklong trek into the mountains.
9. Assess the effectiveness of different weight-loss programs.

YOUR STUDY GUIDE FOR MAGNETISM

"Nature of a Magnet"

Your textbook has these four objectives at the beginning of the chapter:

1. Explain how magnets are similar to objects with electric charges.
2. Use examples of the action of magnets to explain what magnetic poles are.
3. Explain how you can locate a magnetic field.
4. Use two magnets to demonstrate the effect of magnetic poles on each other.

I have prepared this study guide to help you learn these objectives. This guide breaks the objectives into smaller questions or tasks. As you work through them, please:

- Write the page number where you found the answer in the left margin. This will help you find it again when you go back to study.

- Note the number in parentheses before each question or task. This tells you which objective it is matched to.

Thank you.

PAGE

(2)   What is a magnetic pole?
(1)   In what three ways are the magnetic force and electrical forces alike?
(4)   Demonstrate these combinations for attracting and repelling:

N with N _____
S with N _____
S with S _____

(2)   What is a temporary magnet?
(2)   What is a permanent magnet?
(2)   Why does rubbing one end of a steel needle with a magnet magnetize it?
(3)   What is a magnetic field?
(2)   List five items that are attracted by a magnet.
(2)   List five items that are not attracted by a magnet.
(4)   How can you show that a magnet has two poles?

I hope you are not *repelled* by this lesson!

Rather than giving the page number, you can also have students write the page number in the left margin as they complete the task or question. They can then quickly go back to the source of the answer for review.

> **Effective teaching occurs when teachers teach with intended results in mind.**

Make Teaching and Learning Transparent

This chapter has outlined the value of transparency and clarity in teaching and learning. When you design lessons and assignments with crystal clear objectives aligned to assessment criteria, you have created a solid framework for effective teaching. When students understand the purpose of what they are doing and the progress they will make, they are more likely to strive and take responsibility for their own learning. When you and your students are moving toward the same transparent objectives, teaching and learning will be successful in your classroom.

☆ THE EFFECTIVE TEACHER

☑ Uses state or district standards and curriculum guides to formulate lesson objectives.

☑ Uses The Learning Triangle to ensure lesson objectives, instruction, and assessment are aligned.

☑ Knows how to write lesson objectives that are succinct, clear, and state precisely what students are to accomplish.

☑ Ensures that students, parents, and guardians are always aware of lesson objectives.

...IMPLEMENTS!

Improving Achievement

Giving timely feedback is one of the most powerful instructional procedures for unleashing and increasing student performance.

> **Give students timely and constructive feedback information and you will significantly increase student mastery and achievement.**

In Chapter 18, we reviewed John Hattie's research showing that one of the most powerful methods for improving student achievement is to make students aware of what they are to learn.

Tell students what they will be learning (objectives) before the lesson begins and student achievement can be raised as much as 27 percent.[1]

John Hattie's research also found another equally powerful, if not more powerful, method for improving student achievement. The teaching practice that had the greatest effect in raising student achievement was to give students "dollops of feedback."

Provide students with specific feedback (rubrics) about their progress and achievement can be raised as much as 37 percent.[2]

Effective Feedback

Feedback is not an evaluation received at the end of an activity, typically as a percentage score or letter grade. Such scores or grades do not tell anyone exactly what a student has accomplished.

Effective feedback specifically assesses how well a student's work is aligned to lesson objectives. It gives students the assistance and impetus they need to increase their prospects for improvement. Students are far more motivated and receptive to learning when they receive constructive feedback that helps them make progress toward accomplishing objectives.

☆ THE KEY IDEA

Assessment is not what teachers do TO students.

Assessment is what teachers do FOR students.

---

[1] John Hattie, *Visible Learning: A Synthesis of Over 800 Meta-Analyses Relating to Achievement* (New York: Routledge, 2009).

[2] John Hattie, *Visible Learning.*

**Feedback should reaffirm
why students are doing what they are doing
and how well they are doing.**

Making progress toward a goal or objective is what everyone strives for, whether they are on a diet plan, recovering from an illness, making an object, or tackling a project. In the classroom, students seek guidance and validation from teachers. "How am I doing?" is what every student wants their teacher to tell them. They want confirmation that they are doing what they should be doing to progress and succeed.

Progress is a result of effective feedback.

Effective feedback does not always have to be instantaneous, but it does have to be timely. After students have been given ample opportunity to think for themselves, feedback can provide the encouragement they need to go further.

*Feedback is not advice, praise, or evaluation.
Feedback is information about how we are doing
in our efforts to reach a goal.*[3]

Grant Wiggins

Dynamic Duo: Assessment and Feedback

Assessment must be aligned to learning targets or objectives. Feedback must tell students how they can master learning targets or objectives.

Along with objectives and instruction, assessment is what completes The Learning Triangle. **Every lesson must have assessment, a means to check for student understanding of lesson objectives.** That assessment provides the feedback students need to master lesson objectives.

As stated in Unit C, the most misused term in structuring a classroom is "classroom management," referred to by too many as "discipline." The most misunderstood term in lesson planning is "assessment," referred to by too many as "testing." **Assessment is not testing.**

**Assessment is not used to evaluate students.
Assessment is used to elevate students.**

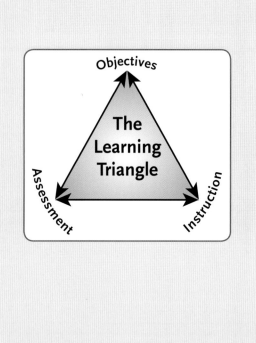

Objectives

The Learning Triangle

Assessment

Instruction

[3] Grant Wiggins, "Seven Keys to Effective Feedback," *Educational Leadership*, vol. 70, no. 1 (September 2012).

Assessment is one aspect of learning; it is not an endpoint. The word should not be in any way intimidating or daunting. The purpose of assessment is not to rank, rate, humiliate, or sort students. **The purpose of assessing and providing feedback based on assessment is to improve instruction and promote student learning.**

Assessments should be happening continually during lessons, day after day, throughout the school year.

Assessments give the teacher insight into how proficient students are in the skill or content being taught.

Assessments tell the teacher what further instruction is needed or how instruction needs to be modified for progress to continue.

Assessments give students the opportunity to see how proficient they are in the skill or content they are learning.

Assessments give them insight into what further efforts they need to make in order to continue making progress.

Assessments should be used to gather information for improving instruction.
They are something we do FOR students, not TO students.

Types of Assessment

There are two kinds of assessments used to inform students of their progress and to further instruction:

- **Formative Assessment:** Rubrics or scoring guides are used to inform students of learning progress and determine the success of a lesson.

- **Summative Assessment:** Tests are used to sum up the lesson and determine a grade. (See Chapter 20 for how to write a test and conduct summative assessment.)

The kind of assessment being discussed in this chapter is formative assessment. It is used to help students make progress, not to grade them. It's simply "checking for understanding." As a teacher, you want to know if students are "getting it." Then you can use the feedback to modify teaching and you can give students the constructive feedback they need to improve learning.

Teachers in Control

Formative assessment is not something you buy; it's something you practice.[4]

Rick Stiggins
Founder,
Assessment Training Institute

There are companies that sell generic, standardized tests in many content areas that claim to be "formative assessment." But they are misusing the term. It is teachers who must be in control of creating and conducting formative assessments because formative assessments are aligned to their own lesson objectives in the context of their own classrooms.

Formative Assessment

- Allows students to see how proficient they are in the skill being taught

- Gives the teacher a reading on student progress so instruction can be tweaked to help students make progress

Formative assessments can be conducted in a variety of ways. Some of the more common are questionnaires, checklists, exit tickets, and rubrics.

Rubrics Chart Progress

A rubric, also called a scoring guide, is one of the most effective techniques used to assess and improve student achievement. Rubrics outline the steps that need to be taken to achieve mastery of lesson objectives. They are a way of measuring progress. **A rubric provides feedback so both student and teacher know what progress is being made on a lesson.**

Letter-Writing : Constructing and Writing a Friendly Letter

Student Name: _____

CATEGORY	4	3	2	1
Salutation and Closing	Salutation and closing have no errors in capitalization and punctuation.	Salutation and closing have 1-2 errors in capitalization and punctuation.	Salutation and closing have 3 or more errors in capitalization and punctuation.	Salutation and/or closing are missing.
Grammar and Spelling	Writer makes no errors in grammar or spelling.	Writer makes 1-2 errors in grammar and/or spelling.	Writer makes 3-4 errors in grammar and/or spelling.	Writer makes more than 4 errors in grammar and/or spelling.
Capitalization and Punctuation	Writer makes no errors in capitalization and punctuation.	Writer makes 1-2 errors in capitalization and punctuation.	Writer makes 3-4 errors in capitalization and punctuation.	Writer makes more than 4 errors in capitalization and punctuation.
Format	Complies with all the elements for a friendly letter.	Complies with almost all the elements for a friendly letter.	Complies with several of the elements for a friendly letter.	Complies with less than 75% of the elements for a friendly letter.
Length	The letter is 10 or more sentences.	The letter is 8-9 sentences.	The letter is 5-7 sentences.	The letter is less than 5 sentences.
Scores:				
Total Score:	/20			

[4] Scott J. Cech, "Test Industry Split Over 'Formative' Assessment," *Education Week*, vol. 28, no. 4 (September 2008): 1, 15.

Ask your students if they keep score during a game. Of course they do, but why do they keep score? They will tell you that they do not want to lose. A scoring guide or rubric lets them know where they are on the leaderboard so that they can make every effort to refrain from losing.

When a doctor conducts tests on you, like a blood test, hearing test, or an x-ray, the purpose is not to grade you and then send you home. Rather, when the test results come back, the doctor assesses them and provides the treatment or medication necessary to help you improve your health. Their goal is to help you progress toward a healthier you.

Similarly, effective teachers use an assessment technique, such as a rubric, to help students chart their progress towards an assignment's objectives. **To make progress, there must be constant assessment for learning.**

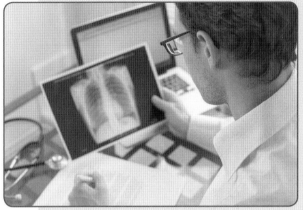

Assessment is key to helping patients make progress on the road to improved health.

Do you remember asking your teachers, "How will you be grading us?" It will come as a surprise to your students— or even as a shock—that a rubric will not be used to *grade* them. It will be used to *help them make progress*. The message you are conveying is that it is your mission to ensure students learn.

> **The effective teacher is constantly assessing and assisting so students achieve at the highest possible level.**

Rubrics Lead to Success

Your preparation for learning is key to student success. Before a lesson begins, tell students that you will be giving them two items:

1. A set of objectives that spell out the purpose of the lesson

2. A rubric that can be used to chart the progress of the lesson

Scoring guides or rubrics are used in competitive sports, such as gymnastics or figure skating. The judges don't arbitrarily grade the athletes. They use a predetermined guide known to athletes and coaches that governs how points are earned when specific skills, moves, or criteria are completed.

Likewise, when students are given rubrics ahead of time, they can clearly see how they can earn a higher ranking based on the rubric's criteria. They can see how to improve their performance, where they need to go, and how best to get there. All the while, the teacher is involved in assessing and assisting each student to achieve at a higher level. With a rubric, the teacher can offer concrete, continuous support. The best motivation students can receive is when they are working collaboratively with their teachers to achieve the same goals.

Students thrive when teachers share expectations for success in the classroom.

Rubrics are road maps to success. Students thrive in classrooms where teaching and learning are transparent and they know what is expected of them. When they have been given lesson objectives and the criteria for assessment, they have been provided with the means to take responsibility for their own learning progress. They themselves can track how well they are doing and the steps required for them to do even better.

> **Give students a scoring guide or a rubric that spells out the criteria for performing a lesson to its exemplary best and students will do their best.**

With safety harnesses attached, the coach pulls or lifts the cable to control the movement of the athlete while teaching and assessing at the same time, over and over again, working toward PROGRESS and ACHIEVEMENT.

Aiming for Self-Assessment

Kathy Monroe is an art teacher in San Jose, California. She uses a "drawing rubric" that students help her create and can easily see to help them aim for higher levels of achievement.

The lesson begins with the objective of drawing a house. Before students begin drawing, she shows them four pictures. She asks which one they think is best and for a word to describe their choice.

One particular year, the class chose the word, "Perfect" and she gave that picture a "4." She then asks which one is next best. The class agreed on the word, "Good," and she gave that picture a "3."

She does the same for the remaining two pictures. The word descriptions change from year to year and the pictures are displayed with their descriptions and point values. The drawing rubric helps students determine what is expected of their assignment.

Students do drawings of houses while using the pictures on display to do self-assessments of them. They ask themselves the following three questions:

1. Where am I going?
2. How will I get there?
3. Where do I go next?

Students have learned to not show Kathy their work and ask how they are doing. If they do, she simply smiles and points to the rubric. **The ultimate aim is to teach students to self-assess their work.**

When students are shown what they are to learn and achieve, the most powerful form of assessment is the feedback they give themselves. Be assured that Kathy gets terrific work from her students!

> *Use frequent assessment to provide corrective actions with varied lengths of instruction to improve concept mastery and up to 95 percent of students can attain mastery.*
>
> Benjamin Bloom

Just Think . . .

Just think what would happen if
teachers taught their students to be responsible learners,
capable of self-assessing their work,
starting in kindergarten,
continuing through high school, and into life.
Achievement would soar.

When Learning Happens

Our major role and responsibility as teachers is to help students make continuous progress in learning. Learning happens when the teacher and students are moving toward the same objectives.

**If YOU know where you are going,
your students will know where THEY are going.**

The effective teacher does these things when creating lessons and assignments:

- Aligns the lesson to district or state standards
- Presents the lesson with objectives that focus the goal of the lesson
- Uses clear instructions and appropriate activities to teach lesson objectives
- Assesses learning using a rubric or scoring guide that is aligned to lesson objectives
- Uses assessments to gather information for teaching what needs to be re-taught

As you develop goals for your lessons, always ask WHAT and HOW. But, don't stop there. The most important part of the entire process is *sharing* the WHAT and HOW with your students. Education is not trickery and clever tactics to stump students. Our goal is to open the wonderment of the world and help students discover the joy and fulfillment associated with learning.

The purpose of designing a lesson is not simply to ensure that students are taught, but to ensure that they learn. With a scoring guide or rubric, both teachers and students have a tool that they can use to assess learning.

Think of The Learning Triangle. Look at the lessons you prepare and ask these three questions:

1. Do your students know **WHAT they are to learn** as a result of experiencing the lesson? (Objectives)

2. Do you know **HOW you are going to help** your students accomplish the goal of the lesson? (Instruction)

3. Do your students know **HOW they—and you—are going to assess their learning** of the lesson? (Assessment)

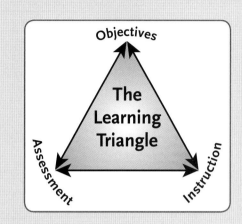

If you cannot clearly answer these questions, you are not ready to teach your lesson. You will only frustrate the students and yourself as you try to figure out what went wrong.

How to Construct a Rubric

Rubrics vary in size and purpose. They can be constructed to assess subject matter, behavior, organization, and virtually anything else that can be measured. Give them titles that help students focus on the purpose of the rubric.

> **A rubric serves as a benchmark.**
> **Students know how they will be measured**
> **and how to measure themselves.**

No matter the type of rubric, most have three parts:

- **Criteria:** The category or trait that will be assessed

- **Point Values:** The most common numerical range of performance level of 1 to 4, with No Score (NS) instead of zero

- **Performance Expected:** Definitions and examples of performance levels with point values so students can see what they need to do to revise their own work and make progress

Rubrics are typically formatted in columns and rows:

- Rows represent criteria, the categories or traits that will be assessed as part of a lesson.
- Columns are headed with a point value, such as 4, 3, 2, 1 and NS (No Score), or descriptive words if they are more meaningful to students.

Each square on the grid represents the intersection of a criteria and a point value, just as two points meet on a graph.

CRITERIA   **POINT VALUE**   **PERFORMANCE EXPECTED**

Title of the Rubric				
	Beginning 1	Developing 2	Proficient 3	Exemplary 4
Criteria #1	Description reflects beginning level of performance	Description reflects movement toward mastery level of performance	Description reflects achievement of mastery level of performance	Description reflects highest level of performance
Criteria #2	Description reflects beginning level of performance	Description reflects movement toward mastery level of performance	Description reflects achievement of mastery level of performance	Description reflects highest level of performance

CRITERIA   **POINT VALUE**   **PERFORMANCE EXPECTED**

Draw, Label, and Describe the Stages of the Water Cycle				
CATEGORY	1	2	3	MY POINTS
Diagram Drawing	Creates diagram with more than one error in the order of the different stages	Creates diagram with one error in the order of the different stages	Creates diagram showing correct order of the different stages	
Diagram Labels	Labels none of the stages of the water cycle correctly	Labels two stages of the water cycle correctly	Labels all three stages of the water cycle correctly	
Diagram Description	Writing does not include any stages and no descriptions are given	Writing includes at least two stages with them being described correctly	Writing identifies all three stages and are described correctly	

Guideline for Creating Levels of Proficiency

- **First, identify the proficient level.** Create the criteria for performing the task or understanding the content at the proficient level first. Put this criterion in the third column with a point value of 3 in a four-column rubric.

- **Then, build the rest of the levels.** Create the criteria for the rest of the columns where 1 would show minimal or beginning proficiency; 2 would show some understanding or performance; and 4 would show an advanced level of performance or understanding.

Geometric Shape Rubric

Topic / Score	1	2	3	4
Geometric Shapes	**Makes No Attempt** to name basic 2-D shapes including circle, square, rectangle and triangle. **Is Unable** to draw an example.	**Inconsistently Names** basic 2-D shapes including circle, square, rectangle and triangle. **Inconsistently** unable to draw an example.	**Names Basic** geometric shapes including circle, square, rectangle and triangle. **Able** to draw an example of each basic shape.	**Instant recall** of basic geometric shapes including circle, square, rectangle and triangle. **Quickly** draws examples of basic shapes.

Just Think . . .

Just think what would happen to learning if students knew what they should learn (objectives) and knew how they would be assessed (rubrics). They would know that they could not fail.

And just think what would happen if that became the culture of the school.

GoBe

Rubric Resources

See examples of other rubrics teachers have created. Find them in the **Go**ing **Be**yond folder for Chapter 19 or scan the QR Code.

Scoring Guides and Rubrics for Everyone

Scoring guides or rubrics are applicable to all grade levels and across all content areas. Here are some examples that can be adapted for the lesson objectives in your classroom and subject areas.

Elementary Reading Task Scoring Guide

Brenna Garrison-Bruden is a principal in Wisconsin. When she was in her elementary classroom, she showed students four different cupcakes and asked which they would like: one with frosting and sprinkles; one with just frosting; an unfrosted one; or a burnt one. Of course, students would all say they wanted the one with frosting and sprinkles. But to achieve the proficiency level of this cupcake, they had to show progress in their reading task.

	 1 = Burnt	 2 = Unfrosted	 3 = Frosted	 4 = Sprinkles
Stays on Task	Wastes a lot of time.	Reads some of the time.	Reads most of the time.	Reads the entire time.
Respects Others	Reads loudly or moves about often, distracting classmates.	Makes some comments, noises, and movements distracting classmates.	Reads quietly. May move around in seat, but doesn't distract classmates.	Reads quietly. Stays focused without distracting classmates.

High School Science Scoring Guide

Karen Rogers, a high school science teacher in Kansas, has designed her scoring guides to be very practical and useful for her students. She makes sure that information is in short, simple doses, making it easy for students to understand and follow.

Karen has some basic scoring guide templates:

- Laboratory Report
- Graphing
- Group Discussion
- Presentations to the Class
- Presentations to the Class (listening)

Karen says, "In my science classes, I use scoring guides for writing lab reports and graphing. Writing a lab report can be overwhelming for students. On my lab report scoring guide, I list the criteria for each component (hypothesis, data, analysis, etc.). That way, students can proceed with their experiments and their reports in a simple, step-by-step fashion."

Her students find value in using the scoring guides.

> Bryan Shephard says he likes them because, "They tell you what you need to know to do the assignment. You don't have to remember all the directions the teacher said. You know how to get 100 percent."

> Nick Jahner agrees because, "With the scoring guides, you can control your grade and know what you are going to get in advance."

> Miles Miller likes them because, "They keep the grading standard (uniform) and they give you the basic idea of what needs to be done."

The scoring guides that Karen Rogers uses can be easily applied to all other subjects where students need to write reports, collect and display data, be involved in group discussions, make presentations to the class, and listen when others are making presentations.

Scoring Guide for State Standards

New Jersey has core curriculum standards for reading, speaking, writing, and media. This is one of the standards:

> All students will understand and apply the knowledge of sounds, letters, and words in written English to become independent and fluent readers, and will read a variety of materials and texts with fluency and comprehension.

To teach this standard, Norm Dannen, a high school teacher in New Jersey, created a lesson using the novel *The Great Gatsby* by F. Scott Fitzgerald.

Karen Rogers' Scoring Guides

Karen Rogers' five scoring guides are available for download. Find them in the **Go**ing **Be**yond folder for Chapter 19 or scan the QR Code.

The Great Gatsby Unit Plan Rubric   English 11 Advanced
Teacher: Mr. Dannen

Student:

CATEGORY	4	3	2	1	NS/0	Total
Content Knowledge 3.1 Reading	The student can easily relate Fitzgerald's idea of "The American Dream" to Jay Gatsby's actions and give three specific written or verbal examples.	The student can relate Fitzgerald's idea of "The American Dream" to Jay Gatsby's actions and give two specific written or verbal examples.	The student can relate Fitzgerald's idea of "The American Dream" to Jay Gatsby's actions, but has trouble giving written or verbal examples.	The student has trouble relating Fitzgerald's idea of "The American Dream" to Jay Gatsby's actions and cannot give any examples.	The student is unable to relate Fitzgerald's idea of "The American Dream" to Jay Gatsby's actions, or give any examples of same.	
Compare and Contrast	The student can easily recognize the similarities and differences between *The Great Gatsby* and Fitzgerald's short story, "Winter Dreams, and can give three specific	The student can recognize the similarities and differences between *The Great Gatsby* and Fitzgerald's short story, "Winter Dreams, and can give two specific	The student can recognize the similarities and differences between *The Great Gatsby* and Fitzgerald's short story, "Winter Dreams, but has trouble giving	The student has trouble recognizing similarities and differences between *The Great Gatsby* and Fitzgerald's short story, "Winter Dreams," and not give	The student is unable to recognize the similarities and differences between The Great Gatsby and Fitzgerald's short story, "Winter Dreams," or give	

Fair and Easy System

Students like the no-mystery approach to learning. One of Norm Dannen's students, Collette Cornatzer, says, "I like scoring guides because they make the student aware of exactly how to do the assignment or write the assigned article, and they plot a very fair and easy-to-understand grading system. A scoring guide creates a backbone for your paper."

Even though scoring guides or rubrics are not used for grading, students view them as guides to their ultimate grade for a lesson.

If a student scores 1 or NS in any of the categories, it doesn't mean the student is unintelligent, lazy, or failing. It may simply mean that it's difficult for a young person who is fifteen years old and hasn't even figured out society today to understand or relate to a period over ninety years ago. This is when the teacher must prescribe a course of action that helps the student achieve proficiency. For example, the teacher and student may go to the Library of Congress website (www.loc.gov) where the student can discover what life was like in the United States during the 1920s. The teacher directs and encourages research on fashion, music, automobiles, sports, and any other interest the student may have, from a variety of sources.

Scoring Guide for Discussion Groups

Diana Greenhouse, a teacher in Texas, uses a scoring guide for her lesson on the novel, *Baseball Fever* by Johanna Hurwitz. The book is about a boy who wants to play baseball even though his father wants him to play chess. The conflict makes for great class discussions.

Diana uses the novel to engage the class in what she calls "Inner-Outer Discussion." This technique was adapted to her fifth-grade class when her daughter came home from high school and reported on the same technique being used by her teacher.

After the class reads the novel, she asks students to think of five discussion questions.

In preparation for the discussion, she sets up a double circle of chairs. The inner circle of chairs faces in, and the

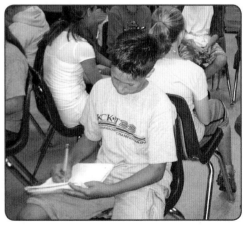

outer circle of chairs faces out. The chairs are back to back, making an inner and an outer circle of seats.

Students in the inner circle are the first discussion group. Students forming the outer circle ask questions they've prepared for discussion, and they take notes. The questions and notes are all turned in to Diana.

The students are handed a scoring guide before the activity begins. It is reviewed and discussed so they are aware of what is expected of them as they prepare for the book discussion.

Diana explains that while the inner circle of students (facing in) is having their discussion, the outer circle (facing out) simply listens. They are not allowed to have verbal input; their role is to be active listeners. When prompted to do so by the facilitator, they ask the discussion questions and take notes. This helps to develop listening skills.

The students in the outer circle are always eager to have their turn at discussion because they have been listening and have a tremendous amount of input bottled up, or written in their notes. Most are very busy writing down important points or scrawling their thoughts.

Everyone has a novel, a notebook with their questions, paper for taking notes, and their scoring guide. Diana randomly selects a discussion group facilitator, and the discussion and learning begin. After twenty minutes, the groups switch roles and a new discussion group begins.

Diana says, "I look forward to these 'Inner-Outer Discussions,' because I enjoy watching my students take charge of the lesson. They are developing good thinking, listening, and speaking habits. My students enjoy the discussions and appreciate the use of the scoring guide because they know exactly what I'm looking for.

"There is total engagement," she continues. "They say they feel a sense of power, and that thrills me because empowering students is one of my daily goals! This is a wonderful activity to observe and my students amaze me every time!"

Literature Circle - Listening and Sharing: Baseball Fever

Teacher Name: **Mrs. Greenhouse**
Student Name: _____

CATEGORY	4	3	2	1
Participates Willingly	Student routinely volunteers answers to questions and willingly tries to answer questions s/he is asked.	Student volunteers once or twice and willingly tries to all questions s/he is asked.	Student does not volunteer answers, but willing tries to answer questions s/he is asked.	Student does not willingly participate.
Comprehension	Student seems to understand entire story and accurately answers 3 questions related to the story.	Student seems to understand most of the story and accurately answers 2 questions related to the story.	Student understands some parts of the story and accurately answers 1 question related to the story.	Student has trouble understanding or remembering most parts of the story.
Thinks about Characters	Student describes how a character might have felt at some point in the story, and points out some pictures or words to support his/her interpretation without being asked.	Student describes how a character might have felt at some point in the story, and points out some pictures or words to support his/her interpretation when asked.	Student describes how a character might have felt at some point in the story, but does NOT provide good support for the interpretation, even when asked.	Student cannot describe how a character might have felt at a certain point in the story.
Respects Others	Student listens quietly, does not interrupt, and	Student listens quietly and does not interrupt	Student interrupts once or twice, but	Student interrupts often by whispering

Baseball Fever Scoring Guide

The complete *Baseball Fever* scoring guide, can be found in the **Go**ing **Be**yond folder for Chapter 19 or scan the QR Code.

Writing Rubric

Our job as teachers is to help students succeed. Besides giving students a rubric to see their progress in achieving a goal, give them guidance on what they need to do to reach mastery of the subject.

Writing Rubric

	4	3	2	1
Focus and Details	One clear, well-focused topic. Main ideas are clear and are well supported by detailed and accurate information.	There is one clear, well-focused topic. Main ideas are clear but are not well supported by detailed information.	There is one topic. Main ideas are somewhat clear.	The topic and main ideas are not clear.
Organization	The introduction captures interest, states the main topic, and provides an overview of the paper. Information is relevant and presented in a logical order. The conclusion is strong.	The introduction states the main topic and provides an overview of the paper. A conclusion is included.	The introduction states the main topic. A conclusion is included.	There is no clear introduction, structure, or conclusion.

HOW TO WRITE TO SCORE A "3" OR "4"

- Make it personal—make the reader cry . . . laugh . . . entertain them!
- Hook the reader in the first paragraph.
- Use figurative language—similes, metaphors, personification, analogies.
- Write descriptively—create images to appeal to the reader's senses.
- Include dialogue.
- Stay on the subject.
- Provide support for your statements.
- Write passionately.
- Write a conclusion that refocuses to the subject.
- Write a rough draft.
- Revise and edit, edit to FINAL DRAFT QUALITY.

GoBe

Writing Rubric

Use the writing rubric and adapt the skill levels to fit your classroom. Find it in the **Go**ing **Be**yond folder for Chapter 19 or scan the QR Code.

Preparation Yields Progress

All parents want to see their children make progress in school. Every student wants to make progress and do well. Every teacher loves to see students make progress.

The solution is simple.
Show students how to make progress.

Give students the rubric for the lesson. With objectives posted and rubrics created before the lesson begins, the teacher's energy is focused on delivering the content and helping all students achieve the objectives of the lesson.

From a student's perspective, it is very important to feel that "the teacher is prepared to teach." A prepared teacher creates lessons that are consistent, continuous, and coherent. Effective teachers are able to give students the constructive feedback and confidence they need to succeed.

7th Grade Position Response Summary Writing

Objective:
Write arguments to support claims with clear reasons and relevant evidence.
    a. Introduce claim(s), acknowledge alternate or opposing claims, and organize the reasons and evidence logically.
    b. Support claim(s) with logical reasoning and relevant evidence, using accurate, credible sources, and demonstrating an understanding of the topic or text.
    c. Use words, phrases, and clauses to create cohesion and clarify the relationships among claim(s), reasons, and evidence.
    d. Provide a concluding statement or section that follows from and supports the argument presented.

	4 Points	3 Points	2 Points	1 Point
Introduction	Introduces the claim in a clear, accurate and organized manner.	Introduces the claim in an accurate and clear manner.	Introduces the claim.	The claim is not clearly stated.
Evidence	Clearly states in logical order three pieces of relevant, accurate and credible evidence to support the author's claim. Combines ideas that work together with smooth transitions.	Clearly states three pieces of relevant, accurate and credible evidence to support the author's claim.	Clearly states two pieces of relevant, accurate and credible evidence to support the author's claim.	States at least one piece of relevant evidence to support the author's claim.
Conclusion	Writes a clear and specific concluding statement that restates the author's claim.	Writes an adequate concluding statement that restates the author's claim.	Writes a weak concluding statement using a literal level of that does not restate the author's original claim.	Does not include a concluding statement.
Mechanics and Grammar	Contains few, if any spelling or grammatical errors.	Contains several errors in punctuation, spelling or grammar that do not interfere with meaning.	Contains many errors in punctuation, spelling and/or grammar that interferes with meaning.	Contains many errors in punctuation, spelling and/or grammar that make the piece illegible.

Name: _____ Period: _____ Score_____

Date: _____

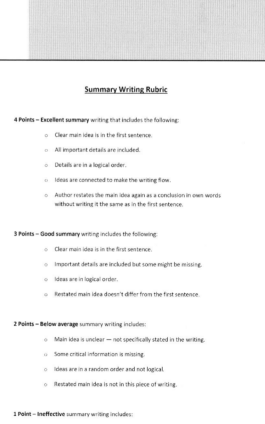

Summary Writing Rubric

4 Points – Excellent summary writing that includes the following:

    ○ Clear main idea is in the first sentence.

    ○ All important details are included.

    ○ Details are in a logical order.

    ○ Ideas are connected to make the writing flow.

    ○ Author restates the main idea again as a conclusion in own words without writing it the same as in the first sentence.

3 Points – Good summary writing includes the following:

    ○ Clear main idea is in the first sentence.

    ○ Important details are included but some might be missing.

    ○ Ideas are in logical order.

    ○ Restated main idea doesn't differ from the first sentence.

2 Points – Below average summary writing includes:

    ○ Main idea is unclear — not specifically stated in the writing.

    ○ Some critical information is missing.

    ○ Ideas are in a random order and not logical.

    ○ Restated main idea is not in this piece of writing.

1 Point – Ineffective summary writing includes:

    ○ The main idea is not present in the 1st sentence of the writing.

    ○ Very few details are included.

    ○ Ideas are not in logical order.

    ○ A concluding sentence with the restated main idea is missing.

⭐ THE EFFECTIVE TEACHER

☑ Constructs rubrics or scoring guides aligned to lesson objectives.

☑ Uses rubrics for formative assessments and feedback, not for evaluation.

☑ Teaches students how to use rubrics for self-assessment.

☑ Uses information from rubrics to give students feedback so that they make continual progress toward lesson mastery.

...IMPLEMENTS!

Students Want to Earn Grades

At the beginning of an assignment, lesson, or unit, tell students that the test has already been written because every test question is correlated to lesson objectives. When lesson objectives were written, the test was written.

> Tests are given to find out
> if students have achieved lesson objectives.

Objectives were the subject of Chapter 18. Chapter 19 was on **Assessment**, the process of using feedback to help students make progress. This chapter is on **Evaluation**, the process of using a **test** to determine a **grade** that a student can earn. Every lesson must have a test to evaluate for student learning. **Therefore, Chapters 18, 19, and 20 are all related and relevant to each other.**

A teacher wrote, "My class always has the highest test scores in the school because I have learned to correlate my test questions to the lesson objectives." This seems so common sense, but it is not put into practice in many classrooms. Students want to know what to expect when it comes to how to earn a grade. John Hattie's research on what motivates students has found the student's expectation of receiving a good grade is the strongest motivation for students to achieve.[1]

> **Lesson objectives tell students what they will learn, what will be taught, and how they will be tested.**

Begin With the End in Mind

You've planned many things backward, such as a wedding, a party, or a vacation. You begin by setting the date for the event, then plan backward with a schedule listing what is to be done leading up to the event.

THE KEY IDEA

Write lesson objectives and tests at the same time to ensure that every test question is aligned to an objective.

> **Teaching and testing are inseparable.**
>
> **Teachers shouldn't test what they didn't teach, and teachers shouldn't teach what they won't test.**

[1] John Hattie, *Visible Learning: A Synthesis of Over 800 Meta-Analyses Relating to Achievement* (New York: Routledge, 2009).

Successful events don't happen by chance. Success is the result of the planning that takes place before the event begins.

Good lesson design works much the same way. The end product for the student is achievement of lesson objectives. To reach that point, the teacher must plan two things in this order:

1. What **method to use to assess** for the achievement of the objective

2. What instructional **strategies to use to teach** the objective

While this approach seems so sensible, there are many teachers who construct lessons by identifying a topic (like the weather) and thinking of fun activities to do about weather (like making cotton cloud pictures). After a week of weather-related activities, it's test time. The teacher recalls all of the activities and creates a test based on the topics that were covered. This piecemeal approach leaves the teacher wondering exactly what he or she was supposed to teach and what students were supposed to learn. In this scenario, achievement of lesson objectives has not been the focal point. It has been about filling in class time doing projects or fun activities.

Backward Design

Grant Wiggins and Jay McTighe have formalized the lesson design process with a framework called Understanding by Design.[2] Backward Design is the part of the process where teachers build effective lessons in three steps. You start by identifying desired results, then how students will be evaluated, and finally what strategies you will use for instruction.

[2]Grant Wiggins and Jay McTighe, *Understanding by Design* (Alexandria, VA: Association for Supervision and Curriculum Development, 2005).

Step 1. Identify Desired Results. What do you want your students to know and be able to do? These are your lesson objectives.

Step 2. Determine Acceptable Evidence. This would be the "test." Evaluate for student performance of lesson objectives with oral questions, observations, dialogue, or with the more traditional quizzes and tests. There should also be a rubric as it will provide acceptable evidence of the progress being made toward the desired outcomes.

Step 3. Plan Learning Experiences and Instruction. What activities, materials, and resources will be used to help students learn and reach the desired objectives?

Objectives Determine Tests

The purpose of a test is to determine if a student has mastered lesson objectives. Therefore, the most effective and efficient time to write the test is at the same time or soon after the objectives have been written. The following three aspects of a lesson must be aligned and correlated with each other before the lesson is presented to students:

1. **Objectives** (learning targets)
2. **Assessment** (rubric)
3. **Evaluation** (test)

The rubric is used to help students make progress in learning the objectives, and the test is used to determine a score or grade for proficiency in lesson objectives.

> **Lesson objectives govern what questions and how many questions are to be written for a test.**

Tests should NOT be used merely to verify coverage of materials. **Tests are used to determine if a student has or has not accomplished and comprehended the stated objectives of the lesson.** Every test question must correspond to a lesson objective. That makes it easy to write a test—write a set of questions for each lesson objective.

However, not all tests need be written tests. A test can be a musical number to be performed, an oral response, or the creation of a project or product. Whatever form it takes, a test must be aligned to lesson objectives.

Two Kinds of Tests: Criterion-Referenced and Norm-Referenced

It is important to define two types of tests and to clarify the significant differences between them. The kind of test most teachers unknowingly write is a norm-referenced test. Tests that teachers should be writing are criterion-referenced test, tests that are aligned to learning objectives.

- **A criterion-referenced test** requires that each question be written to a pre-stated criterion or objective. Since students know what criteria they are responsible for, a percentage grade system should be used. The student knows, for instance, that the standard for an A is set at some percentage.

The only person a student competes against in a criterion-referenced test is himself or herself.

- **A norm-referenced test** is used to determine placement on a normal distribution or bell-shaped curve. Students are "graded on the curve" after a norm-referenced test. Norm-referenced tests are used to determine competitive ranking, such as for positions on a team, entrance into a school, or placement on an organizational chart.

Norm-referenced tests can be useful in certain circumstances, but when you are teaching a lesson you are not teaching for rank or for making comparisons among students. You are teaching for accomplishment, and you want everyone to succeed.

Norm-referenced tests should never be used when evaluating comprehension of subject matter.

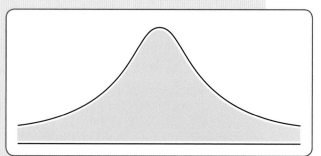

Norm-referenced tests are "graded on the curve." They are not used to evaluate comprehension of subject matter but to determine competitive ranking.

> To teach for accomplishment,
> use objectives and a criterion-referenced test.

Two Kinds of Criterion-Referenced Tests

There are two kinds of criterion-referenced tests: formative tests and summative tests. **Tell students which tests they are taking for practice and which tests they are taking for evaluation.**

- **Formative tests** are like drills and practice tests. They are given during the formative, developmental, or teachable period of time when the student is in the process of mastering a lesson objective. There may not be any need to grade these tests. They simply let you and the students know how well you are teaching and if they are learning the objectives. They are used to determine what remediation is needed to ensure that a student masters the content, skill, or objectives before a final test.

- **Summative tests** are given at the end of a lesson or unit when you want to sum up what the student has learned, and then determine a grade.

It is important to keep teaching transparent. Explain the difference between formative and summative tests. You may want to use some of these examples from daily life.

Two Test Essentials

1. Use the results of each test item to assess for student learning and, if necessary, remediate and correct to achieve student mastery.

2. Grade students on a percentage system. This way they are competing only against themselves to reach a level of achievement or success.

Formative and Summative Tests Around Us

Formative Tests	Summative Tests
Spring training	Opening day of the season
Dress rehearsal	Opening night
Training wheels on bike	Riding alone on two wheels
The bunny hill	The giant slalom
Driver's Ed	Getting a driver's license
PSAT	SAT
Student teaching	The first day of school

Help Your Students Succeed

Give students objectives at the beginning of the lesson so they know what they are responsible for accomplishing.

Students want to know lesson objectives because then they know what they are to learn. Objectives tell them, in bite-size chunks, the purpose of a lesson. Objectives also tell students the basis upon which they will be evaluated, because the test is aligned to those objectives.

If a test cannot be written to assess for learning, then the objectives have not been written correctly to measure for mastery of the content.

You will help your students succeed with this process:

- Write each test question to correlate with a lesson objective.

- Give students the objectives so that they know what they are responsible for learning.

- Explain to students how the test is written; that is, that test questions are correlated to the objectives.

- Explain to students how to study for the tests. They should ensure they understand and have achieved lesson objectives, knowing that the questions will test for mastery of each objective.

- Give or post examples of the tests.

- Consider giving practice, formative tests before you give the actual, summative test. Use the practice test to monitor what help you need to give a student to correct or remediate for learning.

> **Tests do not determine objectives; objectives determine tests.**
>
> **You teach to objectives, not test preparation.**

The effective teacher posts examples of tests. These give students the information they need to study efficiently and the confidence they need to match expectations.

Sample Spelling Pretest

Effective Teachers Give Every Student the Opportunity to Succeed

Benjamin Bloom conducted extensive research in which he noted the norm-referenced test scores of thousands of third graders and then followed them for several years. What Bloom found was that students' third-grade scores could be used to predict, with 80 percent accuracy or better, their scores in the eleventh grade. Achievement ranking therefore, is highly consistent.[3]

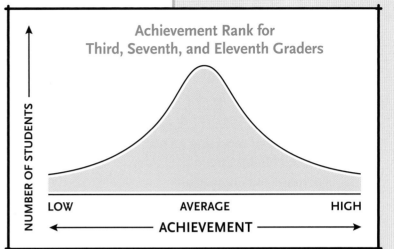

Students who perform well on norm-referenced tests in the third grade are likely to perform well on similar tests in the ninth grade. Conversely, students who perform at or only slightly above average on norm-referenced tests will likely maintain that level of performance all the way through elementary, middle, and high school. Norm-referenced tests, therefore, do not measure ability—what an individual student has achieved or can do. **They only tell you how a student did in comparison with other students.**

When a teacher says, "I need a range of points so that I can grade the class on a curve," this is not a valid reason for giving a test. According to Bloom, the teacher will already be able to predict where most of students fall on such a curve, which ultimately renders that curve pointless. This is true of students as well. When they come into a class, most of them become rapidly aware who will be in the accelerated or the remedial reading group; who will do well and who will do poorly in math; in other words, who will be treated as winners and who will be treated as failures.

This is not what education is about. It's time to change our attitudes and students' presumptions about testing and grading. Teachers should never pigeonhole students at an early age and reinforce, with a succession of bell-shaped curves, the belief that certain students will always be smart, average, or dumb.

**The purpose of teaching is
to help all students succeed,
not to label some students as failures.**

Ranking for students in third, seventh, and eleventh grades is highly consistent if norm-referenced tests are used. The shaded area in the curve is the same for all three grades. This kind of testing can lead to labeling students as below average, average, and above average without regard to the possibilities for progress and achievement that can be attained with quality instruction and sufficient time to master learning objectives.

[3] Benjamin S. Bloom, "New Views of the Learner: Implications for Instruction and Curriculum," *Educational Leadership*, April 1978 (paper presented as a General Session address at the ASCD 1978 Annual Conference, San Francisco).

What We Know About Grades

This is what research has revealed about grades:

- **Grading and reporting aren't essential to instruction.** Grades are not related to teaching or learning well. What is essential is how the teacher continually monitors and assesses for the learning progress of the student.

- **Grades have some value as rewards but no value as punishments.** Teachers should never use grades to shame students. This offers no educational value, and it adversely affects student-teacher relationships.

- **Grading and reporting should always be done in reference to learning objectives, never on a curve.** Grading on a curve pits students against one another and converts learning into a game of winners and losers.[4]

- **Grades are comprehensible if clear standards and objectives are used.** Inconsistency in how tests are formed and grading inconsistency among teachers detract from the clarity of a grade.[5]

---

[4] Adapted from Thomas R. Guskey and Jane M. Bailey, *Developing Grading and Reporting Systems for Student Learning* (Thousand Oaks, CA: Corwin Press, 2001).

[5] Grant Wiggins, "Toward Better Report Cards," *Educational Leadership*, vol. 52, no. 2 (October 1994).

Don't Test for These Reasons

Do not write or administer tests for these reasons:

- Passage of Time
- Material Covered
- Curve Grading
- Period to Kill

Passage of Time. Learning has nothing to do with time intervals, such as the length of a grading period, the due date for deficiency notices, or because "two weeks have passed and it's time for a test." If grades are needed for report cards, structure the assignments, not the tests, to fall within the grading period.

Material Covered. Tests should not be written at a particular juncture simply because "enough material has been covered." Lesson objectives, not the volume of material, determine when to test students.

Curve Grading. It is a mistake to state arbitrarily, "I want each test to be worth 50 points so that I will have a sufficient point spread to grade the class on a curve." There is no research that justifies grading students on a curve, so this method should never be used. Instead, students should EARN a grade based on the percentage of questions, aligned to lesson objectives, which are answered correctly.

Period to Kill. The number of questions on a test should not be determined by the length of the class period. The requirements of each task, or the number of questions necessary to evaluate what each student knows and can do, should determine the length of a test. In short, the length of the test should be long enough to find out whether each individual has accomplished the lesson objectives.

These are examples of ineffective directions for tests:

- The test will cover everything since the last test.
- The test will cover everything in Chapter 7.
- There will be some multiple-choice questions, some true–false, and maybe some fill-ins.
- The test will be worth about 50 points.

Explain the Process

Many students are nervous and full of anxiety when their first assignment is due or when the first test is to be taken. Often, this is because teachers fail to post examples of an ideal assignment or how a typical test looks.

Students feel uncertain and insecure because there are no models or examples. They find out what should have been done or what should have been studied after the fact. Consequently, many students are so disillusioned by an initial failure that they give up trying.

The effective teacher uses these techniques for assignments and tests:

- **Posts** many good examples of past assignments and tests so students can see what they are to do and what the tests look like

- **Explains** how a finished assignment should appear and how test questions are correlated to the objectives of the assignment

Not only do students benefit from seeing and learning from excellent models, they also recognize that you have positive expectations and are guiding them to achieve success.

How to Write a Test for Performance

Step 1. Every test is based on the lesson objectives for each assignment. Have these available as you write the test.

Step 2. Look at the first objective. Write a set of questions for the objective. Avoid writing only one question, because if the student guesses at the answer, you will not know if the student has mastered the objective.

Step 3. Use whatever type of testing method that is appropriate for the subject matter. Questions do not have to be on a written test. They can be oral or physical tasks, whereby the teacher asks the student to perform a skill or produce a finished product.

Step 4. Repeat steps 1–3 for each of the remaining objectives. When you have written a set of questions for each objective, you have finished writing the test.

Matching Objectives to Performance

Example #1

Objective:

List the steps of the scientific method.

Test Questions:

What are the steps of the scientific method?

a. observe, experiment, hypothesize
b. experiment, conclude, study
c. hypothesize, think, observe
d. collect data, state principles, draw conclusions

What is the first step in the scientific method?

a. state the problem
b. collect data
c. conduct the experiment
d. make observations

Example #2

Objective:

Write the plural form of these words ending in y.

Test Activity:

pony	party
battery	decoy
key	sky
	play

Test Example

Look at the example of a test that might have been written for a chapter or lesson on Observation. It has four key parts:

1. Concept. This is the key idea or major point of the lesson.

2. Objectives. These are the tasks the student is responsible for accomplishing.

3. Questions. Each question corresponds to one of the objectives. Note the parentheses to the left of each question. The first number shows which objective the question corresponds to.

4. Remediation. Look at the parentheses again. The second number indicates the part of the textbook where the answer to the question may be found.

(See the section "The Test as a Corrective Tool," page 270, which explains how to use information to help the student study for mastery of the objective.)

Assignment: Observation

Lesson Concept:

Observation, or paying attention, is an important step in the scientific method.

Lesson Objectives:

1. Define all vocabulary words.

2. Explain the importance of studying biology.

3. List the steps of the scientific method.

4. State when and in what order the steps of the scientific method are applied.

5. Explain why the scientific method is useful in daily life.

6. Give reasons why observing and paying attention is important in life.

Lesson Test:

1. Biology is the study of

(1-1A)   a. wild animals.
       b. live plants.
       c. living things.
       d. human beings.

2. Science is

(1-1B)   a. the study of biology.
       b. a method of thinking.
       c. making observations.
       d. paying attention.

3. Studying biology may be important to you because

(2-1B)   a. you may become a doctor.
       b. you will learn about plants.
       c. you will find out about animals.
       d. you will find out about your body.

---

4. Biology is important to you because

(2-1A)   a. you can learn about chemistry.
       b. plants and animals are important to study.
       c. you can explain birth defects.
       d. life is the most precious resource on earth.

5. The first step in the scientific method is to

(3-1B)   a. state the problem.
       b. collect data.
       c. conduct the experiment.
       d. make observations.

6. The steps of the scientific method are:

(3-1B)   a. collect data, state principles, draw conclusions.
       b. observe, experiment, hypothesize.
       c. experiment, conclude, study.
       d. hypothesize, think, observe.

7. The steps of the scientific method can be

(4-1A)   a. used only in the proper order.
       b. used at any time and in any order.
       c. used only with a scientific problem.
       d. used after much data has been recorded.

8. The scientific method can be used

(4-1B)   a. to make observations.
       b. to experiment and collect data.
       c. to state a conclusion.
       d. to accomplish all of the above.

9. The scientific method is used in daily life to

(5-1B)   a. solve problems.
       b. make observations.
       c. make discoveries.
       d. do all of the above.

---

10. Observations are used in daily life to

(5-1C)   a. define science.
       b. help you stay alive.
       c. explain the word biology.
       d. list the rules of the scientific method.

11. In the business world, your boss will want you to

(6-1C)   a. conduct experiments.
       b. talk about science.
       c. write about science.
       d. pay attention.

12. When you don't feel well, your body is telling you

(6-1C)   a. to see a doctor.
       b. to work harder.
       c. to pay attention.
       d. to be careful.

13. Paying attention is a valuable life skill. It can help you

(1-Key Idea)   a. solve problems and make decisions.
       b. memorize the scientific method.
       c. appreciate life and friends.
       d. find the perfect job.

14. Paying attention is an important step in

(1-Key Idea)   a. the scientific method.
       b. the study of biology.
       c. the study of science.
       d. causing problems.

This is an example only. Ignore the subject matter and focus on how the objectives and test questions correlate. Apply the example to your own subject matter.

Students who are lost or left behind need proper remediation to get them back on track. The effective teacher tests and corrects as often as necessary so that all students are given the opportunity to succeed.

The Test as a Corrective Tool

Assume that you have returned from a visit to the doctor. Your friend or spouse asks you, "What happened at the doctor's?" and you respond, "I'm going to have a test." This does not mean that the doctor is going to grade you on a curve. It means that the doctor is waiting for test results, and when the results are studied, the doctor then determines what needs to be done to help overcome your illness.

A criterion-referenced test can be used, in the same way, as a diagnostic instrument. It tells you if a student needs corrective help. If you do not correct and remediate, learning gets worse as the year progresses. It's no different from everything else in life. If you do not seek to correct an illness, or a bad habit such as smoking, your body or your life just gets worse.

Tests are to be given for the students' sake, not the teacher's. The purpose of a test is not to accumulate the range of points needed to grade students on a curve. **The purpose of a test is to help the teacher evaluate what the student has or has not learned.**

The effective teacher tests and corrects,
tests and corrects,
because the effective teacher wants all students to achieve.

It's Simple to Record Grades

Starting with an alphabetical listing of students, assign each student a number, beginning with 1, in your record book. When new students join the class, add their names to the bottom of the list and assign them the next available number.

On all tests, papers, projects, and reports turned in during the school year, students must write their unique number. For consistency, choose one place on papers where this number must be written as a class procedure and routine.

For multiple-choice, true-false, and fill-in answers, give your students an answer form so that all answers are in the same place.

After the forms are collected, ask a student to arrange them in numerical order.

Do not grade tests one at a time, while watching television and snacking. Spread the forms on a large table, perhaps ten across, and correct three to five answers at a time as you move across the forms.

Put the forms back in order ready to be recorded in your grade book.

If a student **MASTERS** an objective, do not assign more work to that student.

Give the student enrichment materials, or ask the student to help another student.

Enrichment work could include puzzles, games, software, or leisure reading.

If a student **DOES NOT MASTER** an objective, give the student remediation or corrective help.

The ineffective teacher, on the other hand, delights in giving out only a few As. The ineffective teacher is satisfied with grading students on a curve and labeling a large percentage of the class as "below average" or "failures." After ten chapters or units of study, many students in classrooms with ineffective teachers have retained only 10 to 20 percent of what has been covered. Poor comprehension and performance occurs because the ineffective teacher rolls through the school year, covering chapters and giving tests because the teacher needs to record points in the grade book. After each test, the teacher blithely moves on to the next chapter without concern for students who have not mastered the material covered.

What do effective teachers do instead?

Corrective Activities

After giving a formative or summative test and determining that a student did not master a certain objective, a corrective activity is assigned. A corrective activity is one that is presented to the student in a differentiated form or with a different explanation so the student can learn the objective through a different approach.

Formative and summative testing followed by corrective activities is not unique to education. A doctor does a laboratory test, prescribes medicine, and then repeats this procedure until the patient is cured. A baseball player watches a video of his or her swing, makes corrections at bat, and repeats this procedure until the batting average improves. A chef tinkers with a recipe, making changes until a perfect dish results.

If a student misses a question, help the student take corrective action. For example, let's assume that the student answered question 6 incorrectly on the test on page 269.

6. The steps of the scientific method are:

       a. collect data, state principles, draw conclusions.

(3-1B)   b. observe, experiment, hypothesize.

       c. experiment, conclude, study.

       d. hypothesize, think, observe.

3 - 1B

Objective	Remediation
Objective correlation: The first number tells you which objective the question correlates with. This tells you that the student has not learned or mastered Objective 3.	**Answer source:** The second number, 1B, tells you that the correct answer may be found in Chapter 1, Section B, of the textbook. Tell the student to review this section, or give the student another form of the same information; learning may be more effective in a differentiated style.

After the student has completed the corrective activity, another formative or summative test should be given to determine mastery. It should be the same kind of test as first given, but the questions must be asked in a different way.

Some authorities, including Benjamin Bloom, believe that you should test and retest until mastery is attained.[6] Others, such as Thomas Guskey, author of *Implementing Mastery Learning*, believe that testing twice is sufficient because much of the content covered in class is spiraled, and the student will be exposed to the content again later on in the school year.[7]

Teachers do not give grades; students earn grades. Through testing and correcting, the effective teacher is seeking 80 to 90 percent mastery for each assignment. If each assignment reaches 80 to 90 percent mastery, after ten chapters or units of studies, most students will have attained 80 to 90 percent mastery. The result is students who are successful, happy, and confident, and a teacher who has time to encourage students to do even better.

Can Rubric Scores Be a Grade?

A rubric is used to help a student make progress towards the quality of work. A test is used to evaluate a student on the quantity of work (how much of the work was done correctly). The two are not the same, yet teachers often ask if a rubric score can be converted into a grade.

[6] Benjamin S. Bloom, "Mastery Learning," *Mastery Learning: Theory and Practice*, J.H. Block, ed. (New York: Holt, Rinehart and Winston, 1971).

[7] Thomas R. Guskey, *Implementing Mastery Learning* (Belmont, CA: Wadsworth, 1996).

There are several mathematical ways to do this, and if not done correctly, it can be dangerously incorrect. For instance, on a 4-point rubric with five categories, such as in the example of the Persuasive Letter Rubric of the book *On My Honor* shown, there are 20 possible points. If the student scores 12 points, that would be 12 divided by 20 to equal 60 percent. If you use 60 percent as the lowest grade in the class (zeroes are not allowed), the student receives a D. Yet, the student is nowhere near failing.

For instance, the following may be fine for percentage mastery on a criterion-reference test, but not with a 4-point rubric.

88 – 100 = A	69 – 78 = C	Below 60 = F
79 – 87 = B	60 – 68 = D	

Rubrics were not designed for grading. They were designed for assessing progress. But for whatever the reason, you are asked to convert a rubric score in to a letter grade, here is a possibility. But, please use it with caution, as rubrics were not designed to be converted to grading.

20/20 = A+	17/20 = B+	14/20 = C
19/20 = A	16/20 = B	13/20 = D
18/20 = A-	15/20 = C	12/20 = D-

Example: Rubric Into a Grade

As shown, a rubric can be converted into a grade, but be very sure that the written rubric has been well designed to assess for the objectives; otherwise, the evaluation will be faulty.

Melody Arndts, a teacher in Pennsylvania uses the following 4-point, 5-category rubric in a reading assignment. Melody uses the rubric for the book, *On My Honor* by Marion Dane Bauer, in which Joel dares his best friend, Tony, to swim in a dangerous river. The boys didn't receive permission from their parents and Tony disappears. At the conclusion of the book, Melody assessed the students using a performance task, in which they had to summarize the most important details of the story and highlighting Tony's disappearance, as it was a major event and an essential theme of the book. She obtained an actual police report from Philadelphia. It gave the students a role

GoBe

No Zeros Allowed

Should you ever give a zero for a grade? Reflect on this by going to the **Go**ing **Be**yond folder for Chapter 20 or scan the QR Code.

[8]Alfie Kohn, "Grading: The Issue Is Not How But Why," *Educational Leadership*, vol. 52, no. 2 (October 1994).

as a writer, the audience, and a format to follow. The students had to draw a picture of the crime scene. Melody said, "The students thoroughly enjoyed it."

Persuasive Letter Rubric
"On My Honor"

	4	3	2	1	Points
Position Statement	The position is **clearly stated** and consistently maintained.	The position is **stated** and consistently maintained.	The position is stated but **not maintained consistently**.	The statement of position is **not stated** or cannot be determined.	
Supporting Information	The **evidence clearly supports** the position.	The evidence clearly supports the position, but there is **not enough evidence.**	The argument is supported, but **lacks sufficient evidence.**	The evidence is **unrelated** to the argument or position.	
Organization	The structure is **clearly developed.**	The structure is developed reasonably well, but **lacks clarity.**	Some attempt to structure the argument has been made, but the structure is poorly developed.	There is a **lack of structure.**	
Tone of Letter	The tone is **consistent** and enhances persuasiveness.	The tone enhances persuasiveness, but there are **inconsistencies.**	The tone **does not** contribute to persuasiveness.	The tone is **inappropriate** to purpose.	
Mechanics and Grammar	The letter has **no** errors in punctuation, capitalization, and spelling.	The letter has **one to three** punctuation, capitalization, and spelling errors.	The letter has **four to six** punctuation, capitalization, and spelling errors.	The letter has **seven or more** punctuation, capitalization, and spelling errors.	

Name _____   SCORE _____

When to Give a Test

To conclude, student learning is presented in lessons, chapters, units, or topics. Small parts of the learning are called assignments. To determine achievement for each assignment, administer a test.

- Each assignment must have a set of objectives that state the specifics of student accomplishment to be demonstrated.

- Each assignment must have a set of questions written for each objective.

- The test must be written at the beginning of the assignment, concurrent with the writing of objectives.

- The test is to be given when the students have finished the assignment.

In the classroom of an effective teacher, students are focusing on the same objectives as the teacher. The preparation and presentation of all lesson materials, reading assignments, worksheets, multimedia, lectures, and activities must be done for one reason only—to teach to the objectives.

Your Students Can Outperform 98 Percent of Other Students

Benjamin Bloom reported on how a teacher can achieve 98 percent mastery. Read how it's done in the **Go**ing **Be**yond folder for Chapter 20 or scan the QR Code.

The Mastery Approach

When I begin a new unit or a topic, I project an outline of my unit on a screen, and it stays up there during the teaching of the unit. On the outline are the lesson objectives. My students see what lesson objectives they are responsible for learning.

I teach to the outline. The students are learning to the objectives, and I am teaching to the performance of the objectives, on the outline. When I finish the outline, I give them the test. And every single question that I write on the test is written to the objectives on the outline.

You see, if you don't know what you want your students to learn, how can you write a test or evaluate to see if they've learned it? My student achievement results are awesome, but then why not? Both teacher and students know what is to be learned. All questions or skills are correlated with the known objectives. That's why my students call it the 'no-mystery approach.'

A high school teacher

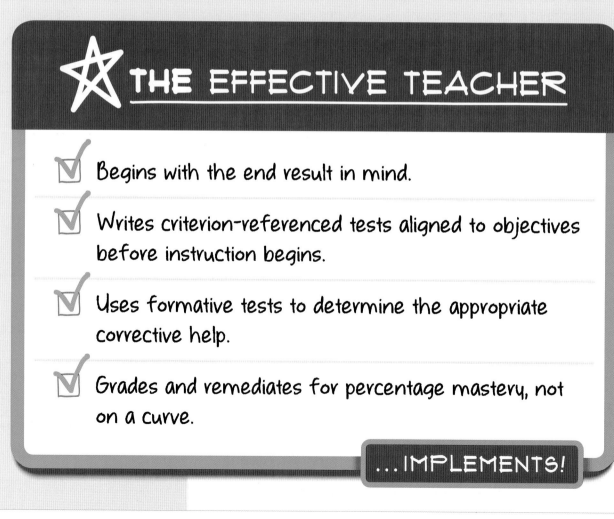

★ THE EFFECTIVE TEACHER

- ☑ Begins with the end result in mind.
- ☑ Writes criterion-referenced tests aligned to objectives before instruction begins.
- ☑ Uses formative tests to determine the appropriate corrective help.
- ☑ Grades and remediates for percentage mastery, not on a curve.

...IMPLEMENTS!

The Purpose of Instruction

Instructional practices and assessment techniques are the key elements in helping students learn, succeed, and master the objectives of the lesson.

> Teachers who work together
> to achieve specific measurable goals
> increase the likelihood of improved student learning.

The Learning Triangle represents a constant flow between each of the points—Objectives, Instruction, and Assessment.

As the teacher teaches to the objective, assessment is taking place to see if the instruction has been effective. If no progress is made toward reaching the objective, new strategies need to be employed to help students master the content.

Just as there is no one way to assess, there is no one way to teach. The teaching techniques used to teach third-grade spelling will differ from the strategies used to teach AP History. A lesson created for a group of special education students will differ from a lesson created for a classroom of Silicon Valley techies.

> The teacher's responsibility is
> to organize an instructional process
> that will help students learn and succeed.

Collaboration to Enhance Learning

Most successful enterprises operate so that their employees feel part of a team. At a restaurant, your meal is a result of a team of people working together, from dishwashers to chefs. In stores, you will notice closed doors with a "Team Members Only" sign. A company that wants your business declares, "Our team will take your design and bring it to fruition from beginning to end." Winning athletic teams will tell you, "We are individuals, but we play as a team."

☆ THE KEY IDEA

Teachers who collaborate create a culture of consistency that enhances learning.

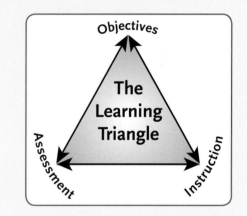

No individual can win a game by himself.

Pele

In 1993, a group of twenty-three doctors in Maine and New Hampshire made an agreement to work as a team by observing each other's operating room procedures and sharing insights. In the two years after their nine months of observation and sharing, they reduced the death rate among their patients by an astonishing 25 percent.

For teachers who have traditionally worked as isolated professionals, the analogy holds a powerful message. If the goal is to lower the "failure rate" of students, teachers are much more likely to succeed with young minds by working collaboratively to analyze student work and make decisions on how to improve instruction to net stronger outcomes.

Effective schools that demonstrate steady progress and high achievement results in student learning do it with teacher learning teams organized by grade level or subject matter.

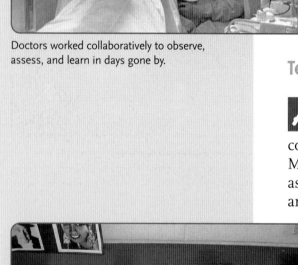

Doctors worked collaboratively to observe, assess, and learn in days gone by.

Team Meetings to Analyze and Improve

At learning team meetings, teachers gather to analyze student progress toward curriculum goals and to collaborate on constructive solutions for improvement. Members bring their respective students' writing assignments, math problems, science projects, artwork, and whatever else students are producing.

If possible, one particularly efficient way to analyze student work is to have members bring in work from a common assignment.

The work is placed on the table and divided into three general piles: excellent, average, and poor. One sample is arbitrarily pulled from each pile and it is then reviewed and analyzed. Suggestions for teaching strategies to implement in the classroom are considered and discussed.

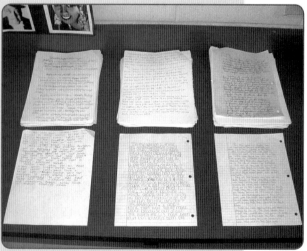

From each stack, one is selected for review and collaboration.

Trust + Collaboration = Improved Outcomes for All

The learning team assesses each lesson sample with simple recurring questions:

- How can we improve or change our instruction to help the student who is doing poor work to do at least average work?

- How do we help the student who is doing average work to do excellent work?

- What tools for learning can we prescribe to inspire each student to move up the achievement ladder?

Teachers also bring their own lesson plans to share and try out on their colleagues. It's somewhat intimidating to do so, but with ground rules in place (as with the Schmoker Model described on page 283) and the principles of brainstorming (where everything presented is accepted without judgment), the focus of the meetings is firmly on enhancing student learning.

The focus of team meetings is always the work on the table and not on the particular student or teacher who produced it.

Teachers gather in learning teams to assess student work and discuss teaching strategies for improvement.

St. Rose: A Top Gain School

At St. Rose Elementary School in Louisiana, the reading scores of every student are posted on a data wall in a room teachers affectionately call "the war room." Like a rescue team with a mission, the teachers are very serious about studying student data and self-assessing their own teaching strategies to help every student become proficient in reading and math.

The school administration and the data team created and maintain the wall to show where students start, how they progress, and where they finish after intervention and further instruction, if necessary. The data wall is housed in a conference room that can only be accessed by staff.

Achievement levels in reading and math for every student in the school can be seen at a glance.

Each grade level has a pocket chart with three colored sections: green at the top, yellow in the middle, and red at the bottom. There is a card for each student with his or her photo.

Cards for students who are at or above level in a certain skill are placed in the green section. The yellow section is for students who are working just below the average level.

The red section is for the students who are working below and far below grade level. The students who are in the red section are monitored weekly to make sure they are moving up (progressing) and receiving all the necessary support to be successful in school.

Some cards also have colored dots that give information particular to the student. The dots indicate intervention, retained the previous year, ESL student, Reading Recovery student, literacy student, math resource program, and Response to Intervention RTI (RTI).

Teachers collaborate and plan strategies to help students make progress in their levels.

The progress of all students is closely monitored for Developmental Reading Assessment (DRA) levels, as well as math skills being taught. Common formative assessments are also given to track the math data. The data helps the RTI committee to group students in order to customize appropriate interventions for each.

It is no surprise that St. Rose Elementary School has been honored by the state of Louisiana as a Top Gain School.

Sisseton Middle School: Success with Consistency

Karen Whitney, the principal of Sisseton Middle School on an Indian reservation in South Dakota, was profiled in Chapter 16 about implementing a Classroom Management Plan with her teachers. She also created and taught her teachers a Classroom **Instruction** Plan using a **Common**

The students in the bottom red section are in greatest need of help. The students in the center yellow section are working at just below average levels. The students in the top green row are at or above skill levels.

Lesson Plan. Within two and a half years after becoming principal, she and her staff became the first public school on an Indian reservation to achieve Adequate Yearly Progress (AYP).

Sisseton Middle School's success can be attributed to an effective principal and a collaborative staff. They have had the persistence to transform a low-performing school with students of diverse ethnicities from low-income families into a school achieving proficient or advanced levels. **The achievement of student proficiency was and continues to be an expectation at Sisseton Middle School.**

The "culture of consistency" was established with

- a common Classroom Management Plan, and
- a schoolwide Common Lesson Plan.

All teachers at Sisseton Middle School use the same Common Lesson Plan format. This makes life easier for everyone, as the teachers know what to teach, and the students know what to learn. The day's agenda and learning targets are always posted in the same location in every classroom. Everyone knows what to do, what is happening, and what to expect—even parents and guardians. When there is cohesion, continuity, and consistency throughout a school, students have the stability and support they need to work, produce, learn, and achieve.

The Common Lesson Plan format (page 282) has eight components that result in a coherent curriculum:

1. **Content Standard(s).** Initially based on South Dakota standards, but could be aligned with Common Core Standards.

2. **Learning Target(s).** Correlated to the standard(s), what does the teacher want students to do, know, and understand by the end of the lesson?

3. **Instructional Strategies.** What will the teacher do, or have students do, that will get them to reach the learning targets?

4. **Assessment.** How will the teacher know that students have met the learning targets? What evidence will there be that they have met the learning targets?

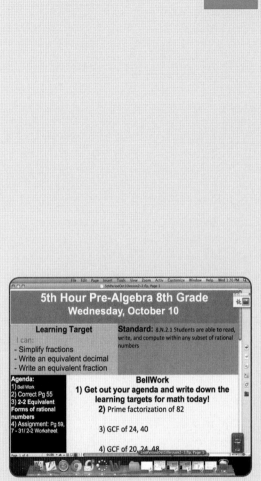

Every teacher posts the day's agenda and learning targets at Sisseton Middle School. Technology allows for easy updates and display.

5. **Evaluation.** How will students be tested for knowledge of the lesson objectives?

6. **Bellwork.** What will students do at the beginning of the class or period to engage them in learning?

7. **Guided Practice.** What will students be doing, with teacher assistance, to practice meeting the learning targets?

8. **Independent Practice.** What will the teacher require students to do independently, while practicing to meet the learning target?

Karen Whitney says, "I am truly grateful for the teachers I work with every day. **My teachers deserve all of the credit for <u>working as a team</u> to create the consistency we have developed at our school.**"[1]

> **The core work of a learning team is to analyze student work with the purpose of improving student learning.**

Practicing Collaboration

The success of schools that are considered proficient or high achieving despite assumptions of being in an under-achieving category actually has little to do with factors such as funding, class size, commercial programs, parent involvement, or tutoring. The facts are that all these factors can be found in varying degrees in both high- and under-achieving schools.

The schools that beat the odds and consistently achieve results for their students are ones where teachers employ these three strategies:

1. They assess and reassess student work.

2. They use the results to teach and reteach.

3. They do not stop until they find a way for every student to grasp each lesson.

Sample Lesson Plan

To see a sample of the completed lesson plan, go to the **Go**ing **Be**yond folder for Chapter 21 or scan the QR Code.

---

[1] Karen Whitney is no longer principal of Sisseton Middle School. She is the superintendent of schools on a large Indian reservation.

Common Lesson Plan Template

Lesson Plan for the week of:		Teacher:		Subject:	Grade:
	MONDAY	TUESDAY	WEDNESDAY	THURSDAY	FRIDAY
Content Standard(s)					
Learning Target(s) (What students know, understand, or be able to do at the end of the lesson.)					
Instructional Strategies (What the teacher will do to teach the content.)					
Assessment (How you will know if students met the learning target. Use both formative and summative.)					
Evaluation (How students will be tested for the learning target.)					
Bellwork (What students do immediately upon entering the classroom.)					
Guided Practice (What students do with teacher assistance.)					
Independent Practice (What students do independently.)					

Teachers are more effective when they work together in teams to enhance student learning. Mike Schmoker, in *Results: The Key to Continuous School Improvement*, reported on the traits of teachers found in schools that produce results:

- They work as a productive team.
- They set clear and measurable goals.
- They collect and analyze ongoing performance data.[2]

The Consortium on Chicago School Research found that in schools where teachers worked as teams, students were taught math above their grade levels. In schools where teachers worked alone, instruction lagged behind. In these schools, eighth-grade math teachers typically taught fifth-grade math.[3]

> "A rapidly growing number of schools have made a momentous discovery: when teachers regularly and COLLABORATIVELY review assessment data for the purpose of improving practices to reach measurable achievement goals, something magical happens: student achievement. How does this come about? Through people working collaboratively as a team in a shared culture."[4]
>
> Mike Schmoker

Many teacher learning teams use Schmoker's Lesson Plan Protocol during the first part of a collaborative meeting. This focuses the discussion on lesson design and is followed by assessing and discussing student work and achievement. All of the information exchanged at the team meeting is recorded in a "Team Learning Log."

Schmoker's Lesson Plan Protocol[5]

1. **Focus** (3–5 minutes)

   - Identify the specific learning objective and the assessment that will be used to determine success of the lesson.
   - Write one learning objective/standard that clearly states the purpose of the lesson.
   - Display the objectives/standards for all team members to see.
   - Ensure the team has a common understanding regarding the assessment.

[2] Mike Schmoker, *Results: The Key to Continuous School Improvement* (Alexandria, VA: Association for Supervision and Curriculum Development, 1999).

[3] *Catalyst Chicago*, "Rate Your School: Here's How to Do It" (July 27, 2005). Available at www.catalyst-chicago.org.

[4] Mike Schmoker, *The Results Fieldbook: Practical Strategies from Dramatically Improved Schools* (Alexandria, VA: Association for Supervision and Curriculum Development, 2001).

[5] Mike Schmoker, *Results: The Key to Continuous School Improvement*.

2. **Assessment**

- Create the assessment aligned with the learning objective/standard.

3. **Quiet Write** (1 minute)

- Quietly and privately brainstorm on paper the elements, steps, or strategies that might go into an effective lesson (a lesson that would help the greatest number of students succeed on the assessment).

4. **Brainstorm** (4–7 minutes)

- As a team, use good brainstorming protocol (no negative comments, any and all ideas are acceptable, piggyback on others' thoughts) to capture twelve to fourteen ideas for all to share.

5. **Selection** (3–6 minutes)

- As a team, select the best strategies, steps, and elements that combine most effectively to promote student success on the assessment.

6. **Outline Lesson** (4–10 minutes)

- As a team, use the best ideas selected in the previous step to build an outline of the lesson.
- Collect related ideas, sequence them, and add or rearrange ideas as necessary.
- Outline the lesson for all to see.

7. **Implementation** (back in the classroom)

- Teach the lesson.
- Assess the results.

8. **Next Meeting**

- Discuss the results of teaching (how many students succeeded), along with the strengths and weaknesses of the lesson or assessment.
- Discuss adjustments to instruction relative to each area of strength or weakness.

> **Collaboration allows teachers to capture each other's fund of collective intelligence.**
>
> Mike Schmoker

District-Wide Collaboration

New teachers at Islip Public Schools work in collegial teams. Their Regent's Diploma rate is, and has been for several years, at 99.7 percent. Read about the school's process in the **Go**ing **Be**yond folder for Chapter 21 or scan the QR Code.

PS 861: The Highest Ranked School in New York

In 2010-11, the Staten Island School of Civic Leadership or Public School (PS) 861 was the highest ranked school in the New York City system of 1,600 schools. They achieved this distinction two years after starting as a new school.

The principal of the school was Rose Kerr, and it was her innovative idea to divide the staff into triads—groups of three teachers who teach two sections at a grade level. Ideally, one of the teachers is a special education teacher. This system is financially feasible because there are no paraprofessionals or aides.

The three teachers are trusted to take ownership of student success and they decide who teaches what, and in what order. They are responsible to each other, and there is ongoing collaboration with common planning periods. They can change the time and order of their prep time and the sequence of instruction depending upon the needs of students. The only time structured for them is the lunch period; otherwise, daily collaborative teaching is embedded.

The teacher triads work like professionals, behave like professionals, and produce results like professionals.

There are two significant characteristics that define the success of the Staten Island School of Civic Leadership (SISCL), and these characteristics are also found in schools in Finland and Singapore, the two most highly regarded school systems in the world:

- **Trust**, the hallmark of Finnish schools
- **Collaboration**, the essence of teaching in Singapore

Teachers working as triads collaborate to produce learning and achievement for all students.

Trust and collaboration ensure a well-oiled learning machine.

The Power of Shared Vision

Asuccessful journey begins with a clear picture of the destination. If you do not know where you are going, then how will you know how to get there or even if you do get there?

The journey to improve student achievement is no different. Everyone involved—principals, administrators, teachers, parents, and guardians—must agree on common goals and together create a map that will ensure students make steady progress toward achieving those goals. They need to collaborate and direct a laser focus on improving student learning. **This concept is known as shared vision.**

With shared vision, knowledge, experiences, and expertise are shared throughout the school. Effort is made to reach consensus around learning goals, assessment, and evaluation. This is accomplished through a collaborative decision-making process by teachers in learning teams and reinforced by strong leadership.

> **In a school with shared vision,**
> **the leader works on getting everyone to work together.**
> **People are connected to, rather than separated from,**
> **each other.**

Ineffective schools have poor leadership, no teacher learning teams, and nothing is shared. There is curricular chaos, where teachers isolated in their classrooms teach wildly divergent topics in the same grade level at the same school. No one knows and no one cares what else is being "learned" throughout the school. Assessment—observation and analysis of how teaching and learning can be improved—is a foreign word in a "culture of isolation." In an effective school, the curriculum is carefully crafted to be coherent, continuous, and consistent. Teachers constantly assess themselves to see if they maintain and nurture a common, shared focus on enhancing student learning in every way possible. They constantly ask themselves if students are being taught, or need to be retaught, the academic content and procedures they need to succeed.

There is only one vision to pursue in education—progress in student learning. Never lose sight of that fact. Travelers never lose sight of where they are going by consulting a compass, a map, or the GPS (global positioning system) for navigation. Think of a compass, map, or the GPS every day and ask repeatedly, **"What is our shared vision? Where are we going? How are we going to get there?"** Every plan and every decision made in a school must lead to improving student learning to prepare them for life.

Collaboration and Consistency Enhance Learning

Effective classrooms and effective schools are consistent. Please go back to page 13, in Chapter 2, and reread the concept of consistency in the classroom. It says, "Students want a safe, predictable, and nurturing environment—one that is reliable and consistent. Students like well-managed classes and classrooms because there is no need to enforce rules and the focus is on learning."

> **The most effective schools have a culture of consistency. There is only one way to establish consistency. Everyone must collaborate and work together as a team.**

Consistency denotes quality and dependability. It is why you buy certain products and use the services of certain people or companies. Consistent does not mean status quo, or never changing. It means that you can depend on getting predictable results because you trust the team of people who have trained, collaborated, and worked together to produce the excellent product or service you enjoy.

The products and services of a school are no different. When everyone at the school has a shared vision of improving student learning, and everyone collaborates to ensure that the focus is always on realizing that vision, then everyone thrives. Behavioral issues are lessened; stress, confusion and frustration are minimized; and you and your students can concentrate on academic achievement and the skills they need to acquire to lead fulfilling lives.

It begins with establishing procedures that (hopefully) everyone in the school—the principal, administrators, and teachers—have all agreed to. They include these things:

- **Greeting** every student at the door
- Having an **agenda** posted
- Using an **opening assignment** to start class immediately
- Teaching and rehearsing basic **procedures**
- Beginning every lesson with a set of **objectives**
- Using a **rubric** to help every student make progress
- **Assessing** to improve teaching and learning
- Displaying **positive** expectations

It continues with collaborative learning teams and continuous assessment to constantly improve teaching strategies and procedures so that everyone is working together to realize the shared vision: progress in student learning.

☆ THE EFFECTIVE TEACHER

☑ Collaborates with colleagues to improve student learning.

☑ Analyzes student work and instruction as part of a learning team.

☑ Contributes to and actively maintains a shared vision throughout the school.

☑ Establishes agreed upon procedures so that teaching and learning are consistent, continuous, and coherent.

...IMPLEMENTS!

Unit

Future Understandings—The Professional

The teacher who constantly learns, grows, and shares becomes a professional educator.

Chapters

Survival or Mastery?

In Chapter 2, you learned that teachers have the possibility to go through four stages in their teaching career—Fantasy, Survival, Mastery, and Impact. Yet many teachers never progress beyond the second stage, **Survival**.

> Self-assessment is how effective teachers become even more effective.

Teachers in the Survival stage are "I" people. Watching out for themselves is foremost on their minds. They look at life as a worker looks at a job, not as a career or responsibility. You keep hearing them use the word "I," as in, "I was hired to teach history, not do these other things"; "I can't teach these kids who come from this neighborhood"; "The contract says that I do not have to stay after 3 P.M. or attend this meeting unless I am paid for it"; or, "I'm tired, I HAVE TO pick up the kids, and I HAVE TO prepare dinner."

They isolate themselves at meetings because improving their knowledge and skills is not part of their job description. To rationalize their behavior, teacher-workers blame people, places, and things, because survival is their goal in life.

Many teachers, however, do attain **Mastery**. Teachers who become effective, master teachers are "We" people. They have student success foremost on their minds. They are relentless in their desire to improve, constantly adding to their knowledge and repertoire of skills. You keep hearing them use the word "we," as in, "We need to work in our learning teams to find a solution to reduce the dropout rate." Or, "Do we have some people who would like to help on the School Improvement Grant proposal?" Or, "We can do it— I know we can do it—so let's all work on analyzing the students' work to see how we can improve student learning."

Their attitudes and abilities are their strengths. They do not dwell on problems by whining about people, places, and things, because they have discovered that life is fuller when doing things with and for other people while tackling the latest challenge, rather than bemoaning the past.

THE KEY IDEA

Effective teachers choose to be professionals who strive to make a difference.

66

The people who get on in this world are the people who get up and look for circumstances they want, and, if they can't find them, they make them.

George Bernard Shaw

99

> Mastery is an attitude, a lifelong attitude
> about aspirations and honing the
> art and craft of teaching.

Impact

Teachers who reach the **Impact** stage, who have the ability to influence students' lives and fulfill the aspirations of their own lives, are adept at "mastery learning," the continuous process of learning. Teachers who understand the concept of mastery learning have the desire to get better and better at something that matters. Mastery learning involves a lifelong commitment to honing the art and craft of teaching with the expectation that you will achieve Impact.

It takes work and effort to be effective. It takes time to go to conferences, read journals, serve on committees, and interact with colleagues. It requires effort to be part of a learning team, give extra help to students who need it, and take classes to improve personal skills and understanding. But rewards and satisfaction go to those who are willing to invest in themselves for the benefit of others. **These are choices they freely make to enhance their own lives.**

When you reach the Impact stage, you will find that you will have gone full circle to the **Fantasy** stage—and fulfilled your fantasy or dream of making a difference in the lives of your students. You'll also become a teacher-leader, leading and coaching teachers, sharing, and living a happier life with a sense of pride and accomplishment knowing that you are contributing to the profession.

Do You Decide or Do You Choose?

Everyone comes into teaching wanting to make a difference in the lives of their students and in their own lives. Yet how is it that some teachers become teacher-leaders while others remain teacher-workers throughout their entire career? It has to do with the distinction between two words: DECIDE and CHOOSE.

Look at the two syllables of the word "decide." The prefix, de-, means "off" or "away," as in defeat, destroy, denigrate, and deemphasize. It is a negative prefix. The stem, -cide, means "cut" or "kill," as in suicide, pesticide, insecticide, and herbicide. To decide is thus to "cut away" or "kill off," not necessarily a positive activity. It means being reduced to one final choice or judgment.

Many people make decisions by deciding. Have you ever dined with someone who cannot select what to order? Everyone at the table waits until someone impatiently barks out, "How long does it take you to decide?" And does the person make a choice? No. Instead the person asks the others at the table what they plan to order. "Oh, you're going to have a turkey sandwich? I'll have the same. No mayonnaise? Oh, OK, make mine the same way." And what happens to people who decide in this way? Deciders become victims because they allow other people to choose for them.

When you study a menu, do you choose or do you decide? People who decide reduce the possibilities available to them and often let other people make their decisions. People who choose see an array of possibilities and take the initiative to make the best choices for themselves.

The same thing happens in teaching. Let's say you are a new teacher and you want to be accepted. So you walk into a seminar, a faculty meeting, or a professional learning community (PLC) meeting with people and someone says,

"Let's sit in the last row (and not participate while I check my phone)." You nod in agreement and follow along, doing what others have "told" you to do. By doing so you have become a victim of their decisions. That is, you have decided to do what the others are doing as if it's the only option without considering what other choices are possible and what's best for you. (Ever notice how hot and crowded it is in the back row?)

In this instance, what you have also decided to do is perpetuate a negative culture, where teachers conspire with each other to do as little as possible to just survive. They behave like the unresponsive and unenthusiastic students they complain about. **The sad reality is that if you do not make the determined choice to be effective and professional, the negative culture will prevail.** You will not get past the Survival stage and both you and your students will suffer.

Survive or Choose

Laura was a teacher—worker. She was typical of the countless number of sweet, kind, average people who teach. She did her work. She taught class, gave assignments, wrote tests, showed videos, passed out worksheets, supervised the cafeteria, attended faculty meetings, and baked cookies for the textbook selection committee she was on for the year. She had a family and sang in the church choir.

She took early retirement at fifty-three, having "put in" thirty years. During that time, she never read a journal, joined a professional organization, or attended a conference.

During her thirty years, Laura never caused any problems, did not abuse her sick leave, and seldom said a word at faculty meetings. She always sat at the back of meetings and knitted. She didn't harm any students, but then she never really lit fires under any of them, either. She did her job and felt, as workers are prone to tell you, "I did my job, didn't I? What more do you want me to do?"

Over a decade later, I saw a familiar face at the mall. I gingerly walked over and said, "Excuse me. Are you Laura? Remember me? We used to teach together." Cordially, she said, "Oh, yes."

I asked her what she had been doing and she mumbled, "Oh, not much. I come to the mall a lot. It's safe here, you know. I see my grandchildren—I have three—and watch television. That's my life. I walk the malls, babysit the grandchildren, and watch television."

Then she asked, "And what are you doing?"

With a smile, I said, "Oh, I'm so happy I chose teaching as a profession. I've written a book, given a presentation at the International Reading Association conference, met my wonderful wife at a teachers' conference, and indulge my taste for fine dining. Life has been very good to me."

I felt for Laura. She was typical of someone who had never tried to move past the Survival stage. She let everything in her life be decided for her. She had never been able to take the initiative and make the choices that would have given her professional satisfaction and fulfillment.

Harry K. Wong

Successful People Choose

In contrast with teacher-workers—the survivors—there are teachers who attain mastery and impact. They become teacher-leaders. **Teacher-leaders do not decide. They CHOOSE!** They enter a meeting ready and willing to work and contribute. They consider all the possibilities and choose a place to sit where they won't miss anything (perhaps front and center), curious to see what new thing they can learn; they make themselves comfortable, whipping out an electronic device from their briefcase (there is usually an empty seat next to them). **These teachers are professionals.**

Effective teachers take the lead in their profession and always strive to improve themselves and others. They are determined, committed, and passionate about achieving results. They enjoy tackling problems, obstacles, and challenges. They see an endless array of possibilities and solutions. They have vision that helps them see beyond their immediate task or job. They understand what choice means and how to exercise it for their own benefit and that of their students.

People who are leaders take control over their lives through the choices they make. They know that the good things in life come from choosing well and they are generally rewarded with whatever they seek to accomplish—whether it be attaining the top of their profession, being secure financially, being popular and admired, professional respect, or personal contentment. They generate their own happiness and well-being, and much of that comes from choosing to serve and share with others.

- They know they are responsible for their choices.
- They know they are accountable for their choices.
- They know that choices give them control over what they do.
- They know that choices have consequences. If something fails, they take the blame. But if it succeeds, they have earned the reward.

The first chapter in this book was "**What** Is an Effective Teacher?" Now you are reading Chapter 22, "**How** to Be an

Taking a Step Towards Success

The margin for success is so thin that getting across it is astonishingly simple. To make that step, go to the **Go**ing **Be**yond folder for Chapter 22 or scan the QR Code.

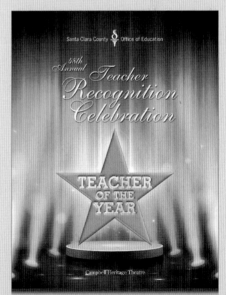

Teachers who are rewarded, and attain Mastery and Impact, know the difference between deciding and choosing.

Are You a Worker or a Leader?

Teacher-workers let other people make their decisions. Teacher-leaders make their own choices. To understand this concept, go to the **Go**ing **Be**yond folder for Chapter 22 or scan the QR Code.

Effective Teacher." You now know what it takes to be an effective teacher and how to go about doing it. You can let others decide for you the type of teacher you will be or you can choose to become an effective teacher. Knowing the difference between deciding and choosing is empowering.

The choices you make will determine your career as an effective teacher.

> Some people go through life
> adding years to their life.
> Others go through life adding life to their years.

Teacher-Workers Decide	Teacher-Leaders Choose
Life's rewards come from what others give me.	Life's rewards come from what I earn.
I expect others to bring me happiness.	I will generate my own happiness.
Life will be better when I get a new X or more Y.	Life is better when I share or help others.
Life would be easier if I didn't have to do all these things.	Life is fine because I want and choose to do these things.
Why do I have to do hall duty?	I enjoy meeting and interacting with students.
All I want is some peace and quiet.	I enjoy challenges; they are the elixirs of life.
I can't do this. I've got to go home and feed the dog.	I'll do this. Then I'll go home and have a wonderful evening with my family.
If I could only win the lottery I'd be set for life and could retire.	I will invest in myself by attending the math conference.
I can't wait for the weekend!	I can't wait for Monday morning!

Choosing to Be an Effective Teacher

Elmo Sanchez teaches in the Miami–Dade County Public Schools. One day, he made a choice.

I was hired to teach fifth-grade reading, language arts, E.S.E. inclusion, and E.S.O.L. Monday, August 8, was the first day of the academic school year. I struggled through my day's lessons. My students spoke throughout the class period and had no sense of direction. I found myself using my "loud and/or angry" voice. I would go home angry and my family felt the direct effects.

At the end of the school year, I reflected on my achievements and failures in the classroom. I labeled myself an "ineffective teacher" because my classroom lacked structure. As a professional, I was disappointed in myself and felt I needed to make changes.

Each year the Miami–Dade County Public Schools has a summer professional development meeting. On Friday, June 9, I remember sitting in the Miami Lakes Educational Center Auditorium and I was captivated. Dr. Wong's classroom management strategies, techniques, and explanations made sense. Then, as he says, I had a "light bulb" moment. What would happen if I could take these strategies back with me to improve the way I managed my class? I could visualize the changes in my head that were going to take place in my classroom the next academic school year. By the end of the seminar, changes were occurring in my mind. I could picture ways of changing my failures into successes.

*After viewing Chelonnda Seroyer's PowerPoint presentation online I began to develop my own PowerPoint presentation. I also read through **THE First Days of School** twice and began to formulate a plan that would suit me as a teacher. It took me about a month to develop my classroom management PowerPoint presentation.*

Picture this: Monday, August 14, the first day of the academic school year. I opened the door at 8:15 A.M. and greeted my students with an extended right arm. Shaking my students' hands, I said, "Welcome to our class; I'm glad you are here." My students greeted me back with warm smiles.

I projected the bellwork assignment as a PowerPoint slide. By the time I closed the door, all of my students were actively working. I could not believe it. After my students completed the bellwork, I began to introduce my students to the PowerPoint presentation I had created. By the end of the day, my students were following the classroom procedures. When the 3:00 P.M. dismissal bell rang, no one got up. They all waited for me to dismiss them. I had control of my class and it was only the first day of school. At the end of the day, peace was with me.

I went home happy and with an upbeat attitude. For the first time in my professional career I had a feeling that was missing from my life for a very long time. My family noticed the difference in me and liked the "new, happier me." I came to love my profession after that first day of school and my students felt safe in the classroom atmosphere that I created.

Last year, I was a stressed out teacher with a chaotic classroom. Now I feel that I'm an effective teacher with a structured classroom. My students are always happy to come to my class. The parents are always asking, "What do you do that causes my child to become so engaged in your class? My child wants to come to your class even though he is sick."

My secret recipe is having a structured classroom with procedures. I'm glad I made a choice to restructure my classroom. I would say that on June 9, my life as a professional teacher was transformed. Thank you for helping me make the choice to be effective!

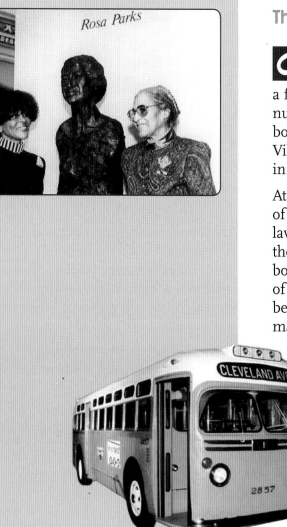

Rosa Parks

The Power of Choice

One of the best examples of the power of personal choice was made December 1, 1955, when Rosa Parks, a forty-two-year-old African American woman, rode on bus number 2857 in Montgomery, Alabama. (Today, you can board that bus at the Henry Ford Museum and Greenfield Village in Dearborn, Michigan, and relive history by sitting in the same seat Rosa Parks sat in that defining day.)

At the time, the Jim Crow law mandated the first ten rows of a bus were reserved for whites. Rosa Parks obeyed the law and sat in the eleventh row. But that day, all the seats in the white section soon filled. When the next white man boarded the bus, the driver (following the standard practice of segregation) told the four African Americans sitting just behind the white section to move further back so the white man could have a seat. Rosa Parks quietly refused.

The driver said, "If you don't stand up, I'm going to have to call the police and have you arrested." Rosa Parks answered, "You may do that"—an enormously polite way of saying enough is enough. What could the threat of jail possibly mean compared to the humiliation and incarceration she and others had been subjected to their entire lives, and for generations before.

Her action on the bus that day was ultimately her personal choice.

After her arrest, local civil rights activists initiated a boycott of the bus system. Among those leading the boycott group was a young Baptist minister who was new to Montgomery. His name was Martin Luther King, Jr.

Because African Americans made up about 75 percent of bus riders, the boycott posed a serious economic threat to the company and the white rule of the community. The boycott lasted 381 days. On November 13, 1956, the U.S. Supreme Court ruled that the segregation law was unconstitutional and the Montgomery buses were to be integrated.

Rosa Parks' quiet resistance ultimately gave every American citizen, regardless of color, creed, or national origin, the

freedom to sit where one chooses to sit, eat where one chooses to eat, worship where one chooses to worship, and learn where one chooses to learn. She left behind an inspirational legacy.

Choose to Be the Hero

The effective, professional educator chooses to always learn and grow. The effective educator is on an endless journey, looking for new and better ideas, new information, and improved skills to further student success.

In Chapter 16, you studied the procedure called SQ4R so you know to teach students to read the beginning and end of the chapter to get a survey of the subject. Hollywood and television producers use the same technique. They are flooded with story plots and scripts from people who want to sell their stories. To quickly sort through them, they do two things:

1. Read the beginning to identify the protagonist, that is, the main character or hero

2. Read the ending to find out what happens to the protagonist

In between is the story line. Producers often comment that many writers have unsatisfactory story lines because of a meager beginning or flat ending.

That's the problem in many classrooms, too. There is no planning to begin the school year with procedures that provide structure and stability. Students aren't focused and lack purpose. Every day is just a jumble of disoriented things to do (as in to kill time) with little learning accomplished.

To make matters worse, many teachers make the monumental mistake of defining classroom management as discipline. There is no learning, because the focus in not on learning—it is on making sure students behave. The essential story line—student learning—is missing.

Remove the barriers to learning with classrooms that are consistent in function and purpose.

Imagine your school year is going to be a movie. You are the protagonist, the main character. Your choices and attitude will create the story line that leads to a happy, tragic, or flat ending. If you are aiming for the happy ending, you know it is your responsibility to be as effective as possible. You will have planned and prepared in order to be proficient in the three characteristics of effective teachers—classroom management, lesson mastery, and positive expectations. You begin the year confidently and enthusiastically.

REMINDER
The single greatest effect
on student achievement
is the effectiveness of the teacher.

As the year progresses, you employ the techniques and methods that research and experience have established as effective—clear objectives, rubrics, continuous assessment, and feedback. You never lose sight of what you want to achieve—student learning. Employing The Learning Triangle is your key to student learning. That's your story line, and you stick to it, day in and day out.

So, what happens to you, the protagonist, at the end of this movie about the school year?

The more effective you are, the more successful your students are. And the more successful they are, the happier you are. It's a happy ending for you and for them! You are truly the hero in the classroom. Each day can have a happy ending. But it is all up to you, as the main character, to make it happen by doing things effectively.

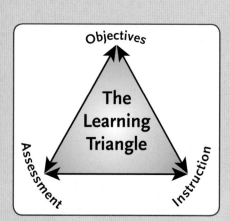

Tell students what they will be learning (objectives) before the lesson begins and student achievement can be raised as much as 27 percent. (Chapter 18)

Provide students with specific feedback (rubric) about their progress and achievement can be raised as much as 37 percent. (Chapter 19)

Teach students with activities that are directly related to the lesson objectives. (Chapter 21)

Assessment for Teacher Effectiveness

A trait of effective teachers is their willingness to self-assess their own work. Self-assessment is not about evaluation; it is about self-improvement. You have the potential to be a highly effective or even more highly effective teacher, but the potential is dependent on your commitment to self-assessment.

Self-assessment is valuable in helping teachers develop strategic thinking. Teachers who learn how to think strategically actively generate, explore, create, and select options that increase the effectiveness of their work.

> **Self-assessment is how effective teachers become even more effective.**

Effective teachers are constantly assessing themselves on how proficient they are in the three characteristics of effective teachers. Self-assessment can be done with **The Effective Teacher Rubric** on page 301. This rubric, as with all rubrics, is not to be used for evaluation. It is to help a teacher make progress and produce better and better student learning. All teachers know that they must have high expectations for their students; however, this is only possible when teachers have high expectations for themselves.

- Place a copy of the rubric in your classroom management or instructional management binder.

- Use the rubric for self-assessment on a regular basis, such as every grading period.

- Strive, at the very least, to be a Proficient and Effective teacher as defined by the rubric.

- To achieve Mastery and be a Highly Effective teacher, review and implement the strategies found in these units:

  Unit B–Positive Expectations
  Unit C–Classroom Management
  Unit D–Lesson Mastery

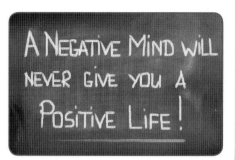

Be Mentally Strong

- Don't practice self-defeating behaviors. Don't waste time feeling sorry for yourself. Make choices.

- Hang on to your power to be in control of your actions and emotions.

- Embrace change and challenge. It will light up your life every day.

- Spend time with people who enhance your life.

- Show genuine joy and excitement for other people's successes.

The Effective Teacher Rubric[1]

Topic / Effect	Mastery and Highly Effective	Proficient and Effective	Partially Effective	Needs Coaching
Classroom Management	Your students take responsibility and know what to do so there is maximum engagement in all classroom activities.	You have a classroom management plan with procedures that structure the classroom.	You have some semblance of organization and structure in the classroom.	You have no classroom management plan and students have no idea what they are responsible for.
Lesson Mastery	You have students who understand how to learn and can self-assess their learning.	You know how to teach to aligned objectives and can use a rubric to help students make progress.	You have an agenda with lesson objectives posted and teach to the objectives.	You just cover materials, do incoherent activities, and there is minimal work being done by the students.
Positive Expectations	You have created a consistent culture in the classroom and throughout the school and students know they cannot fail.	Your students experience consistency and enjoy coming to a safe, organized, and productive classroom.	You have some consistency, but students aren't sure from day to day what is going to happen in the classroom.	Your classroom lacks consistency and the students feel you don't care about them or their learning.

[1]This rubric was created by the Wongs and is based on sixty years of research on the characteristics of effective teachers and the work of Thomas Good, Jere Brophy, Robert Pianta, Charlotte Danielson, Harry Wong, Rosemary Wong, and many others.

Two Effective Teachers

Shannon Dipple and Stephanie Stoebe (page 303) represent the thousands of teachers who have mastered teaching. Not only do they know how to teach—using the three characteristics of effective teaching: classroom management, lesson mastery, and positive expectations—they are identified by one word, "WE."

Shannon Dipple teaches in Ohio. She has mastered teaching and can describe her classroom as effective.

From the second students walk into the room, they have a morning routine to accomplish. They unpack their bags, turn in homework, sign up for lunch, turn in Teacher Mail, sharpen their pencils, and get straight to reading. These procedures have been taught, modeled, and practiced so that every morning they are completed within the first two minutes. This routine is consistent every single day.

My students know what results I want because I have left nothing to chance. They have been taught how to work towards my expectations. Every moment counts, so every moment is defined by a procedure.

A typical day could begin with a math bellwork assignment. Students who finish early can work on a challenge problem. There is no wasted time in Shannon's classroom. She has created procedures that allow her classroom to run efficiently, free from chaos, giving her the freedom to produce results.

Because her professional life has reached the Mastery stage, it has cycled back to the Fantasy stage. Shannon's fantasy is sharing with the profession on her own website at www.k5chalkbox.com.

The Greatest Day of a Teacher's Life

Perhaps the greatest day of a teacher's life is when a former student comes back to visit. There you are, consumed with teaching, when this face suddenly appears in the doorway. It's a former student, but you don't recognize him. You suspect he's a parent.

"Mrs. Riley?" the person asks. Agitated at the disturbance, because class is in session and no appointment has been made, you curtly respond, "Yes, I'm Mrs. Riley."

"Remember me? Keith. Keith Marlowe. I was in your class twenty-three years ago, and I sat right there in that chair. Remember me?"

You don't, but you fake it. "Oh, yes, Keith. How are you?"

"I'm fine, Mrs. Riley. I don't live here anymore. I live two thousand miles away, but I come back to see my parents from time to time. On my way back to the airport, I couldn't help but notice that I had some free time, so I decided to come over here to see if you were still here. And, I'm so

Implementation Guide

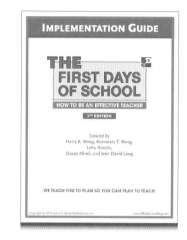

THE First Days of School has an implementation guide. It is free at www.EffectiveTeaching.com. Use it personally or in a peer group to get the most out of every chapter in this book.

The Effective Teacher Rubric

To download and use a copy of The Effective Teacher Rubric, go to the **Go**ing **Be**yond folder for Chapter 22 or scan the QR Code.

I Love Smart Teaching Best of All[2]

I work with kids who are at risk for dropping out of school. I work with students who are struggling to learn English and who receive special education services. Nearly all my students are at least two, sometimes up to seven, grade levels behind in reading. In my reading intervention classes, it is not uncommon for a student to raise their reading level by four grades in a single year. I firmly believe that if I did not have set and practiced classroom procedures, my students would not make the incredible gains that they do.

When a student's life is in turmoil, school is not the top priority; survival must come first. At home, many students do not know what problem, what struggle is going to hit their family next. When at-risk students walk into my classroom and discover that there is a procedure, a "how to" handbook of sorts for nearly any issue that could arise, they are at ease. For some of these students, this type of orderly and smoothly running classroom is the first experience of a life without chaos.

I first met Rodrigo when he was a freshman; he had only been in America for six months. He could barely utter a complete sentence and I often had no idea what he was understanding. One day, we had a new student from Vietnam enter class; I was in the middle of a lesson, but after introducing Nguyen to the class, Rodrigo volunteered to show him around and explain how our classroom ran. Two students. Three languages. One set of classroom procedures that were demonstrated and modeled by a young man who knew what was expected of him. Witnessing this incredible exchange convinced me that having clear procedures and processes in place fostered student success. Not only did I learn that Rodrigo understood quite a bit of information from class, but also that he was able to convey that information to a peer.

Jessie is a young man with autism that I had for three years. At first, he had a paraprofessional attend all his classes with him. He felt comfortable in my class because the notebooks were always in the same spot, the tables labeled, and the agenda for the day on the board. The first class that Jessie ever routinely went to on his own was my reading class. He turned one day to his aide and said, "You know, I got it from here." And from then on Jessie came alone. He first learned to maneuver my classroom, but he soon learned to maneuver the school. His third year in high school, Jessie became my student aide. He was responsible for running errands, posting the agenda for the day, and making sure that all materials were in order. And would he let me know if he was disappointed in a certain period for not following the classroom procedures!

I love teaching. I love teaching with all my heart. But I love smart teaching best of all. Smart teaching means teaching the routines, procedures, and processes necessary to keep our home, our classroom, running smoothly. And you know what? My kids are all very, very smart!

Stephanie Stoebe
Round Rock, Texas

[2] Abridged from Harry K. Wong and Rosemary T. Wong, *THE Classroom Management Book* (Mountain View, CA: Harry K. Wong Publications, 2014), page 223.

happy to find that you are. For you see, Mrs. Riley, I've come here to tell you something. I am who I am, and I am what I am, and I am where I am in life today, because of what you represented to me twenty-three years ago."

Notice that Keith did not say anything about what she taught him. Nor did he say anything about some fun activity he did in class. Keith described Mrs. Riley as a paragon, a role model. She was a significant adult in his life.

He extends his hand to shake Mrs. Riley's and says, "I've come today just to say 'thank you.'"

Keith smiles, nods affirmatively, turns, and is about to walk out of her life forever when Mrs. Riley says, "Keith, please don't leave. I have something to say."

With twenty-eight students watching her, and tears in her eyes, she says, "Keith, we teachers rarely get any validation for what we do. But what you have done today is all we teachers want—the knowledge that we've made a difference in someone's life. Thank you for making my day."

Keith responds, "Thank you, Mrs. Riley. But you made my life."[3]

If you have taught for more than twenty years, you will recall the significance of that teary-eyed, emotional experience of a student's return visit. And if you are just starting out, we wish you the same kind of event sometime down the road.

Choose to Make a Difference

You are the determiner of success in your classroom, not only by the choices you make but, more importantly, through your positive attitude and strong affirmation of your students.

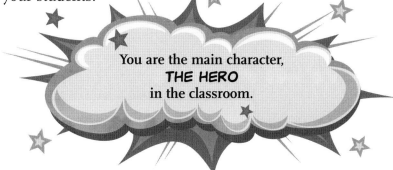

You are the main character, **THE HERO** in the classroom.

A hundred years from now it will not matter what my bank account was, the sort of house I lived in, or the kind of car I drove. But the world may be different because I was important in the life of a boy.

Forest E. Witcraft was a professional Scouter and managing editor of *Scouting*, the journal for Boy Scouts of America. He wrote these insightful words in 1950. His message rings true many decades later and will continue to provide the drive and passion for teachers for another hundred years.

---

[3]Harry K. Wong, "The Greatest Day of a Teacher's Life," *So to Teach: Inspiring Stories that Touch the Heart*, ed. Kathie-Jo Arnoff (Indianapolis, IN: Kappa Delta Pi, 2007).

It is your dedication and leadership ability that will make a difference in your students' lives.

Effective teachers are competent in the three characteristics you studied in Units B, C, and D. To these we now add two more qualities:

1. They have positive expectations for student success.
2. They are extremely good classroom managers.
3. They know how to design lessons for student mastery.

4. **They make choices that enhance their professionalism.**
5. **They are committed to continuous self-assessment.**

> **The single greatest effect on student achievement is the effectiveness of the teacher.**
>
> **Upon the effectiveness of your teaching hangs the success of each of your students.**

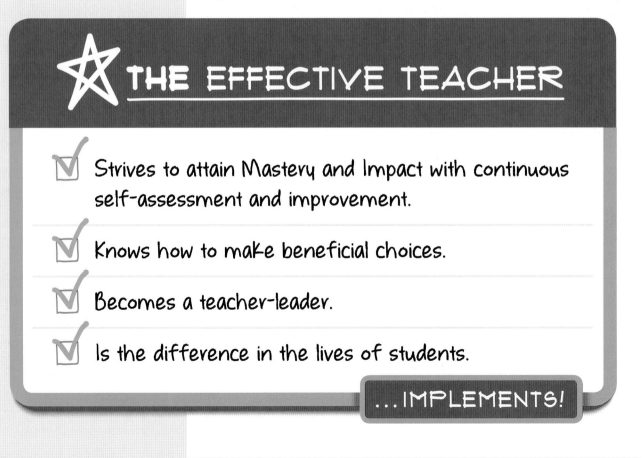

☆ THE EFFECTIVE TEACHER

☑ Strives to attain Mastery and Impact with continuous self-assessment and improvement.

☑ Knows how to make beneficial choices.

☑ Becomes a teacher-leader.

☑ Is the difference in the lives of students.

...IMPLEMENTS!

The Significance of a Teacher

Commitment, dedication, and hard work are the keys to maximizing your potential as a teacher.

> You have the potential to be a very effective teacher.

Ability and talent are not enough. The world loves talent, but pays off in character. Character is the product of ability and talent combined with relentless practice and tempered by years of training.

Teachers can be accurately compared with business executives. Like executives, teachers develop, manage, and evaluate the work and productivity of a relatively large number of individuals on a daily basis. If one compares teachers and doctors, it can be said that teachers actually make more complex and fewer routine decisions than doctors—and they make them far more frequently.

Many teachers go into teaching because of the influence of one of their teachers. This is not true for other professions. Teachers have influence. Teaching is the profession that makes all other professions possible. Ours is the only profession that is totally dedicated to making the world a better place for future generations. They are our legacy.

★ **THE KEY IDEA**

Teachers are a school's greatest assets. Training can maximize teachers' effectiveness so they can realize their potential and that of their students.

Teachers have influence. Teaching is the only profession that is totally dedicated to making the world a better place for future generations.

> **"**
>
> *Nobody can go back and start a new beginning, but anyone can start today and make a new ending.*
>
> Maria Robinson
>
> **"**

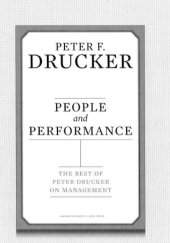

Teachers Are Assets

During the Industrial Revolution, physical capital such as gold, manufactured products, buildings, and money were considered the source and evidence of wealth and economic growth. Things have changed in the modern corporate era. Peter Drucker, the famed management consultant, educator, author, and "business guru," identified people as a company's greatest asset and the "knowledge worker" as the key to the future.

Drucker coined the term "human capital" to describe the value of people to an organization. Human capital refers to what people know (proficiency) and can do (effectiveness). Human capital is not measured by accumulated physical assets, but by knowledge, skills, and attitudes. Companies today depend on their people to create the next great ideas. People are their major assets. University of Chicago economist Gary Becker, its most ardent proponent, won a 1992 Nobel Prize for the idea that human capital has indeed replaced physical capital in today's world.

Companies invest in their assets to make them grow into even greater assets. In the digital age, human capital is what companies invest in to engender wealth and economic growth. Businesses spend $53 billion each year training their people—their assets—to make them worth more to a company. The better their people are, the more successful is the company.

However, ask a school administrator or policymaker to name their greatest asset and they will often refer to money or programs. Rarely do you hear one of them say their effective teachers are their most valuable assets—yet the research demonstrates it over and over again:

**Teacher instructional quality is
the most critical factor by which to improve
student achievement and close the achievement gap.**

Teachers are a school's most valuable resource. The teachers we hire today will be the teachers of the next generation. Their success or failure will greatly influence their students' futures and that of the world. Healthy societies need leaders who model positive leadership for others. What better models are there than the effective teachers who live and work in our communities?

Planning and Executing

If no one has ever approached you and acknowledged your potential, grab this book and go look in a mirror. We are telling you right now, you can do it—you can be the most effective teacher on the planet. We believe in you and believe in your potential. Our passion is to guide you through the process and give you all the skills you need to make it happen.

The cover of this book has the tagline, "We teach you to plan so that you can plan to teach." **Planning is the foundation for all beginnings.** Without a plan, you are planning to fail.

> *Hard work beats talent, when talent doesn't work hard.*
>
> Harrison Barnes

She Was the First to Tell Me

This was a book that I read many, many times growing up in my humble home in Kenner, Louisiana. I wanted to travel, see the world, and help people.

One day, my high school principal, Mrs. Dorothy Donnelly, called me out of sophomore Honors Biology to come to her office. During the course of the conversation, she asked me what I wanted to do. I said, "I want to be a stewardess." She looked me straight in the eyes and said, "My dear, you can do better than that."

I still remember that day so vividly: I wore a purple plaid skirt, green shirt, and matching plaid tie. And her words still echo in my head today. You see, she was the very first adult in my life to tell me that I had potential. I could do or be anything I wanted to be in my life. I had those capabilities.

Now, please, I'm not putting down flight attendants. I fly on airplanes constantly and I want the most effective flight attendant there could possibly be watching over me as I fly safely to my destination.

What I am saying is this—the greatest gifts you can give your students is belief in their power and abilities as individuals; to value them without reference to their gender, race, or background; and to give each of them respect as a person with potential.

This book sits on my desk at home reminding me each day that I do get to live my dream. I get to travel the world, and I get to help people. So, I invite each and every one of you to rise to the level of your potential; release the potential in each of your students; and become the successful— effective—teacher you were meant to be. Go and live your dream of being a very effective teacher.

Rosemary T. Wong

To be effective you need to plan and then plan some more, but most importantly, you need to activate your plan. You will never know what needs to be improved upon, what needs to be changed, what is missing from your plan unless you put your plan into practice. Successful people create plans and execute them. Your success hinges on creating and executing a plan.

> **ex • e • cu • tion**
>
> **the act of carrying out; of doing;
> of producing; of following through**

Professional football is the beloved sport of many Americans. It is game that requires teamwork. To win as a team, players must know their assignments and then execute them when the plays are called. This is why football coaches yell to players, "Execute, execute!" This means to run out the play, follow through, and finish strongly. In a game, that play may be called only once, but that once may be the game-winning play. It has to be executed correctly. Coaches of teams that win will always point to the execution of the plays that created the team's success.

Football coaches of winning teams will always point to the execution of plays that led to success.

Jerry Rice, inducted into the Pro Football Hall of Fame in 2010, is considered by many as the greatest wide receiver to have ever played the game. If he caught a pass during practice, Rice would run it the length of the field just to rehearse another touchdown. As far as he was concerned, the goal of every practice pass was to run it for a touchdown, not to just catch it and stop. He always executed to be as prepared as possible for game day.

Successful corporations crave employees adept at execution to keep their competitive edge. CEO Louis Gerstner, when he retired from IBM, said of his successor, "His real expertise is making sure we execute well." In the business world, every employee is expected to execute according to company standards.

**When people execute, they get things done.
They follow through.**

In many schools, on the other hand, there is no goal line, no game plan, and no focus—just the constant flux of programs, fads, and ideologies. We buy curriculum programs. We buy technology. We run after government money to try the same initiatives that have failed before. This is why little gets done to actually help students learn. **Programs, ideologies, or reform initiatives do not execute.**

Have a Plan; Execute That Plan

Amanda Brooks Bivens teaches in Dyersburg, Tennessee. She was a terrified first-year teacher gathered with five hundred and fifty teachers for a preschool presentation when she saw the PowerPoint presentation that Kazim Cicek used on his first day of school to explain and establish his classroom's organization. (See page 16.) Having never seen anything like it in her college classes, she had a major moment of "Aha!" Rapidly taking notes, she went home to "steal" and modify that presentation so that she could begin her first day as a brand-new teacher with a plan.

Two weeks into the school year, she said, "I couldn't have asked for a better beginning to my career. The first day went like clockwork. It was flawless." At the end of her first year of teaching, she said, "My classroom management plan allowed me to be everything I wanted to be as a teacher and create an environment where students could just learn. I simply taught and enjoyed my students."

At the end of her second year of teaching, her class had the highest state test scores in the school. After her fourth year (bear in mind that research says that 50 percent of new teachers will have dropped out of the profession by now), the district hired her and her teaching partner to conduct an induction workshop for twenty-eight, new teachers coming

Amanda Brooks Bivens' classroom management plan, what she calls her Go-To Guide, made her an extremely effective and successful teacher from the beginning.

into the district. Amanda gave every new teacher a binder of her classroom management plan with sixty-three ideas, techniques, and templates. This may explain why as Amanda began her fifth year as a teacher, and in the first year of eligibility, the staff voted her Teacher-of-the-Year.

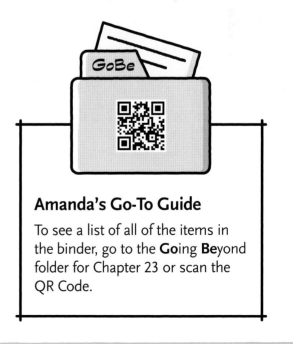

Amanda's Go-To Guide

To see a list of all of the items in the binder, go to the **Go**ing **Be**yond folder for Chapter 23 or scan the QR Code.

An Invitation to Share Your Plan

Our profession is one of sharing. There is ongoing discussion with our professional colleagues about what works and doesn't work in the classroom. Please share your classroom management plan with us so we can help others plan for their success.

Feel free to send your plan to HarryandRosemary@HarryWong.com and we will be in touch about sharing it with the profession. Thank you.

Teachers execute. Teachers get things done. The effective teacher has a well thought out classroom management plan—a plan that is continuously enriched—and uses it to execute an effective classroom environment where the main priority is that students learn.

The Work Ethic

In football they are called "reps," which is short for repetition. Players run plays over and over again to make sure they are executed correctly. In music, it's called practice. Musicians practice over and over again to be sure that the music is executed correctly. In theater, it's called rehearsal. Performers repeat scenes over and over again until the timing and execution are just right.

**Success is not an entitlement;
you have to work at it.**

People who succeed in life do not complain about the hours they have to put in. They complain about the hours that are wasted. The world respects and rewards people who work hard and do their jobs with a degree of courtesy and graciousness. This is what you expect of professionals when you are a customer in a bank, office, or store. The world of business demands that people put in a great deal of effort to complete projects and achieve targets efficiently and effectively. Many immigrant families who come to the United States arrive steeped in the values of the importance of education and hard work. They understand that there are no short cuts to success.

Stanford University psychologist Carol Dweck says, "*Hard working* is what gets the job done. You just see that year after year. The students who thrive are not necessarily the ones who come in with the perfect scores. It's the ones who love what they're doing and go at it vigorously."[1]

In the classroom, teachers are paid to be productive. Just as students are expected to finish work and turn in assignments, teachers are expected to prepare, plan, and produce, day in and day out, to have the impact they should have in the classroom. Students and teachers who are successful always attribute it to hard work—as the famous saying goes, to a great deal of perspiration and only some inspiration. They

[1] David Glenn, "Carol Dweck's Attitude: It's not about how smart you are," *The Chronicle of Higher Education* (May 9, 2010).

believe in the work ethic. They do not eschew memorization and repetition. They are focused on a goal and value the "sweat equity" and perseverance in getting the work done.

Grit

For students to become productive members of society, we need to teach the value of hard work and, just as importantly, the value of persistence. In Finland, they have a term for this. It is "sisu," which is difficult to translate precisely because it means perseverance, resilience, and courage combined. **People who persevere do so because they are determined to achieve success.**

Angela Lee Duckworth at the University of Pennsylvania is a MacArthur fellow. When she was twenty-seven years old, she left her job in management consulting to teach seventh-grade math in New York City. She discovered that some of the strongest performers did not have stratospheric IQ scores. In actual fact, some of her smartest students were not doing well at all.

She left the classroom and went to graduate school to become a psychologist. She wanted to understand why some people succeed more than others. She researched cadets at West Point military academy, spelling bee entrants, corporate sales people, and teachers working in, and students going to, schools in really tough neighborhoods. What she found was that those who performed best were not those with economic opportunities, social intelligence, good looks, physical health, and certainly not the highest IQ scores. **Those who performed best had GRIT.**

Duckworth defines grit as passion and perseverance for very long-term goals. Grit means perseverance, not just for a week, not just for a month or two, but daily perseverance for years, despite failure, adversity, and plateaus in progress. Grit is living life like it's a marathon, not a sprint.[2]

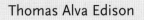

> *If we did all the things we are capable of doing, we would literally astound ourselves.*
>
> Thomas Alva Edison

Open the door to your effectiveness. Apply the techniques of effective teachers with perseverance and you will be rewarded with success.

When it comes to winning, succeeding, and fulfilling a dream, there is no substitute for hard work, willpower, determination, and perseverance.

---

[2] Angela Duckworth, *Grit: The Power of Passion and Perseverance* (New York, NY: Scribner, 2016).

> **You give me effort and I will give you the world.**
>
> William W. Purkey

The Success of Class Valedictorians

Terri Denney of the University of Illinois conducted a long-term study of eighty-one class valedictorians (*Chicago Tribune*, May 29, 1992). He wanted to find out whether they continued to succeed after graduation. The answer is yes. Using standardized tests to measure motivation, he discovered that valedictorians were characterized by their desire to work hard. On the standardized ACT test, which measures intellectual skills, the valedictorians' scores ranged from top of the range to just average.

Denney's conclusion was valedictorians are not necessarily the brightest students. They are the students who work the hardest in school. Most people, with effort, can achieve comparable success. While talent and intelligence are important, commitment, persistence, and a determined work ethic are the qualities that lead to success, qualities all of us can acquire and use to our advantage.

Silver Bullets Do Not Teach

Education policy makers are always looking for "silver bullets." They chase after money to buy faddish programs or technology solutions. They spout buzzwords that are intended to improve learning outcomes and test scores. Since 2002, they have been touting the notion of "21st century skills," stating that our schools must teach the following:

- Creativity and innovation
- Critical thinking and problem solving
- Communication and collaboration

These are all excellent and admirable skills. But there is nothing new about them. They are the same skills that have been taught for centuries. Socrates made good use of them in ancient Greece. They brought forth the Renaissance in the 12th century. They made possible our current era of fast-paced innovation in places like Silicon Valley. These so-called "21st century skills" are currently being done, in real time, by millions of people each day, all over the world. The Internet generation knows how to solve problems by just going online to communicate, collaborate, create, and access information.

Missing from all the rhetoric on 21st century skills is the concept of a "work ethic." This concept is fundamental to the many immigrant families who come to America. They come steeped in the importance of family, respect for others, and the value of hard work. Their accomplishments make our schools look good. They understand that there are no short cuts to success.

When you observe a well-managed classroom with lessons that are mastered, you see effective, knowledgeable, and caring teachers who have worked hard to create a classroom conducive to improved learning.

The REAL Silver Bullet

There is one silver bullet that has always worked to improve student learning, and it has worked for centuries. **It is hard work by dedicated, well-trained teachers.**

As unbelievable as it seems, many school districts do not invest in their greatest assets. They do not develop the potential of their teachers.

More than 80 percent of a school district's budget is spent on teachers' salaries, yet many administrators and policymakers ignore teachers as the schools' most important assets. After they are hired, teachers are summarily dumped into the classroom to survive with no structured, coherent, professional development program.

Teachers may prepare and arrive at a new school with a classroom management plan in hand, but they are left alone to fend for themselves, isolated in their classrooms. It's absurd that some teachers are not even provided with a curriculum. Isolation and lack of support further exacerbate the challenges and problems beginning teachers face.

Tianna was (no longer) a brand-new teacher. She said, "I was hired, given a district USB and a stack of books, and told to go teach."

Another new teacher said, "On my very first day as a brand-new teacher, I was not introduced to the staff. I was not shown to my room and not even shown the bathrooms! I was not told how to get supplies. I was not told how I would fit into the staff and how I could contribute. Needless to say, I left after my first year.

"Looking back, the reason is obvious. There was no culture at this school, so I could not 'fit in' to something that did not exist. It was simply a place where people worked behind closed doors."

Buzzwords and fads distract from the fact that it is well-trained teachers who produce learning achievement.

Ask the fire chief, the store manager, or hospital executive what they do with new employees. Ask the baseball manager, construction foreman, senior partner in a law firm, and managers at coffee shops, fast food restaurants, or pizza chains what they do with new employees. They will tell you that all employees are trained from the day they arrive, and the training continues until the employee leaves.

> *We have too many high-sounding words and too few actions that correspond with them.*
> Abigail Adams

Real Skills

These are the real skills essential for success in today's global generation. They have been around forever.

Ambition	Dedication
Hard work	Diligence
Commitment	Integrity
Determination	Fortitude
Constancy	Responsibility
Loyalty	Steadfastness
Drive	Perseverance

Now, ask a school administrator what they do with a new teacher. Some do absolutely nothing. Most will tell you they assign a mentor to the new teacher, but they rarely monitor the result of the relationship. **Yet we know, and research has confirmed, that the easiest and only way to close the student achievement gap is to close the teacher instruction gap.**

Teach the teachers well and they will teach the students well. It's the teacher! We've known this for decades, yet we refuse to execute and implement the obvious.

> **It's the teacher and how the teacher is trained that produces student achievement gains.**

Effective schools have a culture where they consistently invest in teacher capital.

Teaching Effective Teaching

When Howard Schultz, CEO of Starbucks, came out of retirement in 2008, one of the first things he did was to "bring them back to life," meaning he wanted to "get back to the fundamentals." He closed EVERY Starbucks (over seven thousand of them) on Tuesday, February 26, 2008, from 5:30–9:00 to train every single employee so that they could re-learn how to make the perfect cup of coffee. They used the "Espresso Excellence Facilitator Guide"—a set of procedures—to provide consistency. Here is the amazing part: closing for those three and a half hours cost him approximately six million dollars. He said that was fine because training for perfection was a priceless part of his greater vision.

All of this for cups of coffee . . . and school systems fail to see the benefit of training teachers.

The barista who made this cup of coffee probably had more training than the typical classroom teacher.

Use Coaches, Not Mentors

A growing number of districts now understand that a critical component of a successful comprehensive induction program is a coach. Read why in the **Go**ing **Be**yond folder for Chapter 23 or scan the QR Code.

In education, we almost never have the opportunity to "get back to the fundamentals," meaning teaching effective teaching. Each year, school districts spend billions hiring teachers to replace the teachers they hired and did not train the year before when a fraction of that money could be applied to a structured, coherent, and sustained professional development program. **Teachers stay when they are given the opportunity to succeed.**

To keep new teachers, to close the teacher instruction gap, and to incrementally improve student achievement, provide every new teacher with the following:

- A structured and coherent induction program that flows seamlessly into a sustained professional development program

- A grade-level or content-level learning team they can immediately join and with whom they can collaborate

Which District Would You Choose?

Consider these two examples of school districts. Which would you choose as a place to begin your teaching career?

District A: They offer little help or support and no training. At most you get an assigned teacher (probably an untrained mentor) who may be available, if found. You have to cope.

District B: They have an organized program with trained staff that offers professional development for eight years so that you realize your potential and become as effective as you can be in the classroom.

If you selected District B, it is the Flowing Wells Unified School District in Tucson, Arizona, where they have been producing effective teachers for over thirty years. They are so good at what they do that they have produced more teachers-of-the-year nominees and winners than any other district in Arizona.

That's because Flowing Wells takes novice teachers and turns them into expert teachers. They do this with a well-organized, eight-year, professional development program that begins with a new teacher induction process, which

This bulletin board welcomes all new teachers to the Flowing Wells Unified School District in Tucson, Arizona.

then seamlessly flows into a lifelong professional development program they call Institute for Teacher Renewal and Growth. Student learning results when teachers know how to instruct effectively and administrators are instructional leaders.

Flowing Wells is a small urban district of 5,500 students with high poverty (72 percent free and reduced National School Lunch Program) in a state that is usually ranked forty-eighth in school funding. Despite having to cut their budget, not one dollar of the professional development program has been cut.

The commitment to the professional development process emphasizes the academic standards, vision, and culture of the district.

Teacher Training at Flowing Wells

Whether you are a novice teacher new to the profession or a veteran teacher new to the school district, when you are hired by Flowing Wells you are welcomed, recognized, and immediately made part of the family. A board with pictures of all new teachers is in a separate building called the Professional Development Center (PDC), which has a full-time staff dedicated to professional development. For the past thirty years, the PDC has been a symbol of Flowing Wells' dedication to expending energy, resources, and emphasis on the efficacy of professional development. **Flowing Wells has a plan and they execute the plan.**

There is nothing scattershot or unfocused about what Flowing Wells does. Their professional development program is **comprehensive, coherent, and sustained**.

> **Comprehensive.** There is an organized program consisting of many activities and components that involves many people, including the school-site principal.
>
> **Coherent.** The various components, activities, and people are logically connected to each other—including the school-site principal.
>
> **Sustained.** The comprehensive and coherent program continues for many years.

They use an organized process to take a teacher through five stages of pedagogical expertise:[3]

1. Novice
2. Advanced beginner
3. Competent teacher
4. Proficient teacher
5. Expert teacher

The New Teacher Induction Program is aligned with the Arizona Teaching Standards and takes new teachers through a very intentional process.

- Eight-day induction program
- Classroom demonstrations
- Bus tour
- Mentors
- Coaching follow-up
- Monthly support seminars
- University credit from Northern Arizona University
- Ongoing staff development programs
- Complete support for teacher training

The first three days of the Flowing Wells induction program for any new teachers and administrators (no matter their experience level) are devoted to effective instructional practices. The fourth day of the induction program is focused on classroom management. The reason they only need to focus one day on classroom management—and not until the fourth day—is because there is a culture of consistency in the district that has been in existence for decades. It only takes one day to brief the new teachers on how things are done, and all students know how to follow procedures.

The new teachers are not even taught about classroom management. They are asked to read the chapters in *THE First Days of School* on procedures, and are then debriefed on what they read. Afterwards, they are taken to visit demonstration classrooms to observe master teachers' procedures for their first day. The master teachers actually simulate their first day of school with the new teachers acting as their "students." Together they analyze the procedures and management strategies woven into the simulation, a powerful tool that helps new teachers set their own organizational procedures for their first day of school.

Replicate the Five Stages

To see how Flowing Wells organizes their professional development for optimum teacher growth, go to the **Go**ing **Be**yond folder for the Chapter 23 or scan the QR Code.

[3] David Berliner, "Describing the Behavior and Documenting the Accomplishments of Expert Teachers," *Bulletin of Science, Technology & Society*, vol. 24, vol. 3 (June 2004): 200–212.

Money Well Spent?

Businesses spend $53 billion each year to **train and keep** their employees.

Education spends $7.3 billion each year to **recruit and replace** teachers.

The success of Flowing Wells can be summarized in three points:

1. There is a culture of consistency.

2. There is an organized, coherent, and sustained professional learning program.

3. The teachers work collaboratively.

Districts that are serious about training and retaining teachers must have a comprehensive induction program. **It is better to train a teacher and lose that teacher, than to not train a teacher and keep the teacher.** Effective teachers are made with structured, sustained, intensive professional development programs that allow new teachers to observe others, to be observed by others, and to be part of networks or study groups where all teachers share together, grow together, and learn to respect each other's work.

**Bottom Line:
Trained teachers become effective teachers.
Districts that provide structured,
sustained training for their teachers
achieve what every school district seeks to achieve—
improved student learning.**

Collaboration, Not Isolation

New teachers want more than a job—they want hope. They want to contribute to a group. They want to connect with colleagues. They want to collaborate to achieve the best possible outcomes for their students. They want to make a difference.

Most employees of companies work in teams because teams produce results. People who work in isolation do not produce results. Yet, that is the way most schools are organized. Collaboration is rare. Guskey and Huberman report that teachers working collaboratively will significantly raise their productivity and the quality of their work.[4] Within high-success schools in low-income areas, teachers and principals have built into their regular schedules time for teachers to intensively share each other's ideas and procedures and work together.

[4]Thomas Guskey and Michael Huberman, eds. *Professional Development in Education: New Paradigms & Practices* (New York: Teachers College Press, 1995).

Teachers working in isolation make student achievement a next-to-impossible feat.

We must work together to create a professional culture in which teachers thrive and grow throughout their careers. The results will be quality teaching and improved student learning. Just as the bottom line in businesses is profit, the bottom line in education is academic performance. The ultimate purpose of professional development must be to improve the academic outcome of every student.

Teachers teach more effectively when they work in professional cultures where their opinions and input are valued. In such environments, administrators support teachers as they exchange ideas and strategies, problem-solve collaboratively, and consult with expert colleagues. They are able to help colleagues work collaboratively to solve problems, manage conflict, and promote meaningful choices.

These are the well-documented characteristics about effective schools, effective teaching, and improved student learning:

- **The era of isolated teaching died decades ago.** Good teaching thrives in a supportive learning environment created by teachers and school leaders working together to improve learning in strong, professional learning teams. The young teachers entering the profession come from a "connected" culture.

- **Teachers thrive when they feel connected to their schools and colleagues.**

- **Teachers need and want to belong.** If they do not belong in a positive way, they will belong in a negative way.

- **The trademark of effective schools is a sense of community, continuity, consistency, and coherence.**

- **Effective schools have a high-performance culture,** the hallmark of which is a shared responsibility for learning among all students.

Schools with these characteristics produce the largest achievement gains in student learning ever reported. Such achievements can only happen in schools where teachers work together, assess together, and learn together, all for the goal of improving student achievement.

Teachers in Japan continuously seek to improve teaching through collaborative lesson research.

GoBe

Collaboration in an Urban School District

To see how a principal established a safe, caring, and focused environment when students and teachers love to come to school, go to the Going Beyond folder for the Chapter 23 or scan the QR Code.

Teacher Collaboration in Japan

Shota Matsumoto is typical of every new teacher in Japan. He has been well educated in one of the national schools of education that offers a rigorous curriculum grounded in a subject major of choice. Tokyo itself has fifty school districts (school districts in large cities are small and all children can walk to their nearest school in less than fifteen minutes), and every school district has an induction process.

But here's the best part. When you, like Shota, are assigned to a school, you are immediately immersed in a process where groups of teachers meet regularly over periods of time to work on the design of lessons. You are not alone, nor can you choose to be alone. You are included as a respected member of the teaching staff, a welcome relief if you are a new teacher. In addition, you are continually learning from the other teachers, many of whom are veteran, expert teachers.

Japan has given teachers themselves primary responsibility for the improvement of classroom practice. Run by teachers, the continuous process of school-based professional development starts the minute they begin their teaching careers.

Lesson research (also called lesson study) is a universal and highly valued part of professional development. The process of lesson research is a cycle of collaborative planning, classroom observation, lesson debriefing, and then refinement of lessons. The teachers in the group gather to help put one lesson together. They talk about it, decide what will be created, and then one person will test it out in the classroom. Others observe the "test run," then everyone meets again to debrief the lesson. **They assess the lesson, not the teacher.**

For every lesson research, the focus is on increasing student achievement. Through this practice, communities of teachers enhance their proficiency by thinking deeply together about teaching and learning. **The major premise behind lesson research is if you want to improve teaching, the most effective place to do so is within the framework of a classroom lesson.**

The Best School Systems

In East Asia:
Teachers are supported and collaborate to create effective lessons. Some of their school systems are ranked among the highest in the world.

In the United States:
We chase programs hoping for silver bullet solutions. We let teachers muddle along as best they can.

The Three AREs

Teachers ARE important.
Teachers ARE influential.
Teachers ARE able to make a difference.

Helen Morsink

These practices don't just happen in Japan. Teachers in high-achieving school systems in South Korea, Hong Kong, Shanghai, and Singapore are also included in a collaborative process as soon as they join the school staff. They continue working in different collaborative groups until they leave the profession. There is no other way; that is the culture.

The teachers in these school systems focus on the things that are known to matter in the classroom: a relentless, applied focus on effective learning and the creation of a strong culture of teacher education, collaboration, coaching, feedback, and sustained professional development.

The End of the Book Is the Beginning

You are now at the end of this book. It is the beginning, or perhaps renewal, of your teaching career and the rest of your life. If you are a results-oriented, focused, visionary person, we trust this book has taught you exceptional classroom management and instructional management skills to help you make a significant impact in education and the world.

It cannot be said enough—the **single greatest effect** on student achievement is the effectiveness of the teacher. It's not rocket science—the better the teacher teaches, the better the students learn. **Teachers are a school's greatest asset. They are humanity's greatest asset.** They dedicate their hearts and souls to helping students achieve so they can contribute constructively to society and have happy and fulfilling lives.

Learning from the Best or Chasing Silver Bullets

To learn from the best school systems in the world and to see the shocking list of ineffective programs that have been chased in the United States throughout the decades, go to the **Go**ing **Be**yond folder for Chapter 23 or scan the QR Code.

♪ *And though the path that lies
before you feels so long,
You're a guiding light
And you can empower the life
of every child.*[5]

William Martinez

Norma Freeman was a significant and highly influential teacher in the life of her student, William Martinez. Twenty-five years later, he comes back to personally thank his teacher in story, song, and American Sign Language. Watch this aspirational DVD, *You Have Changed My Life*, found in the back of this book. The potential of every student can be realized with your professionalism, care, and dedication.

[5] As sung in "Standing Strong" on the DVD, *You Have Changed My Life.*

Beliefs of Effective Teachers

- They believe that every student who enters the classroom wants to grow and learn and be successful and has the potential to do so.
- They believe that they are part of a greater community of educators who are proud of their profession and dedicated to their calling.
- They believe that they are both teachers and learners and they choose to grow professionally each year.

You ARE the Difference

As a teacher, you have an awesome responsibility. When students enter your classroom, you may be the only stable adult they will ever see in their lifetime. You are their hope, their dreams, and their advocate to realize their potential. The future depends on them, and they depend on you. A child only has one childhood. Don't waste it. You are their best hope for a brighter tomorrow.

You are the window through which your students see the world. You are the sanctuary their heavy hearts come to each day.

It only takes one person to make a difference and that person is very often you—their teacher. You entered teaching to impact lives, to make a difference. Not only do you make a difference, **you ARE the difference**.

Thank you for your passion to BE the difference. That's why you are given the privileged title of teacher. What you do is nothing short of a miracle that humbles and inspires us all.

You have honored us through the years by sharing what you do so we can in turn share it with others. Our collaborations with you have been rewarding and have contributed to our growth as effective educators as well as to the success of hundreds of thousands teachers.

Best wishes on your journey in the noblest of all professions— being a very effective teacher. Please accept our sincerest thanks for your efforts and for your passion in creating a positive future for the next generation.

Harry and Rosemary

Thank You

**You—the teacher—
gave your students structure.
Structure gave them opportunities and possibilities.
You helped them realize their full potential.**

Students will never come back and thank you for allowing them to read whatever they wanted to read, do whatever project they wanted to do, or spend their time doing whatever they wanted to do. They will come back to thank you for these things:

- You taught them knowledge.
- You taught them skills.
- You were fair and consistent.
- You believed in their abilities.
- You modeled values.
- You gave them positive challenges.

- You helped them succeed in their undertakings.
- You respected their person.
- You gave them hope and inspiration.
- You sent them forth into the world with the belief and confidence that they have the potential to achieve their dreams and be a force in the world.

☆ THE EFFECTIVE TEACHER

- ☑ Is a school's greatest asset.
- ☑ Executes the three traits of effective teachers.
- ☑ Believes every student has potential.
- ☑ Is a member of the noblest of all professions.

...IMPLEMENTS!

BIBLIOGRAPHY

Allday, R. Allan, and Kerri Pakurar. "Effects of Teacher Greetings on Student On-task Behavior." *Journal of Applied Behavior Analysis* vol. 40, no. 2 (Summer 2007).

Allday, R. Allan, Miranda Bush, Nicole Ticknor, and Lindsay Walker. "Using Teacher Greetings to Increase Speed to Task Engagement." *Journal of Applied Behavior Analysis* vol. 44, no. 2 (Summer 2011).

Alliance for Excellent Education, www.all4ed.org.

Alvidrez, Jennifer, and Rhona S. Weinstein. "Early teacher perceptions and later student academic achievement." *Journal of Educational Psychology* vol. 91, no. 4 (December 1999). From Ulrich Boser, Megan Wilhelm, and Robert Hanna. *The Power of the Pygmalion Effect: Teachers Expectations Strongly Predict College Completion.* Washington, DC: Center for American Progress (October 2014).

Anderson, Lorin W., and David R. Krathwohl, eds. *A Taxonomy for Learning, Teaching, and Assessing: A Revision of Bloom's Taxonomy of Educational Objectives.* Boston, MA: Allyn & Bacon/Pearson Education, 2000.

Barber, Michael, and Mona Mourshed. *How the World's Best-Performing School Systems Come Out on Top.* McKinsey & Company, September 2007.

Berliner, David. "Describing the Behavior and Documenting the Accomplishments of Expert Teachers." *Bulletin of Science, Technology & Society* vol. 24, no. 3 (June 2004).

Bloom, Benjamin S. "Mastery Learning." In *Mastery Learning: Theory and Practice.* Edited by J. H. Block. New York: Holt, Rinehart and Winston, 1971.

Bloom, Benjamin S. "New Views of the Learner: Implications for Instruction and Curriculum." *Educational Leadership* vol. 35, no. 7 (April 1978). Presented as a General Session address at the ASCD 1978 Annual Conference, San Francisco.

Bloom, Benjamin S., and David R. Krathwohl, eds. *Taxonomy of Educational Objectives Handbook 1: Cognitive Domain*, 2nd ed. New York: Longman, 1984.

Boyer, Ernest L. "On Parents, School and the Workplace." *Kappa Delta Pi Record* vol. 25, no. 1 (Fall 1988).

Breaux, Annette, and Harry K. Wong. *New Teacher Induction: How to Train, Support, and Retain New Teachers.* Mountain View, CA: Harry K. Wong Publications, 2003.

Brooks, Douglas M. "The First Day of School." *Educational Leadership* vol. 42, no. 8. Alexandra, VA: Association for Supervision and Curriculum Development (May 1985).

Brophy, Jere E., and Carolyn M. Evertson. *Learning from Teaching: A Developmental Perspective.* Boston, MA: Allyn & Bacon/Pearson Education, 1976.

Cardichon, Jessica, and Martens Roc. *Climate Change: Implementing School Discipline Practices That Create a Positive School Climate.* Alliance for Excellent Education, September 2013.

Catalyst Chicago (Chicago Reporter) "Rate Your School: Here's How to Do It." October 1, 2000. www.catalystchicago.org.

Cawelti, Gordon, ed. *Handbook of Research on Improving Student Achievement.* Bethesda, MD: Editorial Projects in Education, 2004.

Cech, Scott J. "Test Industry Split Over 'Formative' Assessment." *Education Week* vol. 28, no. 4 (September 2008).

Child Welfare Information, www.childwelfare.gov.

Cross, C. T., and D. W. Rigden. "Improving Teacher Quality." *American School Board Journal* vol. 189, no. 4 (April 2002).

Danielson, Charlotte. *Enhancing Professional Practice: A Framework for Teaching*, 2nd ed. Alexandria, VA: Association for Supervision and Curriculum Development, 2007.

Darling-Hammond, Linda. "What we can learn from Finland's successful school reform." *NEA Today* (October/November 2010).

Department of Education. *What Works: Research About Teaching and Learning*. Washington, DC: Office of Educational Research and Improvement (March 1986).

Digest of Education Statistics, 2013. U.S. Department of Education, Institute of Education Sciences, National Center for Education Statistics, NCES 2015011 (May 2015).

Duckworth, Angela. *Grit: The Power of Passion and Perseverance*. New York: Scribner, 2016.

Elmore, Richard F. "Why Restructuring Alone Won't Improve Teaching." *Educational Leadership* vol. 49, no. 7 (April 1992).

Emmer, Edmund T., and Carolyn M. Evertson. *Classroom Management for Middle and High School Teachers*, 9th ed. Boston, MA: Pearson Education, 2012.

Evertson, Carolyn M., and Edmund T. Emmer. *Classroom Management for Elementary Teachers*, 9th ed. Boston, MA: Pearson Education, 2012.

Evertson, Carolyn M., and Carol S. Weinstein, eds. *Handbook of Classroom Management: Research, Practice, and Contemporary Issues*, 1st ed. Mahwah, NJ: Lawrence Erlbaum Associates, Inc., 2006.

Feistritzer, C. Emily. "Profile of Teachers in the U.S. 2011." Washington, DC: National Center for Education Information, 2011.

Ferguson, Ronald F. "Paying for Public Education: New Evidence on How and Why Money Matters." *Harvard Journal of Legislation* vol. 28 (Summer 1991).

Fullan, Michael. *Change Leader: Learning to Do What Matters Most*. San Francisco, CA: Jossey-Bass, A Wiley Imprint, 2011.

Glenn, David. "Carol Dweck's Attitude: It's not about how smart you are." *The Chronicle of Higher Education* (May 9, 2010).

Good, Thomas L., and Jere E. Brophy. "Behavioral Expression of Teacher Attitudes." *Journal of Educational Psychology* vol. 63, no. 6 (December 1972).

Good, Thomas L., and Jere E. Brophy. *Looking in Classrooms*, 10th ed. Boston, MA: Allyn & Bacon/Pearson Education, 2008.

Guskey, Thomas, and Michael Huberman, eds. *Professional Development in Education: New Paradigms & Practices*. New York: Teachers College Press, 1995.

Guskey, Thomas R. *Implementing Mastery Learning*. Belmont, CA: Wadsworth, 1996.

Guskey, Thomas R., and Jane M. Bailey. *Developing Grading and Reporting Systems for Student Learning*. Thousand Oaks, CA: Corwin Press, 2001.

Hattie, John. *Visible Learning: A Synthesis of Over 800 Meta-Analyses Relating to Achievement*. New York: Routledge, 2009.

Hershberg, Theodore. "Value-Added Assessment and Systemic Reform: A Response to the Challenges of Human Capital Development." *Phi Delta Kappan* vol. 87, no. 4 (December 2005).

Hughes, Langston. *The Collected Poems of Langston Hughes*. Edited by Arnold Rampersad. New York: Alfred A. Knopf, 2004.

Jensen, Ben, Amelie Hunter, Julie Sonnemann, and Tracey Burns. *Catching up: Learning from the best school systems in East Asia.* Melbourne, AU: Grattan Institute, Report no. 2012–13, February 2012.

Kauffman, David, Susan M. Johnson, Susan Kardos, Edward Liu, and Heather G. Peske. "Lost at Sea: New Teachers' Experiences With Curriculum and Assessment." *Teachers College Record* vol. 104, no. 2 (March 2002).

Kohn, Alfie. "Grading: The Issue Is Not How But Why." *Educational Leadership* vol. 52, no. 2 (October 1994).

Kounin, Jacob S. *Discipline and Group Management in Classrooms.* Huntington, NY: R.E. Krieger, 1977.

Lackney, J. A., and Paul J. Jacobs. "Teachers as Placemakers: Investigating Teachers' Use of the Physical Environment in Instructional Design." Madison, WI: University of Wisconsin, College of Engineering, School Design Research Studio, 1996.

Leithwood, Kenneth, Karen Seashore Louis, Stephen Anderson, and Kyla Wahlstrom. *How Leadership Influences Student Learning.* Center for Applied Research and Educational Improvement, University of Minnesota; Ontario Institute for Studies in Education, University of Toronto; commissioned by The Wallace Foundation. September 2004.

Marzano, Robert. *What Works in Schools: Translating Research into Action.* Arlington, VA: Association for Supervision and Curriculum Development, 2003.

National Association of School Psychologists, www.nasponline.org.

National Commission on Teaching and America's Future. Prepared by Linda Darling-Hammond. *Doing What Matters Most: Investing in Quality Teaching.* Washington, DC: NACTAF (November 1997).

Olson, Lynn. "What Does 'Ready' Mean?" *Education Week* (June 7, 2007).

Perry, Adrian, Christian Amadeo, Mick Fletcher, and Elizabeth Walker. "Instinct or Reason: How education policy is made and how we might make it better." UK: CfBT Education Trust Perspective Report, 2010.

Porter, Andrew. "Measuring the Content of Instruction: Uses in Research and Practice." *Educational Researcher* vol. 31, no. 7 (October 2002). (Updated from an email with author August 2007.)

Postman, Neil, and Charles Weingartner. *The School Book: For people who want to know what all the hollering is about.* New York: Delacorte Press, 1973.

Purkey, William W., and John Novak. *Inviting School Success: A Self-Concept Approach to Teaching, Learning, and Democratic Practice.* Belmont, CA: Wadsworth, 1996.

Purkey, William W., and Betty L. Siegel. *Becoming an Invitational Leader: A New Approach to Professional and Personal Success.* Boca Raton, FL: Humanix Books, 2013.

Richardson, DeRutha. "Projecting Professional Images . . . Through the Eyes of Photo Lenses." March 2007. wwwuk.kodak.com/global/en/consumer/education/lessonPlans/lessonPlan018.shtml.

Rickards, John P. "Stimulating High-Level Comprehension by Interspersing Questions in Text Passages." *Educational Technology* vol. 16, no. 11 (November 1976).

Rivers, June C., and William L. Sanders. "Teacher Quality and Equity in Educational Opportunity: Findings and Policy Implications." Presented at the Hoover/PRI Teacher Quality Conference, Stanford University (May 12, 2000).

Rosenthal, Robert, and Lenore Jacobson. *Pygmalion in the Classroom: Teacher Expectations and Pupils' Intellectual Development.* Norwalk, CT: Crown House Publishing, 2003.

Rowan, B., R. Correnti, and R. Miller. "What Large-Scale Survey Research Tells Us About Teacher Effects on Student Achievement: Insights from the Prospects Study of Elementary Schools." *Teachers College Record* vol. 104, no. 8 (2002).

Ryan, Kevin. *The Induction of New Teachers*. Bloomington, IN: Phi Delta Kappa Educational Foundation, 1986.

Sack, Joetta. "Class Size, Teacher Quality Take Center Stage at Hearing." *Education Week* vol. 18, no. 34 (May 5, 1999).

Sanders, William L., and June C. Rivers. "Cumulative and Residual Effects of Teachers on Future Academic Achievement." University of Tennessee Value-Added Research and Assessment Center (November 1996).

Schmoker, Mike. *Results: The Key to Continuous School Improvement*. Alexandria, VA: Association for Supervision and Curriculum Development, 1999.

Schmoker, Mike. *The Results Fieldbook: Practical Strategies from Dramatically Improved Schools*. Alexandria, VA: Association for Supervision and Curriculum Development, 2001.

Sheffield, Rachel. "Harvard Study: Good Teachers Improve Student Achievement, Earnings, Quality of Life." *Heartlander Magazine*, The Heartland Institute (January 28, 2012).

StandUp For Kids, www.standupforkids.org.

The Annenberg Challenge: Lessons and Reflections on Public School Reform. Annenberg Foundation and Annenberg Institute for School Reform (March 2002).

Tucker, Marc S., ed. *Surpassing Shanghai: An Agenda for American Education Built on the World's Leading Systems*. Cambridge, MA: Harvard Education Press, 2011.

Wang, Margaret, Geneva Haertel, and Herbert Walberg. "What Helps Students Learn?" *Educational Leadership* vol. 51, no. 4 (December 1993/January 1994).

Weinstein, Rhona S., H. H. Marshall, L. Sharp, and M. Botkin. "Pygmalion and the Student: Age and Classroom Differences in Children's Awareness of Teacher Expectations." *Child Development* vol. 58, no. 4 (August 1987).

Wenglinsky, Harold. *How Teaching Matters: Bringing the Classroom Back Into Discussions of Teacher Quality*. Princeton, NJ: Educational Testing Service, 2000.

Wiggins, Grant. "Toward Better Report Cards." *Educational Leadership* vol. 52. no. 2 (October 1994).

Wiggins, Grant, and Jay McTighe. *Understanding by Design*. Alexandria, VA: Association for Supervision and Curriculum Development, 2005.

Wiggins, Grant. "Seven Keys to Effective Feedback." *Educational Leadership* vol. 70, no. 1 (September 2012).

Wiltz, Sue Miller, in conversation with Robert Pianta. "Neither Art nor Accident: New research helps define and develop quality preK and elementary teaching." *Harvard Education Letter* vol. 24, no. 1 (January/February, 2008).

Wise, Kevin, and James Okey. "A Meta-Analysis of the Effects of Various Science Teaching Strategies on Achievement." *Journal of Research in Science Teaching* vol. 20, no. 5 (1983).

Wong, Harry K. "The Greatest Day of a Teacher's Life." *So to Teach: Inspiring Stories that Touch the Heart*. Edited by Kathie-Jo Arnoff. Indianapolis, IN: Kappa Delta Pi, 2007.

Wong, Harry K., and Rosemary T. Wong. *THE Classroom Management Book*. Mountain View, CA: Harry K. Wong Publications, 2014.

Wright, S. Paul, Sandra P. Horn, and William L. Sanders. "Teacher and Classroom Context Effects on Student Achievement: Implications for Teacher Evaluation." *Journal of Personnel Evaluation in Education* vol. 11 (1997).

INDEX

Grateful acknowledgment is made to these people and institutions whose pictures are included in this book:

A/P World Wide Photos, p. 297
Val Abbott
Edward Aguiles
Alain L. Locke School
Bernie Alidor
Stacey Allred
Melody Arndts
Rosemary Aschoff
Lois Austin
Robin Barlak
Chris Bennett
Jennifer Bergeron
Shoshana Berkovic
Cristina Bianchi
Amanda Brooks Bivens
Alicia Blankenship
Melissa Boone
Theresa Borges
Wanda Bradford

Mary Braunstein
Douglas Brooks
Patricia Candies
Deborah Chavez
Cheyenne Traditional School
Kazim Cicek
Maureen Conley
Ayesa Contreras
Jone Couzins
Judy Davis
Jaime Diaz
Eleven Madison Park
Carolyn Evertson
Oretha Ferguson
Jessica Ferguson
Dale Fillmore
Flowing Wells USD
Norma Freeman
Bethany Fryer
Amy Gadbois

Brenna Garrison-Bruden
Heidi Garwood
Steve Geiman
Kirk Gordon
Grand Prairie High School
Diana Greenhouse
Jeff Gulle
Thomas Hatch
John Hattie
Laurie Jay
Julie Johnson
Sarah Jondahl
Judy Jones
Tiffany Landrum
Elecia Lathon
Debra Lindsay
Marvin Marshall
William Martinez
Kathy Monroe
Samara Newnam

Kieu Nguyen
Lena Nuccio
Kasey Oetting
Pacific Elementary School
Janelle Papazian
Angie Perry
Sarah Powley
Riverton Intermediate School
Kathryn Roe
Karen Rogers
Noah Roseman
Charles Russell
St. Rose Elementary School
Elmo Sanchez
Santa Clara COE
Terri Schultz
Kim Scroggin
Chelonnda Seroyer
Denise Showell
Amanda Silvers

Sisseton Middle School
Jane Slovenske
Staten Island School of Civic Leadership
Stephanie Stoebe
Susan Szachowicz
Deb Thompson
Megan Toujouse
Merlyna Valentine
Katie Weber
Casey Weeks
Karen Whitney
Nile Wilson
Kristen Wiss
Cindy Wong

Thank You